European Socialist Realism

Edited by
MICHAEL SCRIVEN and DENNIS TATE

European
Socialist Realism

BERG
Oxford/New York/Hamburg
Distributed exclusively in the US and Canada by
St. Martin's Press, New York

Published in 1988 by
Berg Publishers Limited
77 Morrell Avenue, Oxford, OX4 1NQ, UK
175 Fifth Avenue/Room 400, New York, NY 10010, USA
Nordalbingerweg 14, 2000 Hamburg 61, FRG

© Michael Scriven and Dennis Tate 1988

British Library Cataloguing in Publication Data

European socialist realism.
 1. European literatures, 1940–. Socialist
 realism. Critical studies
 I. Scriven, Michael, *1947*–   II. Tate, Dennis, *1946*–
 809'.04

 ISBN 0–85496–090–2

Library of Congress Cataloging-in-Publication Data
European socialist realism.

 Bibliography: p.
 1. Socialist realism in literature. 2. European
literature—History and criticism. I. Scriven, Michael,
1947–   . II. Tate, Dennis, 1946–
 PN56.S66E93 1988   809'.912   88–2892
 ISNB 0–85496–090ˉ2

Printed in Great Britain by Billings of Worcester

Contents

Preface   vii

Introduction   *Michael Scriven* and *Dennis Tate*   1

Part I: Theorists   11

1. Georg Lukács and Socialist Realism   *Rodney Livingstone*   13

2. Gramsci and Cultural Rationalisation   *David Forgacs*   31

Part II: National Contexts   47

3. Soviet Perspectives on Socialist Realism   *Robert Porter*   49

4. 'Breadth and Diversity': Socialist Realism in the GDR
     Dennis Tate   60

5. Socialist Realism and the West German Novel
     Axel Goodbody   79

6. Socialist Realism without a Socialist Revolution:
     The French Experience   *J.E. Flower*   99

Part III: Textual Analysis   111

7. Persona as Propaganda: Neruda and the Spanish
     Civil War   *Robin Warner*   113

8. Paul Nizan and Socialist Realism: The Example
     of *Le Cheval de Troie*   *Michael Scriven*   128

Part IV: Revitalisation   147

9. Art, Politics and *Glasnost'*: The Eighth Soviet Writers'
     Congress and Soviet Literature, 1986–7 *David C. Gillespie*   149

Select Bibliography   171

About the Contributors   178

Index   179

Preface

The cultural and the political rarely coexist in symbiotic harmony. Their interconnection is rather one of unresolved tension and contradiction. Curiously, this fraught relationship is itself exemplified by the appearance of this particular book at this particular historical juncture. It is perhaps ironic that the economic and political climate of Britain in the late 1980s, so conducive to the fostering of competitive entrepreneurial skills, capitalist accumulation and bourgeois individualism, should spawn a text not only devoted to the collectivist theme of socialist realism, but also produced within a context of supportive and collaborative endeavour. Such are the contradictions of academic life today.

European Socialist Realism is the product of a research project undertaken by members of the European Political Culture group in the School of Modern Languages at the University of Bath between October 1985 and March 1987. As convenors of the research group and editors of the published book, we would like to thank all colleagues who participated in the collaborative process from which *European Socialist Realism* has emerged. In particular, we thank colleagues from the universities of Bristol, Exeter, Sheffield, Southampton and Sussex for their readiness to contribute positively to the discussions on socialist realism held at Bath. We would also like to thank Odile Schmitz and Lynne Lothian for their assistance in the preparation of the typescript.

MICHAEL SCRIVEN and DENNIS TATE
Bath, November 1987

Note on Foreign Language Titles

Classic European works very familiar to English readers in translation (e.g. *War and Peace*) are given with translated title only throughout this volume. Other foreign language works, on their first appearance in each essay, are given both their original title and an English title following in parentheses. When italicised this English title is that given to the official translated edition. When in roman type within quotation marks this is the contributor's own translation of the original title. In all cases the date given in parentheses refers to the first publication of the original language edition.

Introduction

'What seems to be happening now, perhaps this time with a better will, is that Russian writers are once more being enlisted as engineers of human souls.'[1] This provisional assessment of *glasnost'* in Gorbachev's Soviet Union in the spring of 1987 by W.L. Webb, then literary editor of the *Guardian*, may help to explain the origins of this book. It implies that there is nothing intrinsically unacceptable, in the specific cultural context of today's revitalised Soviet Union, about writers dedicating themselves to serving the urgent cause of social regeneration and thereby becoming, in a more convincing sense than in the 1930s, when Stalin thought up the phrase, 'engineers of the human soul'. The phrase itself may therefore not necessarily be so tainted by the associations of ruthless suppression of creative autonomy which any mention of Stalin's name invariably evokes, that it cannot be reinterpreted in a positive sense under significantly different historical circumstances. It may at first seem strange that a British critic as uniquely well-acquainted as Webb has been with the bleaker side of literary life in divided Berlin, post-1968 Prague or Brezhnev's Moscow should employ, without evident irony, part of the terminology of what is normally referred to in inverted commas and/or capital letters as 'Socialist Realism', when its monolithic predictability and literary worthlessness are taken for granted. On closer consideration, however, the very sensitivity displayed by Webb since the 1960s, in his articles for the *Guardian*,[2] to indications of significant change in a wide range of European cultural settings, might be precisely what has persuaded him of the new appropriateness, in the light of a specifically Russian tradition of the writer's social calling which considerably predates Stalin, of the term 'engineer of the human soul' today.

This significant response to cultural change in the Soviet Union offers a timely illustration of two issues which have underpinned our investigations into the unfamiliar concept of *European* socialist re-

1. 'Gorbachev Spring without Retreat', *Guardian*, 20 Apr. 1987.
2. See, for example, his assessment of his first twenty-five years as literary editor, 'Under the Cloud of Unknowing', *Guardian*, 27 Dec. 1984.

−1−

alism. Firstly, whether the handful of concepts which normally serve in the West as convenient shorthand for the 'Socialist Realism' of the Stalin era are restricted in their connotations by the codification imposed on them after the Soviet Writers' Congress of 1934? And secondly, whether there is not a great deal more to the term socialist realism than the patronising inverted commas and the stereotyping capitals suggest? The diverse origins of the core terminology of Stalinist socialist realism — popular appeal (*narodnost'*), class-consciousness (*klassovost'*), ideological orthodoxy (*ideynost'*), partisanship or adherence to the Party line (*partiynost'*) and typicality (*tipichnost'*) — in the writings of the nineteenth-century 'revolutionary democrats' Belinsky, Chernyshevsky and Dobrolyubov, and in the cultural theory of Marx, Engels and Lenin, have been carefully documented in standard reference works such as Vaughan James's *Soviet Socialist Realism* (1973). As they have evolved within a complex historical process and have regularly been subject to fierce interpretative debate, both before and after 1934,[3] they need to be understood, as Geoffrey Hosking has argued, as 'capaciously ambiguous' and 'open to considerable modification and reinterpretation'.[4] It is certainly arguable that Zhdanov's elusive notion of revolutionary romanticism, the substitution of a visionary 'reality in its revolutionary development' for traditional objectivity, is the only striking addition to the cultural vocabulary of Marxist-Leninism to emerge from the 1934 Conference.[5] Even the much-derided positive hero emerged, as Hosking has reminded us, from the venerable heritage of Christian asceticism.[6] Consequently, socialist realism itself is open to quite different definitions, since it can be seen as encompassing a far greater diversity of writing than what was published between the 1930s and the 1950s in the Soviet Union, if it is taken as an umbrella term for an international literary movement with quite distinct national specificities, the myriad 'reflection in the arts of the battle for the creation of a socialist society'[7] which greatly predates

3. It should not be forgotten that, even at the 1934 Congress, which is often assumed to have brought about a total codification of socialist realism, Bukharin's speech was radically different in its emphasis on quality and diversity to Zhdanov's. See *Soviet Writers' Congress 1934: The Debate on Socialist Realism and Modernism in the Soviet Union*, Lawrence & Wishart, London, 1977 (facsimile reprint of *Problems of Soviet Literature*, ed. H.G. Scott, Lawrence, London, 1935) pp. 185–258.
4. G. Hosking, *Beyond Socialist Realism: Soviet Fiction since 'Ivan Denisovich'*, Granada, London, 1980, p. 4.
5. *Soviet Writers' Congress 1934*, pp. 21–2.
6. Hosking, *Beyond Socialist Realism*, pp. 11–17.
7. C. Vaughan James, *Soviet Socialist Realism: Origins and Theory*, Macmillan, London, 1973, p. x.

1934 and has undergone a succession of radical changes ever since.

The argument that there are major achievements of socialist realism which represent a development of nineteenth-century 'critical' realism rather than its antithesis has been strenuously resisted by the majority of Western commentators since the first general assessments of the genre began to appear in the years after Stalin's death. The ideological disillusionment at the brutal termination of the post-Stalin 'thaw' in 1956 left its indelible mark on a pioneering work like Jürgen Rühle's *Literatur und Revolution*,[8] which offered what was in other respects a welcome international breadth of reference. More surprisingly, in the 1970s, in critical works as diametrically opposed in their view of the interrelationship between literature and politics as J.P. Stern's *On Realism* (1973) and Terry Eagleton's *Marxism and Literary Criticism* (1976), there is still a common refusal to reexamine the cold war cliché of socialist realism. Stern insists on a rigid distinction between 'advocacy' of the socialist cause in literature and 'interest' in social issues, in arguing for the irreconcilability of 'ideology' and 'the creative imagination'. The socialist realism which he caricatures as a totally codified and unchangeable doctrine is a 'solipsistic distension' of the realist criteria he acknowledges.[9] Eagleton, from a Marxist perspective, is equally ruthless in his dismissal of Soviet socialist realism as 'one of the most devastating assaults on artistic culture ever witnessed in modern history', so massive a distortion of the Marxist-Leninist heritage as to be clinically excisable from an account of its twentieth-century development.[10] Without seeking for a moment to underplay the horrific scale of Stalin's purges of intellectuals and that callous disregard for creative originality which made Zhdanov, in Eagleton's phrase, a 'cultural thug', we find it surprising that this undifferentiated negative treatment of a cultural process which has had an extensive European impact for a good half-century now should have been taken for granted in literary criticism for so long.

As a counterbalance to the excessive reliance on the theoretical pronouncements of Soviet cultural politicians amongst critics who dismiss socialist realism out of hand, it is important that the individual socialist realist should be given a fair hearing, that due attention be paid, for example, to an author such as Paul Nizan, whose

8. Kiepenheuer und Witsch, Cologne, 1960. The English translation, *Literature and Revolution*, trans. Jean Steinberg, Pall Mall, London, appeared much later, in 1969.
9. J.P. Stern, *On Realism*, Routledge & Kegan Paul, London, 1973, pp. 52–4, 148–50.
10. T. Eagleton, *Marxism and Literary Criticism*, Methuen, London, 1976, pp. 37–8.

relationship to Soviet orthodoxy is infinitely more complex than the cliché of misguided subservience allows, and whose voice has frequently been drowned amidst the cacophany of hostile voices clamouring for his excommunication from the society of the Just. As Geoffrey Hosking puts it in his *Beyond Socialist Realism* (1980): 'The official doctrine was essentially non-committal, a more or less empty shell whose content was to be provided by the writers themselves. Socialist Realism may have been imposed by politicians, but it was *created* by writers'.[11] In this light, the cultural context in which we place major twentieth-century authors such as Alexander Solzhenitsyn and Bertolt Brecht, who are taken by Stern and Eagleton respectively as exemplars of a realism which 'owes nothing' to socialist realism or is 'a valuable antidote to it',[12] also needs fresh scrutiny.

A solid basis for a differentiated assessment of individual authors as socialist realists already exists in the critical writings of Central European Marxists such as Georg Lukács, Ernst Fischer and Brecht himself, who maintained a critical distance from Soviet orthodoxy and sought to prevent the exclusive appropriation of the term socialist realism (whether by its proponents or its sworn enemies) to describe the literary products of Stalinist conformism. However incomplete, and chronologically confusing, the available translations of their criticism into English may be,[13] the reader of Lukács's *Wider den mißverstandenen Realismus* (*The Meaning of Contemporary Realism*) (1958) and *Solzhenitsyn* (1970), or of Fischer's *Von der Notwendigkeit der Kunst* (*The Necessity of Art*) (1957), is presented with substantial arguments for the profound interrelationship of critical and socialist realism as well as for their common interest in exposing the Stalin era to unrelenting scrutiny. He/she also becomes aware of the unresolved nature of the debate on the implications of socialist realism for artistic form, between the poles of the Lukács canon and the Brechtian insistence on 'breadth and diversity', although that is an issue of secondary importance here. As Fischer puts it: 'Against the definition of socialist realism as a method or style, the question immediately comes to mind: whose style, whose method? Gorky's or Brecht's? Mayakovsky's or Eluard's? Makarenko's or Aragon's? Sholokhov's or O'Casey's? The methods of these writers are as different as they can be; but a fundamental [socialist] attitude is

11. Hosking, *Beyond Socialist Realism*, p. 6 (emphasis in the original).
12. Stern, *On Realism*, p. 150; Eagleton, *Marxism and Literary Criticism*, p. 72.
13. The highly selective volumes of Lukács's essays published by the Merlin Press are a case in point, and there is still no substantial edition in English of Brecht's essays on realism.

common to them all'.[14]

The experience of Marxist writers in France is also valuable in highlighting both the progressive emergence of a differentiated view of socialist realism, and the growing realisation of the interconnections to be made between critical realism and socialist realism. The ideological and cultural transformation of a French Marxist critic such as Roger Garaudy, evolving from the blinkered hostility of *Une littérature de fossoyeurs* (*Literature of the Graveyard*) (1948) to the open-minded eclecticism of *D'un réalisme sans rivages* ('A Realism without Banks') (1963), is as much a delayed-action response to the criticisms levelled by Sartre in the 1940s,[15] and by Barthes in the 1950s,[16] against a mechanistic form of socialist realism, as it is a product of a receding cold war socio-political climate. Equally, Lucien Goldmann's pioneering study, *Pour une sociologie du roman* (*Towards a Sociology of the Novel*) (1964), and Pierre Macherey's *Pour une théorie de la production littéraire* (*A Theory of Literary Production*) (1966) have, from differing Marxist perspectives, highlighted the socialist dimension of texts in the critical realist tradition.

The substance of these arguments has not, of course, entirely escaped critical notice in the English-speaking world. Raymond Williams's essay 'Realism and the Contemporary Novel' points to the concept of typicality as a factor linking socialist realism with the mainstream of the realist tradition, and as worthy of unprejudiced re-examination at a time of crisis for realism in the West.[17] Frederic Jameson, in his *Marxism and Form* (1974), argues the case for the essential continuity in Lukács's development as a theoretician of realism (including his 'Stalinist' phase), and for the strength of his 'differentiating and profoundly comparative thought mode'.[18] More recently, Keith Bullivant, in his study of the West German novel, *Realism Today* (1987), has pointed to the central role which the concept of realism evolved by Brecht (and subsequently refined in the German Democratic Republic by Christa Wolf), with its epistemological and Utopian dimensions and its underlying socialist convictions, was to play in the unexpected emergence in the 1970s of a rich vein of realist writing in the Federal Republic.[19]

14. E. Fischer, *The Necessity of Art: A Marxist Approach*, trans. Anna Bostock, Penguin, Harmondsworth, 1964, p. 110.
15. J.-P. Sartre, *Situations II: Qu'est-ce que la littérature?*, Gallimard, Paris, 1948, pp. 277–89.
16. R. Barthes, *Le Degré zéro de l'écriture*, Seuil, Paris, 1953, pp. 49–53.
17. In R. Williams, *The Long Revolution*, Penguin, Harmondsworth, 1965, pp. 300–16.
18. Princeton U.P., Princeton, NJ, 1971, pp. 160–205 (p. 209).
19. Berg, Leamington Spa and New York, 1987, esp. pp. 54–6.

Our map of contemporary European culture, grotesquely distorted for some forty years following the postwar ideological division of the continent, is beginning to take on new contours. The revitalised socialist realism projected by Robert Weimann, the GDR's leading cultural critic, as an integral part of a many-sided creative endeavour to communicate the starkness of the threats to mankind's future in the 1980s, is completely shorn of the doctrinaire, parochial features which have hitherto made it recognisably 'East European'.[20] The Czech exile author, Milan Kundera, has drawn fresh attention to the Central European identity shared by today's Czechs, Hungarians and Poles as the heirs to the early twentieth-century dynamism which produced the unique literary constellation of Hašek, Kafka, Musil and Broch alongside a wealth of other cultural innovations. Although his identification of this cultural identity as 'Western' and his unwillingness to define it in political terms runs counter to the radical distinctiveness which other contemporary writers in Central European states would attribute to it,[21] the publicity given to Kundera's article may help to rekindle the awareness of distinctive national traditions created by authors such as A. Alvarez in the 1960s.[22] Furthermore, there is, as has already been mentioned, the new Soviet policy of *glasnost'*, which is capable of persuading even the most sceptical of commentators to reconsider their deeply rooted assumptions about where the frontiers of socialist realism need to be drawn.

The aim of this volume is to contribute to this process of reorientation by taking stock of socialist realism since the 1930s from a variety of theoretical, nation-specific and textual perspectives, drawing on recent research into the 1930s and 1950s, the decades most affected by entrenched ideological preconceptions. Without seeking to establish any artificial or premature consensus, the authors have looked in an open-minded way at whatever evidence exists for the view of socialist realism as an evolving and creatively innovative force over the past half-century, and have presented their independent conclusions.

In Part I, the evolution of the theory of socialist realism beyond

20. R. Weimann, 'Realität und Realismus: Über Kunst und Theorie in dieser Zeit', *Sinn und Form*, no. 4, 1984, pp. 924–51.
21. M. Kundera, 'A Kidnapped West or Culture Bows Out', *Granta*, no. 11, 1984, pp. 93–118. Compare, for example Franz Fühmann's autobiographical elaborations of his Central European identity, *22 Tage oder die Hälfte des Lebens*, Hinstorff, Rostock, 1973 and *Vor Feuerschlünden: Erfahrung mit Trakls Gedicht*, Hinstorff, Rostock, 1982.
22. A. Alvarez, *Under Pressure — The Writer in Society: Eastern Europe and the USA*, Penguin, Harmondsworth, 1965.

the codification established at the 1934 Soviet Writers' Congress is exemplified through the analysis by Rodney Livingstone of Georg Lukács's writings on the subject. Livingstone's carefully differentiated study indicates why Lukács has enjoyed such a contradictory 'Janus-like reputation' in the eyes of commentators in both Eastern and Western Europe. When Lukács's conception of socialist realism is understood as the logical extension of his sensitive appreciation of nineteenth-century 'critical realist' fiction, it becomes clear that there is no inconsistency between his opposition to ideologically derived, schematic features of the Soviet model and his authoritarian inflexibility in the face of a Marxist modernist like Bertolt Brecht. Livingstone then underlines the dichotomy in Lukács's later writing: the fact that the modifications his thinking on socialist realism underwent in the 1950s (provoking the 'modernist debate') and again in the 1960s (in his essays on Solzhenitsyn) were accompanied by a disturbing ambivalence in his political critique of Stalinism, implying that there were still distinct limits to his tolerance of the autonomy of the committed socialist writer.

Broadening the perspective, David Forgacs contextualises Antonio Gramsci's writings on literature as bearing only an oblique relation to the main body of cultural debate on the Left in the early 1930s, while stressing their growing relevance to the major issues at stake. Centered initially on Gramsci's critical assessment of the 'cosmopolitan' and 'vanguardist' views expressed by Paul Nizan, Forgacs's analysis demonstrates how Gramsci's notion of cultural rationalisation — 'the organisation or acceleration of cultural tendencies for which the necessary cultural premises exist' — constitutes the basis of a challenging cultural policy which is inherently more complex and problematical than that expounded at the 1934 Soviet Writers' Congress, and which could be profitably reworked in the context of today's vastly more modern and technological society.

Our survey of national perspectives on socialist realism in Part II begins, appropriately, with Robert Porter's assessment of the Soviet experience, which identifies the problem created by the proliferation of definitions, both within the Soviet Union and in the Western world, of what socialist realism is, in the light of the literary evidence of the past fifty years. He also focuses attention on the Soviet endeavour to accommodate (retrospectively) the literary traditions of its Central European satellites, such as Czechoslovakia, within its definition of socialist realism. The evident elasticity of Soviet theoretical pronouncements between the 1934 Congress and the threshold of the Gorbachev era leads him to question whether there is anything to be gained in the English-speaking world by debating whether or not contemporary works of undisputed literary quality published in the Soviet Union should be classified as socialist realism, when they have so many features in common with the critical realism of their Western counterparts.

Dennis Tate, in contrast, argues the case for including the outstanding products of recent East German literature within the 'unofficial' definition of socialist realism formulated by Brecht during the German exile debate of the 1930s. Brecht's undogmatic insistence on 'breadth and diversity' of style and content has sustained writers in the GDR in their creative endeavours since the 1960s and compelled cultural politicians there to depart significantly from Soviet stereotypes in order to preserve their own credibility. This can consequently be viewed as providing the central element of continuity in East German literature, building on the sense of a distinctive German cultural heritage which Brecht shared with Lukács, against which the brief periods when the Soviet stereotype was rigidly imposed can be exposed as culturally sterile interludes.

The growing recognition that the literatures of the two German states have much more in common than the cliché of the 'two German literatures' would suggest has led Axel Goodbody to reassess West German realism in the light of the radical cultural tradition it shares with its East German neighbour. Even though the cold war and the political division of Germany effectively severed links between authors in the two states until the 1970s, a process of convergence has been evident since a much earlier stage in their cultural development. A fresh examination of the novels of Heinrich Böll, the 'workers' literature' of the Gruppe 61 and the Werkkreis movement, and the 'political realism' of the 1970s shows that the pursuit of Utopian socialist goals, in conjunction with the integration of documentary and autobiographical elements into traditional structures of the realist novel, constitutes a significant unifying factor in postwar German literature.

John Flower focuses attention on the particular problems encountered by writers in a country where a socialist revolution has yet to be achieved, by tracing the historical development of socialist realism in France during two relatively self-contained periods. The first is the 1930s; the second extends for about twenty years from the late 1940s. Ostensibly centered on the way in which Soviet socialist realist orthodoxy was introduced into a specifically French sociopolitical context, Flower's analysis also highlights a movement in the late 1960s towards a less mechanistic conception of the links between ideology and form, and alludes at the same time to the hidden textual complexity of socialist realism, a complexity invariably simplified by the 'authoritative' critical statement.

In Part III, in the first of two contributions devoted to textual analysis, Robin Warner exposes the deeper structural levels at which ideological elements are embedded in Pablo Neruda's *España en el corazón* ('Spain at Heart') (1936–7). Particular attention is paid to the poet's consciousness of his role as propagandist in the context of the socialist realism debate of the 1930s, and an analogy is drawn between Neruda's approach to committed poetry and the concept of 'revolutionary romanticism' as defined by Bukharin in 1934 in its relevance to poets. However, Warner also shows how the Communist concern to consolidate anti-Fascist alliances during the Spanish Civil War encouraged an active tolerance of certain liberal-democratic values, including the notional creative autonomy of the artist, with the result that the poetic persona of *España en el corazón* is located at the intersection of private and collective viewpoints.

Texts that are designated as 'socialist realist' are rarely assessed on their individual merit, but are more generally perceived in Western circles through the distorting lens of ideological preconception. Michael Scriven's detailed analysis of the textual specificity of Paul Nizan's socialist realist novel *Le cheval de Troie* (*Trojan Horse*) (1935) in which the dynamics of the narrative are revealed as a struggle between two competing discourses, offers a corrective to the gross simplifications and misreadings that can arise from an unwillingness to relinquish convenient critical stereotypes and labels.

Part IV is composed entirely of a contribution which has needed constant updating to keep pace with recent developments. David Gillespie takes stock of the process of *glasnost'* so far, as the ultimate test of whether Soviet theoreticians of socialist realism still have any significant role to play within a dynamically developing cultural movement. The sobering thought that today's Soviet literature is still being mobilised by the political leadership for its own, primarily economic, objectives, even though these objectives may now command widespread public support, runs through a meticulous account of the changes evident in cultural institutions and the publishing media, the easing of the log-jam of unpublished works, the rehabilitation of major figures like Gumilyov, Pasternak and Nabokov, and the progress made in the politically crucial task of unearthing more of the truth about the Stalin era. Gillespie's concluding list of living authors fundamentally critical of the status quo and still awaiting their opportunity to enter into a literary dialogue with a Soviet readership, is a reminder, amidst so many encouraging developments, of how far *glasnost'* still has to go.

It is all too easy to dismiss socialist realism not only as the crude and unmediated interference of politics in the sphere of culture, but also as an anachronism in the contemporary context, the vestige of a dying, if not dead, cultural heritage. Yet the range of subject-matter and critical approach exemplified in these essays demonstrates, on the contrary, that socialist realism remains a potentially dynamic cultural force today. From the sectarianism of the 1930s to the *glasnost'* of the 1980s, from the classicism of Lukács and the oblique originality of Gramsci to the radical challenge of Brecht, from the centrality of the Soviet experience to the intriguingly peripheral developments in Italy and Spain, from the prescriptive dogmatism of Zhdanov to the textual subversiveness of Nizan, this book is a testimony to the continuing vitality of the socialist realism debate.

PART I

Theorists

—1—

Georg Lukács and Socialist Realism

RODNEY LIVINGSTONE

Lukács's writings on socialist realism form a relatively small part of his critical *oeuvre*. In only two periods of his life did he confront in a direct way the issues it raised. The first was in Moscow in 1936–7, when socialist realism was in the process of establishing itself and Lukács was busy formulating his ideas on realism in general. The second phase was the period 1949–56 in Hungary at the time of the 'revisionist debate'. His thinking on socialist realism is an aspect of his larger concern with literary realism in general and with the phenomenon of Stalinism. His writings on the subject share in the ambiguities of his attitudes on both these topics and this is reflected in the Janus-like reputation which he enjoys. In the West Isaac Deutscher's judgement sums up a widely held view: 'Despite the legend that presents him as the hero of intellectual resistance to Stalinism and despite his brushes with the Rákosi regime in Hungary, he may be described as the only Stalinist literary critic of high stature'.[1] In Eastern Europe his ideas have dominated official thinking on literature at various times and have also inspired oppositional groups, like the reformist movement under Wolfgang Harich in the GDR in the 1950s. But he has also been reviled as a traitor to the working class. Thus Hans Kaufmann maintained that far from being the 'representative of literary Zhdanovism' (as Claude Prévost claimed), Lukács, in his *Wider den mißverstandenen Realismus* (*The Meaning of Contemporary Realism*) (1958) 'revealed with the greatest clarity his isolation from the working class'.[2]

1. I. Deutscher, 'Georg Lukács and "Critical Realism"', *The Listener*, 3 Nov. 1966. Deutscher qualifies this by pointing to Lukács's identification with the moderate and rightist elements of Stalinism and in particular with the Popular Front.
2. In his review of *Wider den mißverstandenen Realismus*, 'Lukács' Konzeption eines "dritten Weges"', in H. Koch (ed.), *Georg Lukács und der Revisionismus*, Dietz, Berlin, 1966, pp. 332–39. (*Wider den mißverstandenen Realismus* was republished under the title 'Die Gegenwartsbedeutung des kritischen Realismus' in G. Lukács, *Probleme des Realismus I (Essays über Realismus)*, *Werke*, vol. 4, Luchterhand, Neuwied, 1971, pp. 457–603.) All quotations from German sources in this essay are my own translations, unless otherwise indicated.

Lukács's view of socialist realism is essentially an extension of his definition of realism. The crucial distinction he makes is between realism and naturalism. This in turn rests ultimately on Hegel's distinction between pictorial and conceptual representation.[3] In this distinction only the pictorial mode is artistic. Art which is conceptual in nature — and this includes naturalism, as well as the methods of montage, reportage and documentary — inevitably leads to a loss of authorial perspective and ends up in a 'fetishism of the facts'. The essence of this fetishism is that the writer simply reproduces the empirically given surface manifestations of reality, but fails to reveal the 'overall process' with its real and essential driving forces. Above all, the naturalist renounces the attempt to depict social and historical causality, contenting himself with *how* things are, not *why*. The revelation of this overall process is the preserve of realism. Realism uses the pictorial mode. It concentrates on the concrete fates of individuals in their various interactions. However, these individuals go beyond individuality and become types representative of their class and society at a particular historical conjuncture. The idea of the type is crucial to Lukács's understanding and it differs from the Soviet conception in that 'the individual must contain class features as individual ones'.[4] They must not simply derive from a theoretical concept which they then illustrate. Lukács uses this distinction normatively. The realist writer experiences life and gives it shape so that the reader experiences it as life. The naturalist writer does not experience; he observes and then describes what he sees. Whereas the realist writer participates actively in life (Lukács has Goethe and Stendhal in mind), naturalist writers like Flaubert and Zola are the victims of the defeats of the bourgeoisie in 1848 and the increasing division of labour which turns the writer into a specialist. A further drawback of naturalism is its subjectivism, which derives directly from its partial view of reality. Realism can claim to be objective because of its totalising view.[5]

'Erzählen oder Beschreiben?'

These ideas receive their most cogent formulation in the essay 'Erzählen oder Beschreiben?' ('Narrate or Describe?') which ap-

3. See E. Mozejko, *Der sozialistische Realismus*, Bouvier, Bonn, 1977, pp. 183–203.
4. See G. Lukács, 'Reportage or Portrayal?', in idem, *Essays on Realism*, trans. D. Fernbach, Lawrence & Wishart, London, 1980, p. 50.
5. For more detailed accounts of Lukács's view of realism see G.H.R. Parkinson, *Georg Lukács*, Routledge & Kegan Paul, London, 1977.

peared in 1936.[6] In making this distinction between narration and description Lukács embraced the nineteenth-century bourgeois novel, which he opposed polemically to the decadent art of 'late capitalism'. It is astonishing, therefore, to see that in the final section of this essay he simply maps the same dualism on to Soviet writing. He maintains that whereas Soviet society is progressive, Soviet art has not yet overcome the vestiges of the tradition of a decadent bourgeoisie, which continue to act as a brake on its development. These vestiges are to be seen in socialist realism, above all in the survival of observation and description, as opposed to experience and narration. Instead of realist narration, they provide 'monographs of a kolkhoz or a factory. Human beings are mainly no more than accessories, the illustrative material attached to the connections between things'. Thus socialist realism shares with other modernist trends a fetishistic 'domination of men by things' (p. 235). In this context Lukács refers with disapproval to an unnamed Soviet writer (in reality Tret'yakov) who had conceived the idea of a 'biography of things', an idea that might well have appealed to Walter Benjamin, but which held no charm for Lukács.

Lukács describes the plot of a typical socialist realist novel as follows: 'In a factory saboteurs are at work. There is fearful chaos. Finally, the Party cell or the GPU discovers the source of the sabotage and production booms, etc' (p. 236). He objects not to the content of such works but to their treatment. Too many authors confuse the theme with the plot, or rather plot is replaced by the exhaustive description of everything that has a bearing on the theme. This distinction is in essence a repetition of the one between realism and naturalism, for such novels really do no more than illustrate themes; characters and events have no organic interconnections, no internal logic of their own. As an example he cites Gladkov's *Energiya* ('Energy') (1928–38) in which one of the characters writes a detailed diary which has no consequences at the level of plot and so remains a mere 'document'.

A further problem concerns the narrator. Anachronistically, but doggedly, Lukács clings to the omniscient narrator of nineteenth-century fiction. He deplores the modernist practice of describing events from the point of view of the participant, a 'bewildered

6. The German original, 'Erzählen oder Beschreiben?' is available in G. Lukács, *Probleme des Realismus I*, pp. 197–242. The translation by Arthur Kahn, 'Narrate or Describe?', in G. Lukács, *Writer and Critic*, Merlin, London, 1978, pp. 110–48, entirely omits the part of this essay devoted to socialist realism (Section VII). Subsequent quotations are therefore my translations from the German, with page references included in my text.

observer'. For in such cases there is no internal link between the characters. In the novels of modernism man does not manifest himself as the master of things, but 'as their audience, as the human components of a monumentalising still-life'. Thus man becomes submerged beneath things at the very moment when his mastery of them is asserted by socialism. What such novels lack is 'the human energy in struggle with the external world which can only find expression in a struggle which is really given shape' ['gestaltet'] (p. 240).

He concludes with the assertion that just as naturalism 'dimished the reality of capitalism', so too its vestiges in Soviet art 'diminished the greatest revolutionary process in human history' (p. 240). The writers themselves sense this diminution of both art and reality and respond to it with an act of overcompensation. Following an idea of Franz Mehring's, he maintains that they attempt to make up for their feeble efforts by compounding naturalism with symbolism. Symbolism is the dialectical consequence of naturalism. Here too he cites an incident from Gladkov's *Energiya*. Someone says: '"Drive the train on to a new track." Yes, thought Miron, gazing into the blue dawn sky, yes, on to a new track . . . Life is constantly breaking fresh ground!' (p. 241). In Lukács's eyes revolutionary romanticism involves a similar act of overcompensation for the sterility of socialist-realist writing.

Whilst, on the one hand, Lukács identifies much socialist realism with naturalism, the other side of the story is that even where he views it positively, he does not look at it in its own terms or accept that it represents a revolutionary break with the past. Instead he theorises it in terms of classical or critical realism. Moreover, good socialist realism largely conforms to the criteria laid down for classical realism. Most of the writers singled out for praise — Gorky, Makarenko, Fadeyev, Sholokhov and Platonov — either antedate socialist realism proper or are marginal to it, or even, as in the case of Solzhenitsyn, may be construed as a version of *anti*-socialist realism. In discussing them he deploys the standard concepts, such as positive hero or partisanship, but reinterprets them so as to fit in with his views on classical realism. What seems to survive is the notion that the good socialist-realist writer is in all essentials similar to a traditional bourgeois realist except that he writes as a conscious socialist.

Maxim Gorky

These points emerge from a scrutiny of his essays on Gorky. Lukács emphasises his links with the heritage of classical realism, even describing him as its 'guarantor'. A further link is that he is acclaimed because he stands for the 'culture of life',[7] as opposed to the purely literary culture (to be found in a writer like Leonid Andreyev). Thus Lukács maintains his view of literature as a reflection of life in contrast to a literature which somehow just feeds on the writer's subjectivity. It is Gorky's *Volkstümlichkeit*, his links with the life of the people, that enable him to become a realist and so to escape the *fin-de-siècle* dichotomy of the bourgeois ivory tower versus a narrow practicism or agitprop literature. He is celebrated as the first master of socialist realism because 'he shows as an artist how the contradictions of bourgeois art can be overcome in reality, in artistic praxis'.[8] In other words, he succeeds because he is both a realist and a socialist. A further link with tradition is the suggestion that, like Balzac, he has created a *comédie humaine*, in his case it is the comedy of pre-revolutionary Russia.

Moreover, just as Balzac had shown the present as historical, Gorky becomes the chronicler of class upheavals in Russia because he shows how 'a man becomes the man of a particular class'.[9] That is to say, class is not the Fate which it was under capitalism. Thus at a time when bourgeois realism is breaking down because of the increasing reifications of social processes under capitalism, Lukács sees Gorky as the true successor to the bourgeois tradition. Whereas bourgeois writers succumb to these reifications in the various brands of naturalism or modernism, Gorky is able to create a new imaginative totality. This achievement has its formal aspect. Although realism is not really a style or technique for Lukács, in Gorky's hands it generates new formal features. His starting-point is the brutal atomism of Russian life which Gorky called 'zoological individualism'. Gorky dissects this social inertia into an 'unbroken sequence of movements, minute efforts, desperate explosions, elations and depressions'.[10] This is reproduced by means of small dramatic moments full of an inner dynamic, both tragic and comic, and creates in his novels a long chain of small, internally dramatic

7. 'Der Befreier', in idem., *Probleme des Realismus II (Probleme des russischen Realismus)*, *Werke*, vol. 5, Luchterhand, Neuwied, 1964, pp. 287–97 (p. 288).
8. Ibid., p. 296.
9. "Die menschliche Komödie des vorrevolutionären Rußland', ibid., pp. 298–336 (p. 299).
10. Ibid., p. 326.

scenes. Lukács subsequently discerns the same formal innovation in Sholokhov's *And Quiet Flows the Don* (1929). He contrasts both with the epic breadth of Tolstoy. In using this 'facet' technique Gorky shows us how human beings become fragmented. It is a technique appropriate to the formative phase of socialist realism. *Mother* (1906) is seen as a turning-point. It shows the liberating effect of proletarian revolution, not just as a future perspective, but as a present reality. It is this that creates the new totalisation, and the achievement Gorky is credited with is that 'he is the only writer of his age who is able to depict the fetishised world of capitalism in a wholly unfetishised way'.[11]

The Positive Hero

Lukács also notes that a further effect of *Mother* is that it makes possible the depiction of the positive hero. This is a concept he regards with as much suspicion as revolutionary optimism and happy endings. He accepts it in a limited way, but only if it grows organically from the narrative. The problem of the positive hero is obvious: how to give him life.[12] In the Russian context this problem was exacerbated by the entire tradition, as Andrey Sinyavsky has pointed out.[13] According to Sinyavsky the great literary tradition had been critical. In socialist realism it was expected to be affirmative. The quintessential Russian hero was, arguably, Oblomov, the superfluous man. In socialist realism the superfluous men became the villains, while the heroes joined the vanguard. Lukács, who really wants literature to be critical, expresses a preference for the middle-of-the-road heroes of the bourgeois novel, noting that characters who were fully developed tended to occupy secondary roles. With the concept of a positive hero the problem was to move these fully developed characters on to centre-stage, to create positive heroes out of 'conscious Communists'.

One solution embraced by Lukács is to suggest that in socialist realism the novel will tend towards epic. In epic, heroes like Achilles do not develop, yet they still retain our interest. In his discussion of Sholokhov, Lukács struggles to present the positive characters as the

11. Ibid., p. 328. The importance both of this facet technique and of *Mother* as a turning-point was first pointed out by Parkinson in his *Georg Lukács* (see pp. 114–16).
12. See E. Mozejko, *Der sozialistische Realismus*.
13. Abram Tertz [Andrey Sinyavsky], *Der Prozeß beginnt*, Fischer, Frankfurt, 1966, p. 137.

heroes, even while he is evidently more absorbed by the negative characters, Gregor and Aksinia. In the upshot Lukács's conception of the positive hero amounts to its subversion. It includes Ivan Denisovich and Matryona, characters in Solzhenitsyn's works who are not 'positive' at all in the sense implied by official doctrine. His view here is connected with the fact that he sees the novel essentially as the reflection of the forces whose conflicts drive the motor of history. Since these conflicts are mirrored in the characters the latter will inevitably tend towards the tragic.

This emerges very clearly from his dicussion of Platonov's *Bessmertiye* ('Immortality') (1936). Platonov, a deeply original writer, most of whose life was spent under a cloud of official disapproval, had become more or less unpublishable after Averbakh's critique of *Usomnivshiysya Makar* ('Makar the Doubtful') following its appearance in 1929. Lukács courageously caused two of his stories to be published in *Literaturny Kritik* in 1937, accompanying them with an anonymous article denouncing the cult of optimism and the political determination of artistic value.

In *Bessmertiye* there are two points of interest. The story concerns a railway worker, Levin, who lives for the railway, but his attitude towards his work has none of the sterility which characterises the specialist in capitalist industry, where the specialist is the product of the division of labour. In socialism technology is inseparable from man, according to Lukács. Man controls the technology instead of being controlled by it. Levin sees his task as the education of his fellow-workers, who are peasants or semi-peasants, teaching them how to be good railway workers. His method of education is not to impose discipline, but to follow up what he regards as disruptive influences in their personal lives. In other words, he is not just concerned to see that people do their work well, he also strives to ensure the satisfaction of private needs which may be affecting their work adversely. Lukács stresses the educational aspect of the story, the importance of the role of a man like Levin in transforming the lives of others.

However, what interests Lukács most is that Levin is not depicted as an ideal figure, a positive hero. He is characterised by a certain asceticism. Over-modestly, he regards himself as a transitional figure to be superseded by history. This asceticism is criticised in the story. It is suggested that Levin is right to believe that socialism has not yet brought about the full development of personality, but he is mistaken in his view of himself as someone to be sacrificed to the society of the future, a mere 'fertiliser of history'. Hence Lukács praises Platonov for showing the contradictions inevitable in the hero at this stage of social development and for insisting that even the educator has to be educated. It is clear that in his eyes the contradictions in human character are more important than the ideological imperative to present 'positive' heroes.

Some twenty years later, in *Wider den mißverstandenen Realismus*, Lukács repeats and extends his critique of the positive hero, again referring to Platonov. Castigating the Stalinist dogma that Communism is imminent he deplores the tendency to depict exceptional actions and people as typical. He refers to an unnamed work in which 'an otherwise interesting novel is marred by a scene in which a woman on a collective farm rejected the prize of a lamb she had herself brought up because communal property is dearer to her than private property'.[14] In another story 'a group of Komsomols set out to win a harvest competition; they succeed in this by giving up their lunch-hour. Only the strict orders of the supervisor can make them take some food and have a proper rest. The supervisor regards their zeal as an indication of the imminence of communism'.[15] Lukács's objection to such scenes is not that they are untrue, but that they are untypical. Exceptional cases are presented as the norm. 'This is no more than wishful thinking.'[16] The typical situation in the USSR is that men have to be educated for Communism. In this context he refers to Platonov's critique of the asceticism and self-sacrifice which schematists hold up as true Communism. Under Stalin, he remarks, asceticism 'was imposed on the population by bureaucrats who were not inclined to adhere to it themselves'.[17]

We may add that Lukács's doubts about the positive hero and his attempt to divert the novel into epic are reinforced by his reluctance to accept that the Soviet Union is a non-antagonistic society. His view is rather that it is premature to dismiss the reality of conflict in Soviet society and that for individuals there will always be 'insoluble conflicts ['ausweglose Lagen']'.[18] He infers from this that critical (i.e. bourgeois) realism will have a relative justification in the USSR for a long time to come and will gradually merge with socialist realism.

The Revisionist Debate

In 1945 Lukács returned from Moscow to Budapest. In theory at

14. Lukács, *The Meaning of Contemporary Realism*, trans. J. and N. Mander, Merlin, London, 1963, p. 129.
15. Ibid., pp. 129–30.
16. Ibid., p. 130.
17. Ibid., p. 132.
18. Idem, *Werke*, vol. 4, p. 585.

least, the People's Democracies were set up originally, as their name suggests, on the basis of a continuation of Popular Front policies, in other words, a collaboration between the Communists and progressive elements of the Left. Lukács was more or less predestined to become a major spokesman for this position on cultural matters, for he had consistently advocated such an alliance ever since the Blum Theses of 1929. In literature this implied the approval of the progressive bourgeois humanist tradition. That in turn meant the outright rejection of the socially critical realism of the 1920s and, of course, of modernism. The task of such a revival of the literary heritage, therefore, was not to shock the reader, but to educate him. For whereas modernism alerts the reader to what is being done in art and to the way in which art functions, realism renders form invisible . It is thus ideally suited to manipulation. In its Lukácsian form the manipulative potential of realism is overlooked and the emphasis is placed on education. For example, in his essay on Fadeyev's *Razgrom* (*The Nineteen*) (1927), the Leninist hero is presented as an ethical model, while other personality types are rejected. However, with the restatement and reinforcement of Zhdanovism in 1946, largely as a response to the cold war and the perceived need to achieve a greater degree of cultural uniformity and discipline, Lukács's realist canon was felt to be too broad and permissive. In consequence he was subjected to a series of fierce attacks in the so-called 'revisionist debate' of 1949–52. These attacks focused on the issue of partisanship.

Lukács's critics directed their fire at the doctrine of the 'triumph of realism' which they saw as central to his thought. According to this idea the realism of a work prevails despite the intentions or attitudes of the author. Balzac's works, for example were models of realism despite Balzac's own legitimist attitudes. Lukács had used this idea, which derived from Engels's letter to Miss Harkness, first published in *Die Linkskurve* (the journal of the BPRS, the German League of Proletarian-Revolutionary Writers) in 1932, as a weapon in his attack on naturalism and modernism. Now, his main critic, Joseph Revai, a former pupil, focused on 'Erzählen oder Beschreiben?'. According to Revai, Lukács in the 1930s criticised both Western decadence and Soviet literature. Soviet critics did likewise whilst always assuming the superiority of socialist realism over bourgeois literature, an assumption which Lukács signally failed to share. 'At the very moment when the Party intensified the struggle against capitalism and the turning-point had come, at that very moment — in Spring 1949 — Lukács turned to the right and began to fight not for socialist realism, but essentially against it.' In Revai's opinion, the Soviet writer was not a 'neutral observer, but a fighter',[19] and he criticised Lukács's view of partisanship because it implied independence from the Party. Another critic, Alexander Abusch, saw Lukács as the theoretician of the Popular Front. He accused him of making absolute the standards of bourgeois realist literature, though 'fortunately', he added (this was after the crushing of the Hungarian uprising in 1956), 'the immortal and glorious rescue action of the Soviet Army has provided him with the opportunity for a profound self-criticism'.[20]

Perhaps the most carefully reasoned criticism was that of J. Elsberg:

> The adherents of this view are of the opinion that the truth of life and the laws of objective reality are as it were automatically precipitated in art, that is to say, by virtue of the nature of art and of artistic talent. It is this methodology which essentially characterises Lukács's works too. Lukács is of the opinion that reality, namely the age itself, dictates truth to the artist who obediently reproduces it in his works. The writer submits unconsciously to this dictation. . . . We cannot avoid the conclusion that the methods used by Georg Lukács have their ideological roots in *objectivism*. The objectivist, however, is the enemy of the partisanship which must be the guiding principle of Marxist-Leninist literary scholarship and criticism. Objectivism is the manifestation of revisionism.[21]

Lukács responded initially to this criticism by admitting that his knowledge of Soviet literature was not what it might be and that he lacked the experience to comment on it. Subsequently, however, he produced the series of essays on major and minor writers which are contained in *Der russische Realismus in der Weltliteratur* ('Russian Realism in World Literature') (3rd edn, 1952). Then in 1956 (after the Twentieth Congress but before the Hungarian uprising) he wrote *Wider den mißverstandenen Realismus* which, although chiefly an attack on Western modernism, devoted its final section to a comparison of socialist realism with critical realism, that is, the best of progressive bourgeois realism in the twentieth century. In these and other essays Lukács responds to the charge of objectivism by restating his views on partisanship. His original position had been set out in 1932 in '"Tendenz" oder Parteilichkeit?' ('"Tendency" or Parti-

---

19. J. Revai, 'Die Lukács-Diskussion des Jahres 1949', in Koch (ed.), *Georg Lukács und der Revisionismus*, pp. 13, 18.

20. Quoted in F. Benseler, *Georg Lukács: Die Moskauer Schriften*, Sendler, Frankfurt, 1981, p. 152.

21. See H.T. Lehmann (ed.), *Beiträge zu einer materialistischen Theorie der literarischen Produktion*, Ullstein, Frankfurt, Berlin and Vienna, 1977, p. 558.

sanship?'), where he gave his approval to a partisanship which, like the positive hero, emerged organically from the narrative. He explicitly rejects 'tendencies tacked on literary works from outside',[22] and goes on to say: 'The fact that the Stalin-Zhdanov theory later called precisely that sort of tendentiousness partisanship, that it turned an article written by Lenin in 1905 into the Ten Commandments of this "partisanship", did nothing to prevent me, even subsequently, from defending the right position'.[23] In short, Lukács rejected the accusations brought against him and even went further. In the essay on Virta he exhumes a distinction first made by Marx in which the objectivity of Shakespeare is preferred to the subjectivity of Schiller. Since he accused Stalin of subjectivity, his defence of this notion of partisanship became a coded attack on Stalinism.

In *Wider den mißverstandenen Realismus* Lukács replaces the term with 'perspective'. The essential distinction between critical (bourgeois) realism and socialist realism is one of perspective. In critical realism the writer writes with false consciousness; his political principles are one thing, his grasp of reality another. The 'triumph of realism' ensures that his work reflects reality despite his explicit views and, as it were, behind his own back. In socialist realism the writer possesses true consciousness; his perspective is the 'struggle for socialism'. Lukács is anxious to emphasise that the possession of a socialist perspective does not confer on the writer an automatic superiority. Socialist realism, he insists, is a possibility rather than an actuality. The 'study of Marxism' and 'even Party membership' are not in themselves sufficient. 'It is no easier to translate true socialist consciousness of reality into art than bourgeois false consciousness.'[24] This makes it clear that in Lukác's view the purchase on reality and the need to reflect reality outweigh any ideological allegiance. What he expects from art is 'above all the consciousness of the totality of society in its movement and including its direction and its various stages'. Faced with a leadership which was forcing the pace and which insisted on the superiority of the Communist point of view, Lukács called for a constant confrontation with reality, and an awareness of the real social process. To that extent the reproaches of objectivism levelled against him were understandable, though he would have rejected the suggestion that his position was un-Marxist. Lukács always insists on the primacy of reality over

22. Lukács, preface to *Müvészet és társadalom* ('Art and Society') Magvető, Budapest, 1968. Published in English in *New Hungarian Quarterly*, vol. XIII, no. 47 (Autumn 1972), pp. 44–57. I quote from this English translation.
23. Ibid., p. 49.
24. Idem, *The Meaning of Contemporary Realism*, pp. 96–7.

ideology, of objectivity over subjectivity, even where subjectivity is Marxist. Hence even though socialist realism does away with the conflict between reality and consciousness and even though socialist realism has true consciousness, the problem does not seem to disappear entirely. As opposed to the schematism of Stalinism Lukács insists that conflicts between consciousness, ideology and reality must be resolved in favour of reality — for literature is primarily a matter of knowledge, not propaganda. In this respect Lukács is on the same side as Marxists like Brecht. Where he differs from Brecht and other Marxist modernists is in his insistence that literature should reflect reality in the sense which limited the idea of realism to its nineteenth-century version. It is this that places him in the orthodox camp.

Stalinism

Whereas the essays written between 1949 and 1952 appear to be designed to make up for his failure to praise Soviet literature, Lukács himself evidently conceived them as restatements of his earlier views and, by implication, as coded ripostes to his critics. His own objections to official socialist realism and to Stalinism were made increasingly explicit as time went on. A comparison between the editions of his essays on Russian realism makes this clear. In 1952 *Der russische Realismus in der Weltliteratur* contained an enthusiastic essay on Kazakevich's *Vesna na Odere* ('Spring on the Oder') (1949) a patriotic account of the Battle for Berlin which won a Stalin prize. Lukács dropped this, however, in Volume 5 of the *Werke* (*Probleme des Realismus II*) (1964) on the grounds that it was a 'literary failure'. It was replaced by the essays on Platonov and on Solzhenitsyn's *One Day in the Life of Ivan Denisovich* (1962). Evidently the later edition appears much less conformist than the first. However, Lukács insists, as usual, on the essential continuity of his views and backs this up in the 1964 Preface with references to his 'tactical retreat' in the 1952 edition. Similarly, he comments on the apparent newness of his polemic against 'revolutionary romanticism' in *Wider den mißverstandenen Realismus* (1958), pointing out that his views were substantially identical with the earlier ones, but that there was no longer any need to express them in 'Aesopian language'. Even if Lukács exaggerates his earlier nonconformity there is substantial evidence to suggest a strong element of continuity.[25] It is possible therefore to

25. In his book on Lukács, *From Romanticism to Bolshevism*, New Left Books, London,

summarise his view of Stalinism in fairly general terms, ignoring the question of historical development. Broadly speaking, Lukács supported Stalinism through the 1930s and 1940s because of the priority of the fight against Nazism. However, he rejected the cult of personality, which he saw as the cause of the growth of bureaucracy, the treason trials and the demerits of socialist realism.[26]

His objections to Stalinism focused on its method, by which he meant its exclusion of mediations. What this meant was that theoretical propositions were applied absolutely, without regard for actual circumstances. The consequence was a reversal of the relations between science and political decisions. Whereas in Marxism proper science provides the material for agitation, under Stalinism the needs of agitation determine what science should say. Hence he accused Stalinism of subjectivism. Over and above its massive political drawbacks this subjectivism also had serious repercussions in literature. 'The truth about Socialist Realism is that its content and form were seriously distorted during the Stalinist period.'[27] Stalin's subjectivism creates a variety of naturalism. In naturalism the absence of mediations is the product of the inability to rise above the merely factual nature of individual experience. In Stalinism the particular case is a mere illustration of an abstract truth. But both are variants of the same fallacy. Likewise, just as symbolism was the bad conscience of naturalism, so revolutionary romanticism was the bad conscience of socialist realism.

Lukács's most outspoken denunciations of Stalinism are to be found in his two essays on Solzhenitsyn. In *One Day in the Life of Ivan Denisovich*, Lukács writes, it appears at first as though the camp is not placed in any social or historical context and as if Ivan Denisovich's struggle is with nature. In reality, however, he is in conflict with society. What Solzhenitsyn succeeds in doing is 'to take an uneventful day in a camp and erect it into the symbol of a past which has not yet been overcome and which has never been given literary shape'. His achievement is to present 'the concentration camp as the symbol of ordinary life under Stalin'.[28] These are strong words and for once Lukács is quite unambiguous.

Moreover, Lukács is quick to argue that Solzhenitsyn's approach is neither symbolist nor naturalist. Instead he sees Solzhenitsyn as

1979, Michel Löwy argues convincingly that Lukács stolidly maintained his position throughout the various changes of official Party policy.

26. For an account of Lukács's views on Stalinism see ibid. and Parkinson, *Georg Lukács*.

27. Lukács, *The Meaning of Contemporary Realism*, p. 133.

28. Idem, *Werke*, vol. 5, Luchterhand, Neuwied, 1964, p. 550.

'the first and most important precursor of a new creative epoch' of socialist realism.[29] He is careful to insist, however, that his works revert to the socialist realism of its first creative phase in the 1920s. Like Gorky and Sholokhov, Solzhenitsyn devises a new form to do justice to the new situation and the new content: their earlier facet technique is replaced by a form based on a uniform setting, a microcosm: the camp or the cancer ward. But most importantly, in his hands socialist realism retains its critical function. It is this, above all, which makes Solzhenitsyn sound in his account like a representative of critical realism, particularly since he seems to lack a socialist viewpoint. Lukács criticises Solzhenitsyn for what he calls his plebeian standpoint — the spontaneous protest against inhuman conditions, reminiscent of that of Platon Karataev in *War and Peace*: 'Solzhenitsyn rightly depicts the diversity of the ideological consequences of Stalinism. Nevertheless, objectively his whole critique confines itself in the last analysis to the damage done to the integrity of individual human beings'.[30] Solzhenitsyn achieves neither the standpoint of the old bourgeois comic genius (from Sterne to Raabe), nor the insight of socialism. It is for this reason that he treats Solzhenitsyn as a precursor rather than a new pinnacle of achievement.

The Limitations of Lukács's Critique of Stalinism

Lukács's criticism of Stalinism focuses on method. In other words, even though it does have evident political implications, its basis is philosophical. Hence it both resembles and forms the basis of his criticism of socialist realism as something comparable to and derived from naturalism. Although his utterances become increasingly outspoken, it is irritating that he hardly ever goes beyond what is politically acceptable at any given time. The Platonov essay was undoubtedly a courageous act, but the essays on Solzhenitsyn fall within the period of the 'thaw'. The criticisms expressed in *Wider den mißverstandenen Realismus* always base themselves on positions adopted in the Twentieth Party Congress. Whilst acknowledging the reality of his claims that his messages are often coded and whilst recognising the danger of overstepping the line, it is often difficult to discern the differences between his position and what was generally acceptable. This claim is borne out by a more detailed examination

29. Ibid., p. 552.
30. Idem, *Solzhenitsyn*, trans. W.D. Graf, Merlin, London, 1970, p. 86.

of two of his essays. This makes it clear that his approach implies a marked reluctance to scrutinise the specific social and historical pressures that brought Stalinism into being, with the consequence that although Stalinism is criticised in general terms, he does not care to examine particular aspects of it too closely.

Sholokhov's *Virgin Soil Upturned* (1935) depicts the forced collectivisation of agriculture of 1929–32. It faithfully records the pandemonium created in the countryside by Stalin's determination to eliminate the two million kulaks and collectivise the whole of the Russian peasantry.[31] The turning-point in the novel is the unexpected reversal of the policy as signalled by Stalin's edict 'Golovokruzheniye ot uspekhar' ('Dizziness with Success') of March 1930, in which he admitted that the programme had gone too far, but threw the blame on the minor officials and Party agents who had been entrusted with implementing the original policy and who were now accused of having shown an excess of zeal. Henceforth the collectivisation would proceed more slowly and would take the milder form of 'cooperatives' which would not deprive the peasants of every last chicken. Whilst the resulting confusion is vividly depicted in the novel, it is confined to the village of Grenachy Log. There, Stalin's representative, Davidov, makes the switch as quickly as Stalin himself, and like him, throws much of the blame on a subordinate. Davidov admits to minor mistakes, but no blame is attributed to Stalin. The confusion in the village is not extended to Sholokhov's depiction of the leadership. Historically, Stalin's edict took the Politburo and the Central Committee completely by surprise. They had not been consulted about it and protested at being made to appear the main culprits. Stalin was even forced to issue a statement making it clear that his edict represented not just his personal view, but that of the Central Committee as a whole. Sholokhov shows nothing of these disagreements among the leadership or of the larger political context. Lukács also ignores the violence of the change of policy. He focuses instead on the ethical attitudes of the characters, especially that of Makar Nagulnov, the secretary of the local party, who is cast in the role of the villain. No hint is given in Lukács's account that Nagulnov's errors are directly attributable to Stalin's instructions (though Sholokhov himself is more ambiguous). Instead, Lukács ignores the rights and wrongs of collectivisation itself and concentrates on Nagulnov's allegedly sectarian, ultra-Left attitude. By implication, then, Lukács endorses Sholokhov's own disin-

31. For an account of this process see I. Deutscher, *Stalin*, Penguin, Harmondsworth, 1970, Chapter 8.

clination to point the finger at the leadership. Indeed, there is room for doubt about Sholokhov's position while there can be none about that of Lukács. It might be added that Lukács had always argued against modernists like Brecht that it was perfectly possible for the accurate description of a village to symbolise the historical process affecting society as a whole. In *Virgin Soil Upturned* we see how a fairly faithful account of conflict and confusion at the village level fails to extend this picture to the larger political scene, to the supreme Soviet, where all is sweetness and light. A similar criticism could be made of Lukács's views of Nicolai Virta's account of the impact of the NEP (New Economic Policy) on the countryside in 1921.

We find a similar evasion in Lukács's account of Alexander Bek's *Volokolomskoye shosse* ('Volokolamsk Highway') (1944), a novel depicting the defence of Moscow in the winter of 1941. Lukács's approach to the text is to enquire why the Germans were victorious everywhere in the West, but were defeated by the Russians. He finds the answer in the superiority of Soviet strategy but also in the greater discipline of Soviet soldiers. He views the book as a novel of education in which discipline and the need to overcome the fear of battle are paramount issues. According to him, fear is overcome not by the cult of heroism or the acceptance of routine (as in Tolstoy's Nicolai Rostov) but by the Party's educational campaign. Likewise with discipline. Unlike the Prussian Army, where discipline was achieved by ensuring that the soldier feared his sergeant more than the enemy, discipline in the working class was strengthened and controlled by the class-consciousness of the Party. It was strict, but essentially humane. Lukács explicitly endorses the punishments which are handed down in a number of harsh episodes. In one, a corporal, Barambayev, is sentenced by the narrator, Momysh Uli, a battalion commander, to be executed for having shot himself in the hand. Bek is alive to the problems of such severe punishment. He describes two scenes, in the first of which Barambayev is reprieved after the intervention of his soldiers. In the second, the execution is carried out. Bek endorses this, but gives almost equal emotional support to the more lenient outcome. Panfilov, the general in command of the division, also accepts the execution but makes it clear that a court-martial would have been the better solution.

Unlike Lukács, Bek puts the question of discipline in a larger context. The book questions the received military wisdom of defending every inch of territory, a strategy that had led to some stunning German victories. Instead General Panfilov advocates a policy of flexible response, which involves tactical withdrawals and unexpected counter-attacks or outflanking manoeuvres. This was a sensitive issue, since it raised the question of the legitimacy of retreat. In the sequel written in 1960, *Rezerv generala Panfilova* ('General Panfilov's Reserve'), Panfilov is reprimanded and humiliated while Momysh Uli, who carries out Panfilov's ideas, is relieved of his command. The historical context is provided by Stalin's order of 28 July 1942, which comes after the events described in the novel, but which gives an indication of the moral climate in which decisions were taken. The order established military tribunals empowered to impose the death penalty for cowardice and, by equating retreat and surrender with treason, effectively disinherited Russian prisoners of war. Even troops who broke out of encirclement were treated with suspicion, disarmed and interrogated by Special Branch agents. With desertion common, all escaped prisoners were similarly questioned and at best sent to penal battalions.[32] It is evident that the problem of discipline has to be seen in the context of the general strategy of defending every inch of territory. This in turn raises the questions about the training of the troops, the expertise of the officers and the role of the political commissars in the Army. The need for ferocious discipline was bound up with the general conduct of the war. Lukács endorses the strict discipline without raising such questions, let alone criticising the Supreme Command. It was not until years later that writers like Simonov were able to ask questions about why the war had begun so disastrously for the Soviet Union. It is perhaps understandable that, writing in 1950, when victory was still fresh in the mind, Lukács should have set himself the task of explaining not early Soviet defeats, but the ultimate triumph. Nevertheless it is telling that he should have written a positive review of Kazakevich's *Vesna na Odere* (referred to above) which attributes victory to Stalin's wisdom. Even though he dropped this essay from the *Werke* edition, the piece on Bek is written in the same affirmative manner, and Bek's own critical sub-text is ignored.

Conclusion

Lukács's essays on socialist realism highlight the fundamental ambiguities in his critical position. His dogged defence of a conception of socialist realism which is barely distinguishable from critical realism embodies his determination to preserve the humanism of the West-

---

32. See D. Piper, 'The Soviet Union', in H. Klein, J. Flower and E. Homberger (eds.), *The Second World War in Fiction*, Macmillan, London, 1984, pp. 131–72 (esp. pp. 138–40).

ern bourgeois tradition. However, this humanism is given a 'Left' interpretation: that is to say, it is held to be more radical than the partial, one-sided 'sectarian' literature of a socialist realism dominated by explicit ideology. During periods of 'thaw' Lukács is confident enough to abandon his coded language and make explicit criticisms of the Stalinism which underpins the doctrine. But, equally, he was no dissident. He endorsed major features of Stalinism, and even when he disagreed, he believed that criticism should be carried out from within. Hence, to radicals like Brecht or Ottwalt, he appeared to speak with the voice of the Party. In Lukács, Brecht remarked, every judgement contains a threat. This identity with Stalinism is perhaps intensified by the authoritarian streak in Lukács's character, which may have been strengthened in its turn by the difficulties of the balancing-act he was compelled to perform. The uneasy compromises of Lukács's later works are brilliantly captured by the title Adorno gave to his essay on Lukács, 'Erpreßte Versöhnung' ('Reconciliation under Duress').[33]

---

33. T.W. Adorno, 'Erpreßte Versöhnung', *Noten zur Literatur*, vol. 2, Suhrkamp, Frankfurt, 1965, pp. 152–87.

—2—

Gramsci and Cultural Rationalisation

DAVID FORGACS

Gramsci's writings on culture and literature in the Prison Notebooks (1929–35) bear a somewhat oblique relation to the main body of cultural debate on the Left in the early 1930s. There is no mention of socialist realism, no direct engagement with the question of realism versus modernism, or with that of proletarian literature as against Popular Frontism, no discussion of relations between the Communist Party and fellow-travellers, no theorisation of the impact of the newer communications technologies — cinema and radio — and only the barest suggestion of their revolutionising effect on culture as a whole.

With Gramsci, indeed, we are dealing with a very different set of parameters of cultural analysis and strategy. For example, Gramsci places an emphasis, which is unique at this time, on the need to look at the culture of a nation as a whole formation, from the high culture of its intellectual elites to the local and particularised subcultures of its pre-literate communities, from its canonical works of literature to its popular fiction and orally transmitted stories. Furthermore, Gramsci's discussions of culture belong to a larger project of political analysis and strategy in the prison notes as a whole, and they lose much of their meaning if they are isolated from it. This project is at once more wide-ranging and long-term — that is to say more 'strategic' — than the political projects to which many of the contemporary Left discussions on culture were linked, caught up as they were in conjunctural and tactical offensives between Communists, Trotskyists, bourgeois democrats and radicals, or in the twists and turns of Soviet and Comintern policy itself. At the same time it is more concretely political than the cultural projects of other 'Western Marxists' — notably those of Lukács and the Frankfurt School — which in this period, as Perry Anderson argues in *Considerations on Western Marxism*,[1] are characterised precisely by their

---

1. P. Anderson, *Considerations on Western Marxism*, New Left Books, London, 1976.

abstract character, their retreat from immediate political considerations.

It would, nevertheless, be wrong to think of Gramsci's cultural
writings as being entirely *sui generis*. In reality they take up but
displace onto a different plane many of the issues at stake in those
debates going on elsewhere in Europe. Thus Gramsci is also concerned with the relations between art and politics, with the problem
of artistic freedom, the coercion of the artist and the imposition of a
particular cultural line, with questions of form, style and subject-
matter, with questions of overall cultural strategy, with the relations
between socio-economic transformation and political and cultural
change. It is just that the particular conditions of isolation in which
he was writing — first the relative provincialism and insularity of
Italian culture itself during the Fascist period, at least with respect
to the debates of the European Left, then his lack of contact in prison
with intellectuals and with cultural discussion among Marxists —
separate him from the terms in which these debates are being con-
ducted on the outside. Moreover, on the rare occasions that he does
hear of them, it is in a mediated, fragmentary and distorted form.

A convenient point of entry into Gramsci's cultural writings, and a
good illustration of all these points, is his response to an article of
1932 by the French Communist intellectual Paul Nizan. He knew
this article not in its original form but as it was reported and
paraphrased by a hostile reviewer in *Critica Fascista*, one of the
periodicals he received regularly in prison.

In this article, 'Littérature révolutionnaire en France' ('Revolutionary Literature in France'), Nizan defined the kind of literature
which he considered revolutionary. Revolutionary literature was
not the same, he said, as proletarian literature. If proletarian literature means literature written by the proletariat, about the proletariat and read by the proletariat, then it is not necessarily
revolutionary. Indeed, given the fact that both State education and
the means of cultural production and distribution are directly or
indirectly in the hands of the bourgeoisie, so that the bourgeoisie
controls the cultural spaces available to the proletariat and hands
them down a debased popular culture — sports newspapers, detective magazines, erotic fiction — then it is likely, Nizan says, that for
a long time to come many revolutionary writers will be 'rebellious
sons of the bourgeoisie'.[2] Revolutionary literature, moreover, must

2. P. Nizan, 'Littérature révolutionnaire en France', in *Pour un nouvelle culture*, ed. S.

not be thought of as being confined to depictions of the proletariat. What is essential is that it should adopt a proletarian point of view, in other words be written from the critical standpoint of Marxism. 'Revolutionary literature will express all its objects, including the proletariat, with the weapons of Marxist philosophy, of Marxist revolutionary criticism.'[3]

Nizan goes on to review the main literary currents in France in order to see where such a revolutionary literature is to be found. He writes off populism, a kind of literature, he says, where bourgeois writers investigate the lives of the working class in the same way as travel literature represented 'savages', namely as exotic subject-matter to be contemplated with fascination, pity and a reassuring sense of one's own charity and humanity. He likewise disposes of so-called 'Left' literature, which he says amounts to no more than a moralistic denunciation of the human misery created by capitalism. He characterises as 'revolutionaries by intention' that group of writers, which includes Emmanuel Berl and André Malraux, who are tempted by the revolution but frightened of committing themselves, and finally he rubbishes Henri Barbusse and the group of ex-Communists around the journal *Monde*, who consume their political energies in attacking the party which expelled them. What is left after this process of elimination is the group to which Nizan himself belongs, the Association des Ecrivains et Artistes Révolutionnaires (AEAR) — an international association which then included among its members Dos Passos, Anna Seghers, Aragon and Buñuel. The tasks of the AEAR, as Nizan defines them, are

> to denounce capitalism in general, in all its forms, in its regime, its codes of behaviour, its army, its priests, its police, its values, its philosophy, its fine arts, to expose to the proletariat the capitalist enemy as it really is. To struggle concretely against imperialism, war, Fascism, the social-democratic traitors, to defend the Soviet Revolution. To describe the proletariat no longer in a 'humane' but in a revolutionary way.[4]

The line pursued by this group of artists, Nizan believes, is so closely tied to the aims of the proletariat that, as the class struggle and the world crisis intensifies, as war draws nearer, the most honest of the 'pre-revolutionary' writers from the other literary groups will be drawn to it, whereas the unreconstructed petty-bourgeois mem-

---

Suleiman, Grasset, Paris, 1971, p. 35. All quotations from French sources in this essay are my own translations.

3. Ibid., p. 36.
4. Ibid., p. 41.

bers of the same groups will show their true colours and go over to the Fascist camp.

Although Gramsci only read about this article at second hand in a polemical account, he appears to have gleaned a fairly good impression of what Nizan wrote. Moreover, in one respect — as a fellow-Communist concerned, like Nizan, with helping to bring about 'integral renewal of cultural premises' — he explicitly states his sympathy with Nizan against the Fascist critic who reports and criticises his article. At the same time, however, Gramsci is critical of two interrelated aspects of Nizan's approach: its 'cosmopolitanism' and its vanguardism.

Gramsci locates 'the cosmopolitan dangers of Nizan's conception' in the latter's advocacy of the cultural line of the AEAR at the expense of all the other more or less radical and progressive tendencies in French national culture. His criticism of this position is linked to his belief that integral cultural change, like the revolutionary process of which it is a part, has to pass first through a national stage, and that this stage involves the winning of allies in the population at large. This belief is, in turn, rooted in Gramsci's whole political experience and outlook. All the capitalist countries, in his analysis, are stabilised to varying degrees by the rule of a hegemonic bloc of social forces. The term 'hegemony' designates, in this usage, a class alliance, or power bloc, between the bourgeoisie and the social strata which give it their active support. A hegemonic bloc also secures the consent of the social strata subjected to its domination, by making a number of political and material concessions to them. For Gramsci, a subaltern class (the proletariat) which seeks to be hegemonic must, along with its own intellectuals and with intellectuals from the classes who have allied themselves to it, build its own oppositional bloc by securing the active support of other 'subordinate social groups'. Only in this way can it succeed both in winning and maintaining power. One of the terms Gramsci uses to describe this oppositional bloc is 'national-popular'. The error of Nizan's approach, in Gramsci's view, is precisely to have ignored the national-popular perspective, and the molecular process of struggle and alliance-building which it involves, and to have backed instead a political and cultural strategy in which revolutionary intellectuals, whether of middle- or working-class origin, simply pursue the most 'advanced' line in isolation from the masses.

From this point of view, many of Nizan's criticisms of groups of French intellectuals should be reconsidered: the *Nouvelle Revue Française*, 'populism' and so on, including the *Monde* group; not because his criticism is politically off-target, but because the new literature must necessarily manifest itself 'nationally', in relatively hybrid and different combinations and alloys. One must examine and study the entire current objectively.[5]

Gramsci by the same token dissents from Nizan's view of literature as having a direct political function. Nizan in his article had stated: 'All literature is propaganda. Bourgeois propaganda is idealist, it conceals its game. . . . Revolutionary propaganda knows it is propaganda, it publicises its aims with complete frankness'.[6] For Gramsci, on the contrary, literature is different from propaganda. The writer, as he puts it, necessarily has 'a less precise and sectarian outlook than the politician'. This is because the artist produces fixed images, images of people and things as they are at a given moment in time, whereas the politician imagines people both as they are and as they should be. Or, to put it another way, art is descriptive, politics is prescriptive, art is cognitive, politics is practical. If art cannot be directly mobilised to a political end, then a revolutionary cultural policy cannot just take the form of backing the most correct line, the kind of art that represents one's political views in an unmediated way. It must, rather, take the form of encouraging all the cultural currents that are moving more or less in the direction of a revolutionary transformation of society. Gramsci argues that Nizan's strategy only takes account of the needs of the most advanced cultural strata, those able to read and understand the writers of the AEAR. However, if the point is to help bring about the cultural transformation of the people as a whole, this selective, vanguardist strategy is quite inadequate. One has to start by looking at where people actually are in cultural terms before talking about where one would like them to be. In Gramsci's words:

> moral and intellectual renewal does not develop simultaneously in all of the social strata. On the contrary it is worth repeating that even today many people are Ptolemaic and not Copernican. There are many 'conformisms', many struggles for new 'conformisms' and various combinations of that which already exists (variously expressed) and that which one is working to bring about (and there are many people who are working in this direction). It is a serious error to adopt a 'single' progressive strategy according to which each new gain accumulates and becomes the premise of further gains. Not only are the strategies multiple, but even in the 'most progressive' ones there are retrogressive moments.

5. A. Gramsci, *Selections from Cultural Writings*, trans. W. Boelhower, ed. D. Forgacs and G. Nowell-Smith, Lawrence & Wishart, London, 1985 (hereafter *SCW*), p. 100
6. P. Nizan, 'Littérature révolutionnaire', p. 34.

Furthermore, Nizan does not know how to deal with so-called 'popular literature', that is, with the success of serial literature (adventure stories, detective stories, thrillers) among the masses, a success that is assisted by the cinema and the newspapers. And yet it is this question that represents the major part of the problem of a new literature as the expression of moral and intellectual renewal, for only from the readers of serial literature can one select a sufficient and necessary public for creating the cultural base of the new literature. . . .

The most common prejudice is this: that the new literature has to identify itself with an artistic school of intellectual origins, as was the case with Futurism. The premise of the new literature cannot but be historical, political and popular. It must aim at elaborating that which already is, whether polemically or in some other way does not matter. What does matter, though, is that it sinks its roots into the humus of popular culture as it is, with its tastes and tendencies and its moral and intellectual world, even if it is backward and conventional.[7]

While it may be conceded that Gramsci corrects Nizan's cosmopolitanism and vanguardism, his own position is vulnerable to the objection that it goes too far in the opposite direction. For how can a concept of cultural change which supports multiple strategies, including some 'retrogressive' ones, and which bases itself explicitly on 'popular culture as it is' guarantee a progressive outcome, let alone a revolutionary one? There seems to be a strong element of unpredictability, of *laissez-faire*, and a consequent lack of direction about this position.

So far, however, I have given only half the picture. If one looks elsewhere in Gramsci's cultural writings, one finds this tendency being checked by what appears to be a counter-tendency. The other half of the picture is the side of Gramsci that deals with what can be termed 'rationalisation', with the planning and organisation of cultural change in a rational way.

In a series of notes written between 1933 and 1935, Gramsci deals with the question of artistic spontaneity and discipline, individual freedom and collective endeavour. As in the note on Nizan, he distinguishes between political activity and artistic activity, propaganda and art. 'When the politician puts pressure on the art of his time to express a particular cultural world, his activity is one of politics, not of artistic criticism.'[8] By the same token, an artist who tries to express a particular political world in a merely factitious way, in other words by simply 'willing' its content, will not create a work of art because his writing will not be the expression of a 'living

7. *SCW*, pp. 101–2.
8. Ibid., p. 109.

and necessary world'.[9] It should be remarked in passing that this distinction between a merely 'external', 'willed' content and a fully realised work of art, like Gramsci's more general distinction between art and political activity, is steeped in the aesthetic categories and assumptions of Benedetto Croce.

What might at first glance appear to be a simple defence of the autonomy of artistic creativity in relation to politics is in fact part of a more complex argument. For what Gramsci is really concerned with here, and in the related notes, is not the autonomy of art in any absolute sense but on the contrary cultural initiatives and policies which attempt to give a specific direction to art. As he puts it: 'Is the concept that art is art and not 'willed' and directed political propaganda in itself an obstacle to the formation of specific cultural currents that reflect their time and contribute to the strengthening of specific political currents? It seems not; indeed it seems that such a concept poses the problem in more radical terms'.[10] Gramsci wants, in other words, to understand how and how far cultural change can be consciously directed and what the limits of such a 'formation of specific cultural currents' are. That is to say, he wants to know under what conditions and for what reasons cultural initiatives do or do not achieve their desired ends and how real cultural change occurs or fails to occur. His coordinates on this investigation are the Fascist culture around him and the socialist culture he would like to see.

On the first of these, Gramsci is interested in why the various attempts made under Fascism to 'revolutionise' Italian culture have been unsuccessful, why the Italian intellectuals have on the whole remained traditionalist and refractory. Essentially, his conclusion is that one cannot 'will' a revolution in the cultural superstructure unless a real social transformation, in other words a fundamental transformation of the productive base of society and of social relations as a whole, is also under way. In Italy, no such transformation is taking place in the 1920s and 1930s. Fascism is merely a 'passive revolution', a recomposition of the dominant power bloc and an authoritarian hardening of the State. It is not a transformation of society, since it leaves the fundamental class relations intact: indeed it consolidates class polarisation. Rather, it is a strategic response 'from above' to the social conflicts produced by modernisation in a semi-traditional society and to the crisis of bourgeois hegemony and the liberal State. Consequently, there is in Fascist

9. Ibid.
10. Ibid., p. 108.

Italy no major reconstruction of culture and of moral life as would occur in a period of real social upheaval and change, as occurred in France during the late eighteenth century, as Gramsci saw occurring, to some extent at least, in the United States in his own time, and as would occur in a phase of preparation and transition to socialism.

It is into this discussion that Gramsci introduces the concept of rationality. Taking his lead from contemporary discussions in the press about rationalism and functionalism in architecture, he asks: 'What in literature corresponds to "rationalism" in architecture? Clearly, literature based on a plan or on a pre-established social course, in other words "functional" literature. It is strange that rationalism is acclaimed and justified in architecture and not in the other arts'.[11] Then, noting that any talk about rationalism or planning in the arts tends to raise in people's minds the spectre of coercion, he goes on:

> How people do blather against this coercion! Nobody sees that it is merely a word! Coercion, direction and planning are nothing more than a terrain for selecting artists. They are to be chosen for practical purposes, in a field in which will and coercion are perfectly justified. As if there has not always been some form of coercion! Just because it is exerted unconsciously by the environment and by single individuals, and not by a central power or a centralised force, does it cease to be coercion? Ultimately, it is always a question of 'rationalism' versus the individual will. Therefore, coercion is not the issue, but whether we are dealing with an authentic rationalism, a real functionalism, or with an act of the will. This is all. Coercion is such only for those who reject it, not for those who accept it. If it goes hand in hand with the development of the social forces, it is not coercion but the 'revelation' of cultural truth obtained by an accelerated method. One can say of coercion what the religious say of predestination: for the 'willing' it is not predestination, but free will. In fact there is opposition to the concept of coercion because it involves a struggle against intellectuals, especially traditional and traditionalist intellectuals who are prepared at most to concede that innovations can be brought in little by little, gradually.[12]

The concept of rationalism and rationalisation in Gramsci is bound up with some of the central themes and preoccupations of the Prison Notebooks: the construction of a national-popular hegemonic bloc; the question of the leadership of this bloc by intellectuals and by that 'collective intellectual' the Communist Party; and the relation between socio-economic base and political and cultural superstructures. The concept of rationality is intimately linked, above all, to Gramsci's discussion of the historical process, and in particular

11. Ibid., pp. 129–30.
12. Ibid., p. 130.

the dialectic of freedom and necessity by which, as Marx wrote: 'Men make their own history, but not of their own free will; not under circumstances they themselves have chosen'.[13] In examining the relation between historical necessity and consciously willed activity, Gramsci returns on several occasions to the passage in Marx's 1859 Preface to *Towards a Contribution to a Critique of Political Economy* where he talks about the links between the development of the productive forces and the emergence in consciousness of the attitudes necessary for bringing into being new relations of production. Marx says that 'mankind only sets itself such tasks as it is able to solve; since, looking at the matter more closely, it will always be found that the task itself arises only when the material conditions for its solution already exist or are in the process of formation'. In the margins of this passage, as it were, Gramsci notes that a situation of historical 'necessity exists when there exists an efficient and active *premise*, consciousness of which in people's minds has become operative, proposing concrete goals'.[14]

Likewise, for Gramsci, a situation is rational when the material and ideological premises exist for the achievement of a desired end. Gramsci sees in the historical process itself a form of rationality. When the contradiction between forces and relations of production has developed to such a point (the premise) as to make possible a revolutionary transformation of society (the goal), then such a transformation is both historically necessary and rational. 'Necessary' here does not mean inevitable: the whole direction of Gramsci's prison writing is against any 'mechanical' determinism. It means rather that the historical conditions exist in which consciousness of the contradictions can emerge. If such a consciousness does indeed emerge in these conditions then it will be 'rational', because it will be in accordance with achievable ends.

Turning back to Gramsci's application of this to freedom and innovation in art, we find that he in fact separates two different meanings of freedom. The first is Romantic in origin:[15] freedom means the freedom to break existing artistic rules, to be different from everyone else, to put a premium on originality and creativity for their own sake. Freedom in the second sense is linked to the

13. K. Marx, 'The Eighteenth Brumaire of Louis Bonaparte', trans. B. Fowkes, in Marx, *Surveys from Exile*, ed. D. Fernbach, Penguin, Harmondsworth, 1973, p. 147.
14. A. Gramsci, *Selections from the Prison Notebooks*, trans. and ed. Q. Hoare and G. Nowell-Smith, Lawrence & Wishart, London, 1971 (hereafter *SPN*), pp. 412–13.
15. *SCW*, pp. 124, 125.

concept of rationality. It means freedom to act in accordance with historical necessity, in terms of rational interests and achievable goals. Corresponding to these two senses of freedom are two types of conformism. The first is that 'artificial conformism' rejected by the Romantics: a set of external and factitious rules. The second is what Gramsci calls 'rational conformism', which he argues is compatible with the exercise of free will.

> There is also a 'rational' form of conformism that corresponds to necessity, to the minimum amount of force needed to obtain a useful result. The discipline involved must be exalted and promoted and made 'spontaneous' or 'sincere'. Conformism, then, means nothing other than 'sociality', but it is nice to use the word 'conformism' precisely because it annoys imbeciles. This does not mean that one cannot form a personality or be original, but it makes matters more difficult. It is too easy to be original by doing the opposite of what everyone else is doing; this is just mechanical. It is too easy to speak differently from others, to play with neologisms, whereas it is difficult to distinguish oneself from others without doing acrobatics. Today people try to be original and to have a personality on the cheap. Prisons and mental asylums are full of original men with strong personalities. What is really difficult is to put the stress on discipline and sociality and still profess sincerity, spontaneity, originality and personality. Nor can one say that conformism is too easy and reduces the world to a monastery. What is 'real conformism', what is the most useful and freest form of behaviour that is 'rational' in that it obeys 'necessity'? Everyone is led to make of himself the archetype of 'fashion' and 'sociality', to offer himself as the 'model'. Therefore, sociality or conformism is the result of a cultural (but not only cultural) struggle; it is an 'objective' or universal fact, just as the 'necessity' on which the edifice of liberty is built cannot but be objective and universal.[16]

This passage is interestingly parallelled by one in which Weber deals with the concept of purposive rationality (*Zweckrationalität*):

> It is obvious what is mistaken about the assumption that 'freedom' of the will, however it is understood, is identical with the 'irrationality' of action. The characteristic of 'unpredictability' — equal to but no greater than the unpredictability of 'blind, natural forces' — is the privilege of the insane. On the contrary, we associate the strongest empirical 'feeling of freedom' with precisely those actions which we know ourselves to have accomplished rationally, i.e. in the absence of physical or psychic 'compulsion'; actions in which we pursue a clearly conscious 'purpose' by what to our knowledge are the most adequate 'means'.[17]

16. Ibid., pp. 124–25.
17. Quoted in K. Löwith, *Max Weber and Karl Marx*, Allen & Unwin, London, 1982, p. 45.

Yet despite this parallel formulation, Gramsci's rationality is actually closer to what Weber called 'value rationality'. Like Marx, Gramsci sees the historical process itself as unfolding towards greater rationality, which he understands as generally good and progressive. Weber himself either saw rationality as 'value-free' and equated it with calculability, or he saw it as a negative historical tendency and equated it with bureaucratisation and loss of freedom.

Gramsci's notion of cultural rationalisation therefore has the meaning of the organisation or acceleration of cultural tendencies for which the necessary historical premises exist. Artists who contribute to the formation of a new culture do so at once freely and in conformity with this social end. The difference between the kind of cultural policy which this implies and the cultural policies of Stalinism, notably the exhortations given to artists by the 1934 Soviet Writers' Congress to produce socialist realism and be engineers of human souls, should not need to be spelt out. As Gramsci indicates at several points in his notes on literature, it is not possible to create a new art directly, by political order or fiat. One can only create the cultural conditions, the 'terrain of selection', in which this new art will emerge. And it is these cultural conditions that are amenable to rationalisation, not individual artists or works of art themselves.

But has Gramsci really exorcised the spectre of 'social coercion'? Not entirely, I would suggest. For his tendency to view rationality as essentially good and historically progressive leads him, firstly, to equate the rational with the socially beneficial and, secondly, on this basis to see as universally rational certain forms of thought and social organisation which are in fact historically specific and contingent.

This notion of what one might call 'universal' rationality in Gramsci's thought occurs at several places in the Prison Notebooks. I shall mention just two here which seem to me particularly significant. The first is the idea of rationalised production and a rationalised social structure which one encounters in the notes on 'Americanism and Fordism'. Rationalised production refers here to the Ford system of organising and controlling the labour process to maximise productivity and output, a system which combines coercion (exclusion of unionised labour, rigid timekeeping and discipline) with persuasion (high wages, social benefits for employees and their families). Fordism extends into the regulation of workers' private lives, through the promotion of regular and abstemious habits, religious observance, a stable family life. In this way Fordism succeeds 'in making the whole life of the nation revolve around production'.[18] Complementing this rational organisation of production is a 'rational demographic composition' of American society, by which Gramsci means the absence of residues of a feudal mode of production, and those parasitic intermediate strata which constitute such a significant part of European social structure, notably in a semi-traditional society with a bloated service sector like Italy. The rationality of the America epitomised by Fordism consists, for Gramsci, in the more or less direct relationship between the sphere of economic production and the spheres of the superstructures. In old Europe, this relationship is highly mediated. Americanism is clearly for Gramsci, once shorn of the specifically capitalist relations of production and exploitation that characterise Fordism, a model of the more rational social and economic order that is achievable under socialism.

The problem with Gramsci's thinking here consists in the idea of a rational 'core' in Fordist production techniques and in American society that can be extracted from the exploitative husk of capitalist property relations. In economic production, there are different kinds of rationality according to the kind of social arrangement one wants to achieve. Productive techniques and technologies bear inscribed within them the relations of production which they serve. The typical Fordist arrangement of serial production across the factory floor, with parts moving on belts or on chains and the worker staying in the same place, or related notions like speed-up, embody power relations of control and surveillance that are specific to the rationale of capitalist exploitation and valorisation, and are thus not automatically and unproblematically transferable to socialism. The same applies to the rationalisation and regularisation of social mores (sexual behaviour, prohibition, etc.) which one finds in the America of the New Deal era.

The second area where the notion of a universal rationality occurs, and seems to be equally problematic, is Gramsci's discussion of the relations between language and dialect, philosophy and folklore, high literate and oral popular culture, Western culture and other cultures. In each case, a notion intrudes that the first term of each pair (the standard language, philosophy, literate high culture, Western culture) is more elaborated and systematic and consequently more 'universal'. In other words the difference between them is not one of different kinds or systems of 'rationality', but of intrinsically greater and lesser rationality and universality. Hence the cultural transformation which Gramsci envisages, the process of

18. *SPN*, p. 285.

intellectual and moral reformation, involves in his view both a process of diffusion, of radiation out from intellectual 'centres' to 'peripheries' (town to country, high to low culture, language to dialect, philosophy to common sense) and at the same time a converse and dialectically related process of 'raising' by which people pass from 'feeling' to 'knowledge', from common sense towards philosophy, from dialect to language.[19] Both the idea of diffusion and that of raising would seem to depend on the assumption of a rational axis or centre around which the whole process of cultural change revolves. And yet it is precisely this notion that one needs to call into question, by suggesting that there are many different kinds of rationality, relative to different ends, and that in a process of cultural change, each cultural manifestation in society needs to develop within the limits of its own rationality, without being coerced by any body outside it.[20]

This brings us back to the note on Nizan. For it was precisely such a notion of multiple lines of cultural development that Gramsci invoked in his criticisms of Nizan's cosmopolitanism and vanguardism. And it was precisely such a notion, as we have seen, that laid itself open to the objection that it would lack direction unless the various lines were in some way coordinated.

This coordination, it can now be seen, comes from Gramsci's notions of rationality and rationalisation. For if a given cultural line or tendency is really the expression of 'a living and necessary world', this means that it is tending, for Gramsci, in the direction of historical development itself, and can therefore be rationally 'accelerated' by the intervention of a coordinating agency. The most important coordinating body for Gramsci is, of course, the Communist Party, since it is the party that most fully expresses and organises the tendency of the historical process. Rationality for Gramsci means both the necessary tendency of the historical process itself and the conscious organisation (rationalisation) of that process by planned intervention and leadership. Hence, when Gramsci's conception of cultural change oscillates, at first sight inexplicably, between opposing poles — pluralism and centralism; undirectedness

19. See for instance: '"Language", Languages, Common Sense', ibid., pp. 348–51; 'Passage from Knowing to Understanding and to Feeling and vice versa', ibid., p. 418; 'Sources of diffusion of linguistic innovations', *SCW*, p. 183; and 'Observations on folklore', *SCW*, pp. 188–91.

20. A fundamental essay on these normative elements in Gramsci's thought is A. M. Cirese, 'Gramsci's Observations on Folklore', in A. Showstack Sassoon (ed.), *Approaches to Gramsci*, Writers and Readers, London, 1982.

and strategic direction; lack of regulation and planning — on closer inspection it can be seen that the gap between the poles is constantly bridged and traversed by his concept of rationality.

It does not follow from this that Gramsci's concept of rationality *effectively reconciles* these poles. Nor does it follow — and I have argued in this sense above — that we are obliged to accept it on Gramsci's terms. I believe, however, that it is important, firstly, to see that *for Gramsci* the concept of rationality did indeed negotiate these contradictions and produce an internally coherent structure of politics and, secondly, that *for us* the concept is problematic and we need to go beyond it.

Firstly, then, we must understand the concept of rationality in Gramsci's writings in order to see through interpretations of his thought which suggest that he had, as it were, two political souls in one body: liberty and authority, democracy and dictatorship, pluralism and the one-party State, council democracy and the democratic centralist party. The view was for instance put forward by the veteran socialist philosopher Rodolfo Mondolfo that, when Gramsci became a Communist, such Leninist notions as strict party discipline and decisive class leadership became overlaid upon the earlier libertarianism to be found, for instance, in his advocacy of the factory council movement and his sympathies with the anarchists. Thereafter, according to Mondolfo, he moved back and forth between the two in a way which rendered highly contradictory and problematic such central concepts as hegemony.[21] Yet this 'two souls' view misses the point that it was precisely Gramsci's mature belief that leadership and discipline could act in accordance with a process of general human liberation, and that when they did so they would be 'rational' and would win popular consent.

Secondly, however, having understood this, it is equally important to register its limitations. Such a notion of rationality depends crucially on the belief that the historical process is tending towards a determinate outcome and that this outcome is implicit in the actions of social masses and their political agents. This belief (the 'absolute historicism' that was the object of an important critique by Althusser)[22] leads in turn, to the belief that the party which most fully expresses this historical tendency can rationally interpret, support and further the aspirations of the masses in a planned and

21. R. Mondolfo, 'Intorno a Gramsci e alla filosofia della prassi', 'Le antinomie di Gramsci', in idem, *Umanismo di Marx. Studi filosofici 1908–1966*, Einaudi, Turin, 1968, pp. 279–304, 398–409.
22. L. Althusser, 'Marxism is not a Historicism', in idem, *Reading Capital*, New Left Books, London, 1970, pp. 126–35.

conscious way. This belief is, of course, deeply at odds with other formulations by Gramsci himself: namely the expanded notion of the Party, the need to create a mass of 'organic intellectuals' of the working class in order to overcome the division between intellectuals and masses that leads to bureaucratic involution and centralisation of power, the need to build alliances of social forces, the need for an effective mass political movement to articulate the demands of many diverse social groups. Yet the point about Gramsci is precisely, *pace* Mondolfo and others, that this conception of the Party and of politics sits *side by side* in his writings with those more historicist and centralist conceptions and is *theoretically reconciled* with them.

Since Gramsci's time, many of us who are Marxists, including some of us who are Communists, have become more uncertain and more sceptical about the possibility of such a 'rational' understanding and acceleration of the historical process. This process seems more complex, moving not in one direction but in many simultaneously, looping back on itself or even appearing to go temporarily into reverse. At the same time, the process of struggle seems no longer to involve a single historical mass but many exploited and oppressed groups whose demands cannot be easily or obviously reconciled and coordinated with one another, least of all by a tightly knit and centrally disciplined party of the Leninist type. Gramsci was moving between two conceptions of the revolutionary process — as consciously directed and as evolving in all its multiple contradictory strands — and between two related conceptions of the revolutionary party— as disciplined vanguard and as mass organisation. He did not move beyond them into a new one. This is what we now need to do.

Gramsci's legacy as a cultural theorist is therefore at once extraordinarily rich and deeply problematic. For the reasons I have set out here, I believe that it cannot merely be taken over wholesale as a model of cultural analysis and strategy. On the other hand, it is far too important to be simply passed over. We need to shear off those parts that are usable, not compromised by the notion of a universal rationality — such as his recognition and mapping of a whole cultural formation, his brilliant critique of cultural vanguardism, his interest in all manifestations of popular cultural activity in the context of a project of radical social change. These parts of Gramsci's cultural writings must now be reworked in terms of a vastly more modern and technological culture and a changed political strategy and practice. Yet this sort of creative reworking is the sort of undogmatic Marxism of which Gramsci, I like to think, would have been happy to approve.

PART II

National Contexts

—3—

Soviet Perspectives on Socialist Realism

ROBERT PORTER

While there has been some tampering with the official definition of socialist realism since the term was first coined, in essence it has not changed, either as a theory or as a method, over the years.[1] The current *Bol'shaya sovetskaya entsiklopediya* (*Large Soviet Encyclopaedia*) (1978) defines the term as follows:

> Artistic method of literature and art representing an aesthetic expression of a socialistically recognised conception of the world and man, conditioned by the epoch of the struggle for the establishment and creation of socialist society. The depiction of life in the light of the ideals of socialism conditions both the content and the fundamental artistic-structural principles of the art of Socialist Realism. Its appearance and development are connected with the spread of socialist ideas in various countries, with the development of the revolutionary working class . . . Socialist Realism constantly widens frontiers, acquiring the significance of the leading artistic method of the contemporary epoch. This widening, by force of its conditioning [determining] principles, opposed the so-called 'realism without banks' of R. Garaudy, which is in essence directed at the destruction of the ideological bases of the new art.

There have been, of course, more 'off the cuff' definitions, including the scurrilous 'socialist realism is praise for the Soviet leaders written in language they can understand', Fadeyev's reported 'The

1. For the record, one may recall that the term was first coined in 1932, but was officially adopted at the First Congress of Soviet Writers in 1934 and defined as follows: 'Socialist Realism, the basic method of Soviet *belles lettres* and literary criticism, demands of the artist truthful, historically concrete representation of reality in its revolutionary development. At the same time, truthfulness and historical concreteness of artistic representation of reality must be combined with the task of ideologically remoulding and training the labouring people in the spirit of socialism', Stenographic record of the First Congress of Soviet Writers, Moscow, 1934, p. 716. As with the other translations from Soviet texts which I have made in this essay, it is worth, I think, preserving the tone of the original at the expense of stylistic elegance.

devil only knows' and Sholokhov's'that which is written for the Soviet government in simple, comprehensive [sic], artistic language' (*New York Times*, 11 May 1958).[2] Two Western scholars have done much to convince one that socialist realism as practised under Stalin is well-nigh dead, if not buried. Max Hayward's 'The Decline of Socialist Realism' (1971)[3] and Geoffrey Hosking's study *Beyond Socialist Realism*,[4] as their titles imply, indicate that Soviet literature has moved a long way from the stereotypes of the 1930s. Rosalind March, however, in her recent book *Soviet Fiction since Stalin* (1986), is less convinced:

> The bureaucratic organisations controlling literature have not changed much since Khrushchev's time, but an important development has been that since 1971, the Congress of the Writers' Union has taken place every five years (rather than every four years) — that is just after the Party Congress which also occurs every five years. The purpose of this change was to make it difficult for writers to adopt any independent initiative. Traditional views of 'socialist realism' continue to be propounded in official publications on Soviet literature, in speeches by literary functionaries . . . and party leaders. The bulk of literature published in the USSR still conforms to socialist realist canons . . . . In the 1970s, however, some Soviet theoreticians have adopted a more flexible approach to the official doctrine, in an attempt to account for the widening gap between the theory of socialist realism and the practice of many Soviet writers, which had become largely apolitical, more akin to the 'critical realism' of nineteenth-century Russian literature. This can be largely attributed to the growing scepticism or indifference of Soviet writers towards ideology, and the greater sophistication of editors and censors.[5]

Elsewhere (p. 21) she suggests that Hayward and Hosking have been premature in their assessments and that socialist realism is still with us.

What does seem to be the case is that socialist realism is still 'on the statute book', that, when necessary, it can be invoked to deal with difficult writers, that its interpretation is sufficiently elastic to embrace the magic and grotesque of, say, Bulgakov's *Master i Margarita* (*The Master and Margarita*) (1966) or Orlov's *Al'tist Danilov*

---

2. Quoted in H. Swayze, *Political Control of Literature in the USSR, 1946–1959*, Harvard University Press, Cambridge, Mass., 1962, p. 270.
3. M. Hayward, 'The Decline of Socialist Realism', *Survey*, vol. 18, 1972, pp. 73–97. Repr. in his *Writers in Russia, 1917–1978*, ed. P. Blake, Harvill Press, London, 1983, pp.149–83.
4. G. Hosking, *Beyond Socialist Realism*, Granada, London, 1980.
5. R. Marsh, *Soviet Fiction Since Stalin*, Croom Helm, London, 1986, pp. 17–18. Page references are indicated in my text.

('Danilov the Violist') (1980) and the religiosity and mysticism of Rasputin's *Proschaniye s Matyoroy* (*Farewell to Matyora*) (1976), while on occasion delighting in Solzhenitsyn's traditional brand of realism (*One Day in the Life of Ivan Denisovich*, 1962) or rejecting it as fantasy (*The Gulag Archipelago*, 1974). A good deal of literary criticism in the Soviet Union seems to be able to avoid the term to a large extent, while still insisting on the civic responsibilities of the writer. In his aforementioned article 'The Decline of Socialist Realism', Max Hayward discussed Ovcharenko's attempt to broaden the canons of socialist realism; Ovcharenko argued that while socialist realism was the *basic* method of the artist as stated in the 1934 definition of the term, Soviet literature was younger and broader than socialist realism (p. 169). Incidentally, Ovcharenko was stung into replying to Hayward's interpretation of his book (see note, p. 118).

It is certainly the case that there exist clear antecedents in the nineteenth century for socialist realism, witness Belinsky's advocacy of a utilitarian art, or Chernyshevky's enactment of it in his novel *Chto delat'?* (*What is to be done?*) (1863). Lenin exclaimed of this book: 'Now this is real literature. It teaches, guides and inspires!'[6] Would it be unfair to see embryonic positive heroes and attainable Utopias elsewhere in nineteenth-century Russian literature, in works more universally recognised as great art than Chernyshevsky's? Dostoevsky sought to create the perfect man in *The Idiot* (1869), while Tolstoy's Levin or Karatayev possess a moral cohesion that has inspired many a third-rate Soviet novelist. It fell to Gorky, of course, to build the bridge between the nineteenth and twentieth centuries, both in his own works and more particularly in his own pronouncements on socialist realism, when he contrasted it to the 'critical realism' of the nineteenth century.

Thus it is an oversimplification to say that socialist realism was grafted on to twentieth-century Russian literature. Rather it developed with it. The dangers that it held were already there long before the Revolution. The writer turned moralist meant decline; this was true of Gogol, Tolstoy, even Turgenev. A similar pattern of eclipse may be discerned in Solzhenitsyn's work. Blok spoke of 'one drop of politics' that might remain in his great poem of the Revolution, *Dvenadsat'* (*The Twelve*)(1918). Fortunately, it remained only 'one drop'.

There have been at least two serious attempts 'near home', so to speak, to disestablish socialist realism as practised — one by the

6. Quoted in C. Vaughan James, *Soviet Socialist Realism*, Macmillan, London, 1973, p. 20.

dissident writer and critic Andrey Sinyavsky, who, under the pseudo-
nym Abram Tertz published abroad his now famous essay 'Chto
takoye sotsialisticheskiy realizm?' ('What is Socialist Realism?')
(1967). He sees socialist realism as being very akin to eighteenth-
century classicism, in that it involves a pattern to which the artist
must conform and the artist must depict a projected reality, not real
reality: 'The river of art has been covered by the ice of Classicism.
As a more defined, rational, teleological art form it has ousted
Romanticism'.[7] Sinyavsky's own creative works derive directly from
the fantastic/grotesque tradition in Russian literature, from Gogol
through to Bulgakov and Voynovich. For his ideas on socialist
realism and his attempts to give flesh to his theories he earned a
seven-year sentence in a labour camp. Serving his sentence and then
settling in Paris, Sinyavsky came to identify the profession of writer
with that of criminal. In 1974 he wrote:

> At this moment the fate of the Russian writer has become the most
> intriguing, the most fruitful literary topic in the whole world: he is either
> being imprisoned, pilloried, internally exiled or simply kicked out. The
> writer nowadays is walking a knife-edge; but unlike the old days, when
> writers were simply eliminated one after another, he now derives pleasure
> and moral satisfaction from this curious pastime. The writer is now
> someone to be reckoned with . . . . We shall not be far wrong if we say
> that the major topics [of Russian literature today] are prison and labour
> camps.[8]

Well, the labour camps produced Solzhenitsyn, and his work in
the 1960s produced an erudite but convoluted reassessment of
socialist realism by Georg Lukács. In two essays (1964 and 1969) he
discusses in turn Solzhenitsyn's novella *One Day in the Life of Ivan
Denisovich* (1962), and *The First Circle* (1968) and *Cancer Ward*
(1968).[9] He argues that the novella as a genre is either the harbinger
of a new social and literary era or marks the decline of such an era.
He sees Solzhenitsyn as taking us through to a new dawn of socialist
realism:

> The world of socialism today stands on the eve of a renaissance of

7. A. Tertz, [Andrey Sinyavsky], 'Chto takoye sotsialisticheskiy realizm?', in idem
   Fantasticheskiy mir Abrama Tertsa, YMCA, Paris, 1967, pp. 401–46 (p. 438). See
   also T.R.N. Edwards, *Three Russian Writers and the Irrational*, Cambridge University Press, Cambridge, 1982, pp. 122, 134, for a discussion of Sinyavsky's view.
8. A. Tertz, [A. Sinyavsky], 'The Literary Process in Russia', trans. M. Glenny, in
   Kontinent I, André Deutsch, London, 1976, pp. 73–110 (pp. 75–6).
9. G. Lukács, *Solzhenitsyn*, trans. W.D. Graf, Merlin, London, 1970, Subsequent
   page references are indicated in my text.

Marxism, a renaissance whose task it will be not only to eliminate Stalinist distortions and point to the way forward, but above all adequately to encompass the new facts of reality . . . . In literature, socialist realism faces a similar task . . . I believe . . . that it is also wrong to attempt to give socialist realism a premature burial. (p. 16)

Contemporary discussions of realism, and above all of socialist realism, pass heedlessly over the real basic question, not least because they lose sight of the contrast between realism and naturalism. In the 'illustrating literature' of the Stalin era, an official naturalism, combined with an equally official so-called revolutionary romanticism, was substituted for realism. (p. 17)

Lukács concludes that Solzhenitsyn's socialist realism is political at a certain level, but that 'his works are surely just as political in the final analysis as are those of Beaumarchais or Diderot, Goethe or Tolstoy' (p. 79). He thus seems to be echoing Blok's words about in the long run three being only 'one drop of politics' in true works of art.

Of the three basic ingedients of socialist realism (*narodnost'* — popular-mindedness or awareness of the people; *klassovost'* — class-mindedness; and *partiynost'* — party-mindedness), party-mindedness is the most important. Based on Lenin's famous article of 1905, 'Partiynaya organizatsiya i partiynaya literatura' ('Party Organisation and Party Literature'), the notion has come to mean unswerving allegiance to the demands of the Party; and of course, these can vary according to political circumstances. We shall see how the party line may shift and how this can affect the literature produced. However, to conclude the discussion of the theoretical side of socialist realism, one must consider socialist realism abroad.

Summarising the Soviet view, Vaughan James writes:

Socialist Realism is a world-wide artistic phenomenon that arose under the influences of the great social changes at the end of the nineteenth century and the beginning of the twentieth — the sharpening contradictions within capitalist society, the crisis in bourgeois culture and the rise of a socially conscious proletariat. It is therefore the reflection in the arts of the struggle for the victory of socialism. (p. 85)

Further: 'Outside the Soviet Union, elements of Socialist Realism may be seen in the work of a whole variety of artists: Anatole France, Barbusse, Rolland, Léger, Picasso, Neruda, Nezval . . . Brecht' (p. 86).

Be this as it may, many of the artists abroad, once championed by the Soviet establishment, have subsequently fallen from grace, or are discussed in a one-dimensional way in the Soviet media. In the newly established socialist countries of the postwar years there were particular problems. Countries like the German Democratic Republic, Poland, Hungary and Czechoslovakia had cultural traditions far different from that of Russia. They had all experienced the Renaissance, albeit in various forms and to differing extents, and had thrown aside medieval dogma in favour of the freedom of the individual centuries before Russian literature came of age. In the interwar years the left-wing avant-garde enjoyed a certain prominence in the face of growing Fascism. After 1945 the left-orientated artist then had to conform to the Soviet model — like Mayakovsky after 1917, he had to 'step on the throat of his own song'. One might venture to say that the act of contortion was more difficult for writers coming from a tradition different from Mayakovsky's, and that the results could not be as successful.

Let us examine briefly the case of Czechoslovakia. At first sight it might seem that here was a country ripe for socialist realism. Firstly, it was industrialised and relatively rich, yet it had suffered the horrors of Nazi occupation. Secondly, owing to Czech history, its literature was peculiarly plebeian. German was the language of the towns and cities. Czech was the vernacular, spoken in the villages. This had been the case since the end of the Thirty Years War and until the so-called National Revival got under way at the end of the eighteenth century. Thus modern Czech literature was — and still is — denied the 'high style' and the truly epic qualities of many other European literatures. Alois Jirásek wrote a string of second-rate historical novels that might appeal to a sixteen-year-old Czech patriot, but not to a more sophisticated and cosmopolitan readership. On the other hand, there was — and still is — a robust earthiness about Czech literature, which could lend it great appeal to a proletarian readership. However, earthiness can shade into irreverence, which in turn can become anti-authoritarianism. The best of Czech literature could present the Soviet literary establishment with a real dilemma. Jaroslav Hašek is a case in point.

The Good Soldier Švejk (1921–2) is generally perceived in Western Europe as an essentially grotesque work, a mock epic, a twentieth-century picaresque novel. It is anti-militaristic, anti-institutional and, like its author, in the main, anarchistic. The military drop-out has a long literary pedigree going back at least to Falstaff. However, Švejk is triumphant in his ineptitude and touches on universal truth in his naïvety and lack of guile. To an extent these comments do not entirely refute the Soviet view of this novel.

However, some of the leading minds of Czechoslovakia have been keen to interpret *The Good Soldier Švejk* in terms of the irrationality of the modern world. They point to Hašek's great contemporary and fellow-citizen of Prague, Franz Kafka. The philosopher Karel Kosík writes as follows:

> Švejk's 'odyssey under the honourable escort of two soldiers with bayonets' takes him from the Hradčany garrison jail along Neruda Street to Malá Strana and over the Charles Bridge. It is an interesting group of three people: two guards escorting a delinquent. From the opposite direction, over the Charles Bridge and up to Strahov, another trio makes its way. This is the threesome from Kafka's *Trial*: two guards leading a 'delinquent', the bank clerk Josef K., to the Strahov quarries, where one of them will 'thrust a knife into his heart'. Both groups pass through the same places, but meeting each other is impossible. Švejk was let out of jail — as is the custom — early in the day, and he and his guards make the journey just described before noon; while Josef K. was led in the evening hours by two men wearing top hats, 'in the moonlight'.
> But let's imagine that these two groups were to meet.[10]

Kosík goes on to argue that these two authors complement each other and concludes that Kafka depicts the materialism of our everyday existence whereas Hašek shows that man transcends materialism.

Yet Hašek is perceived by the Soviet etablishment as a socialist realist writer.[11] His colourful biography, at least in part, shows him to be a committed Bolshevik, a life-long fighter against the bourgeoisie and its values. The advent of the October Revolution demonstrated to Hašek the unconquerable strength of the ideas of Marxism-Leninism, even if sometimes he did not 'always correctly understand' the significance of these events (p. 37). Hašek graduated to socialist realism (p. 54). *The Good Soldier Švejk* differs from satirical works of critical realism (for example, those of Saltykov-Shchedrin) in that it is socialist realist, demonstrates the superiority of the man of the people over privileged figures and affirms the optimistic certainty of the complete abolition of existing social forms (p. 77). That there is no revolutionary proletariat in the novel is explained by the book's strict regard for realism, for the 'concrete historical' conditions of the time; there were at the time no conscious revolutionary manifestations in Czechoslovakia (p. 80). *Švejk* is above all, in Soviet eyes, an anti-war novel, to be classified with Barbusse's *Le Feu* (*Under Fire*) (1916), Renn's *Krieg* (*War*) (1928),

---

10. Kosík, 'Hašek and Kafka', *Cross Currents*, no. 23, University of Michigan, 1983, pp. 127–36. Subsequent page references are indicated in my text.
11. The following remarks are taken from N.P. Yelanskij, *Yaroslav Gashek*, Prosveshcheniye, Moscow, 1980. Subsequent page references are indicated in my text.

Remarque's *Im Westen nichts Neues* (*All Quiet on the Western Front*) (1929) and Hemingway's *A Farewell to Arms* (1929). Barbusse's and Hašek's works are socialist realist, the others cited here are examples of critical realism (p. 89). Anti-war novels of critical realism see the reasons for war as man's age-old bestial nature, whereas socialist realist anti-war novels see the reasons for war from a Marxist-Leninist viewpoint, they are the inescapable result of the class nature of society (p. 90). In *Švejk* there is revolutionary optimism (p. 92). Finally:

> Communist party-mindedness ['partiynost''], the broad grasp of reality on an international scale from the point of view of the struggle between socialism and capitalism, the optimistic nature of the satire, the aesthetic socialist ideal from which satirically and humorously the various contemporary events and figures are depicted — all these qualities of the majority of Hašek's stories and *feuilletons* of the 1920s give one grounds to consider them and *The Good Soldier Švejk* to be satire of Socialist Realism. (p. 109)

Here, in essence, we have the basic ingredients of socialist realism spelt out for us: *partiynost'*, *klassovost'* and *narodnost'*, together with a good dose of optimism.

Bulgakov's *Master i Margerita* has been accommodated in a similar fashion by being presented as a satire on the shortcomings of Soviet life in the 1920s and 1930s. Perhaps one day Voynovich's masterpiece *Zhizn' i neobychaynyye priklyucheniya soldata Ivan Chonkina* (*The Life and Extraordinary Adventures of Private Ivan Chonkin*)(1975), a work frequently and with justification compared to *Švejk*, will be published in the Soviet Union and accommodated in a similar way. However, socialist realism would be hard pressed to countenance the elements of the absurd and the existential questions raised in these essential *comic* (as opposed to satirical) works. Because *Švejk* makes us laugh, it does not mean the work is optimistic. Comedy recognises the tragedy of man and works for him as a defence mechanism. Satire at its most civic-minded seeks merely to correct the evils in what is assumed to be a basically sound society. If Josef K. and Švejk had met on Charles Bridge it would have been a meeting of guilt and innocence produced by a common culture. It is doubtful if either of these human states or their combination could eradicate evil as understood by the politician.

The 'front rank' socialist realists of Czechoslovakia, Marie Majerová, Marie Pujmanová and Ivan Olbracht, have never enjoyed world status, despite their official promotion, their utter sincerity and the relative popularity of the Communists in Czecho-

slovakia in the immediate postwar years. Moreover, many of Czechoslovakia's leading writers of the 1960s who found themselves in
the 'dissident' camp after 1968 and therefore, presumably, deemed
anti-socialist and anti-realist, have enhanced the reputation of
Czech literature, and *not* just by their political stance. Milan Kundera in his novels and articles since 1975, when he emigrated, can be
accused equally of castigating Western values and those of the
socialist counties. Likewise, Ivan Klíma and Václav Havel, still in
Czechoslovakia, or Josef Švorecký, now in Canada, would all look to
Hašek for inspiration, and laugh through their tears at what they see
as his being hijacked by Soviet critics.

The Soviet press today contains a good deal of lively literary
debate (as well as a good deal of dross) and not infrequently it
avoids the hackneyed terminology of 'classical' socialist realism
(party-mindedness, positive hero, even the term socialist realism
itself). There are extensive discussions in the *Literaturnaya gazeta*
under such headings as 'Kuda polozhitel'nyy geroy?' ('Wither the
Positive Hero?') or 'Fantastika: zrelost' ili starost'?' ('The Fantastic:
Maturity or Old Age?'). Naturally, there is also an enormous
coverage of political events. The issue for 26 February 1986 (no. 9)
devoted no less than eight full pages (out of sixteen) to Gorbachev's
speech to the Twenty-Seventh Party Congress. A small part of the
speech was given over to literature and art:

> The moral health of society, the spiritual climate in which people live is to
> a large extent determined by the state of literature and art. Our literature,
> reflecting the birth of a new world has actively participated in its
> formation as it shapes the man of this world, the patriot of his Homeland,
> the genuine internationalist . . . . Only literature — ideological, artistic,
> national ['ideynaya, khudozhestvennaya, narodnaya'] — educates
> people to be honest, strong in spirit, capable of taking upon themselves
> the burden of their time.[12]

Two weeks before looking to the Twenty-Seventh Party Congress,
there was a lengthy article by Yuriy Surovtsev in *Literaturnaya gazeta*
on literary theory and it raised (again) the question of socialist
realism:

> Let's admit honestly: the theory of Socialist Realism in recent years has
> lived a somewhat hindered ['pritormozhennyy'] life in our
> country. . . . I'll just touch on, only touch on,. . . one of those so to speak
> ticklish questions. Are all the works written today in our country, works
> of Socialist Realism? . . . There's no need to be afraid of asking this

12. *Literaturnaya gazeta*, no. 9, 26 Feb. 1986, p. 9.

question out of fear that afterwards, in the West say, people will start shouting about the 'end' of Socialist Realism!... I think that in our judgements on Socialist Realism we have perhaps forgotten that it is not just a method, but a trend as well ['napravleniye'], an historical-literary, historical-cultural artistic movement.... These new criteria, advanced by Lenin in his article of November 1905, 'Party Organisation and Party Literature', continue to act today and to *broaden* Socialist Realism as an objective and natural *world* literary-artistic trend.[13]

In short, the article seems to cling to the established terminology while striving to broaden its application, as well as guard against works that might be politically uncomfortable. The article mentions no contemporary works of fiction and fails to discuss in detail any work of literature.

In September 1984 the Union of Writers of the USSR celebrated its fiftieth birthday. President Chernenko addressed the gathering and awarded the Union the Order of Friendship of Nations. He told those present that the approach of literature to life should consist in . . . , 'to use words well-known to you, Socialist Realism'. He also said: 'Yes, comrades, a lot of ineptitudes, utter nonsense, is written and talked in the West in order to subvert the meaning of the party approach to art. . . '.[14] It may be that what has been said in this article is the sort of thing President Chernenko had in mind; or could it be the case that the vocabulary and style of thinking forged by some twenty years of 'hard-line' socialist realism under Stalin can no longer really match the art that is being created in the Soviet Union and abroad?

When one examines some of the literary criticism addressed to specific works the comments can be more illuminating and the points of reference more imaginative. The theoreticians will allude to Lenin, and then Gorky, Fadeyev, Sholokhov, Fedin and other 'classics' of socialist realism. The reviewer of a novel may additionally refer to Rasputin, Abramov, Tendryakov, to such characters as Darya Pinigina or the Pryaslin family, Aitmatov's Old Momun and his grandson — such recent works seem to be regarded as modern classics by Soviet writers and readers, and few fair-minded people would deny the high quality of the works referred to. At the same time it is difficult to see how the term socialist realism can *usefully* be applied to them. They contain authentic characters, they raise serious topical and moral issues, they possess a rich and varied style, a subtle structure — in short are 'artistic' (*khudozhestvennyy*), as

13. *Literaturnaya gazeta*, no. 7, 12 Feb. 1986, p. 2. Yuri Surovtsev's italics.
14. *Literaturnaya gazeta*, no. 39, 26 Sept. 1984, p. 2.

Sholokhov and Gorbachev require — but the same might be said of many works written abroad by people who are not socialists; and in the West the term 'realism' has become debased. In his book *The Rise of The Russian Novel*, Richard Freeborn quotes as follows:

> Realism is not only vague and elastic, but also pretentious in the implicit claim it makes to determine reality. No apologist for his own vision will tamely let the 'real' be appropriated by some other; and so it is forced into new postures, encouraged in new pretences, until everyone has his different claim upon it. This is the situation we are now, with competing critics pulling the word a dozen different ways.[15]

One feels that these remarks might equally apply in Eastern Europe, given the wide variety of works that the term 'realism' is expected to embrace.

Mundanely, one might conclude that whether a work is regarded as socialist realist or not depends on the political loyalty of the writer concerned (more than on the intrinsic qualities of the work). Many pages of *The Quiet Don* (1928–40) portray the Whites sympathetically or suggest the supremacy of universal human values over the virtues of ideology, yet this epic is seen as one of the pinnacles of socialist realism; Sholokhov through the successive reigns of Lenin, Stalin, Khrushchev, Brezhnev, Andropov and Chernenko never faltered in his adherence to the Party line, even if his humanistic principles did.

A final illustrative anecdote: in the early 1960s Voynovich published some poems in the *Moskovskiy Komsomolets*, the Moscow Komsomol (youth organisation) newspaper. One of the poems is about the girls at a local dance attended by Red Army men preferring the officers to the privates. The then Minister of Defence Marshal Malinovsky happened to see the poem, and consequently denounced the work as a shot in the back of the Red Army. In Voynovich's own words: 'I thought that a Minister of Defence of a nuclear superpower had more important business to attend to than the analysis of a young poet's verses. All the more so, given that this was shortly after the Cuba crisis. I then came to have real doubts about the defence capability of the USSR'.[16] No one has doubts about the capability of Russian literature — with or without socialist realism.

---

15. D. Grant, *Realism*, Methuen, London, 1970, pp. 54–5. Quoted in Freeborn, *The Rise of the Russian Novel* Cambridge University Press, Cambridge, 1973, p. 7 (footnote).
16. *Posev*, no. 9, 1983, p. 31.

—4—

'Breadth and Diversity': Socialist Realism in the GDR

DENNIS TATE

Any account of socialist realism in the context of the German Democratic Republic needs to acknowledge the uniqueness of the cultural and political circumstances under which East German literature has evolved. Two basic points should be noted at the outset. Firstly, its origins are to be found in the distinctively German cultural debate of the 1930s about the nature of a committed socialist literature, which took a markedly different course to the debate in the Soviet Union. Its protagonists were all in exile from Hitler's Germany, some (such as George Lukács and Johannes R. Becher) apparently close to the sources of cultural authority in the Soviet Union, while others (notably Bertolt Brecht and Anna Seghers) found themselves in relative isolation and with far less opportunity to articulate their responses to the conception of socialist realism established at the First Soviet Writers' Congress in 1934. They were all critical, albeit to varying degrees, of the Soviet model, but accepted the need for compromise with the authority of Stalin and Zhdanov, whether by expressing their dissent in carefully coded form in work actually published at the time, or by withholding their views until the overriding political task of defeating German Fascism had been accomplished.

Secondly, since 1945, the development of literature in what was initially the Soviet Zone of Occupation has been immensely complicated by the division of Germany. East German authors have been obliged to strike a difficult balance, under frequently changing circumstances, between their allegiances as socialists ideologically rooted in Eastern Europe and intellectuals convinced of the radical potential of their German cultural heritage. They have consequently experienced periods of intense crisis over the issue of whether their work is primarily a contribution to a developing national literature, which will only be fully appreciated as such if a reunified socialist Germany is created, or the product of a quite different kind of literature in a newly established state — the GDR having come into existence in the autumn of 1949 — drawing its main inspiration from the contemporary culture of its East European neighbours.

The failure to acknowledge these special historical and geopolitical features of literature in the GDR can produce seriously distorted accounts of how socialist realism has developed there. Some Western commentators, most recently Georg Buehler in *The Death of Socialist Realism in the Novels of Christa Wolf*,[1] have uncritically assumed that the original Soviet model was imposed by administrative fiat on East Germany in 1945 and became the sole point of reference for authors who, like Wolf, served their literary apprenticeship in the 1950s before rising to prominence on the following decade. Buehler's quest for 'an all-encompassing, satisfactory definition' of socialist realism (p. 29) is based on a check-list of five criteria, derived from Soviet sources of the 1930s — 'objective reflection of reality', 'partiality', 'national orientation', 'the typical' and 'the positive hero' — which he believes will allow him 'to determine to what degree the work at hand conforms to or deviates from the precepts of socialist realism' (p. 32). Having established this schematic framework, which assumes that there has been no significant development in the theoretical discussion (whether in the GDR or the Soviet Union) over half a century of historical upheaval, Buehler methodically performs the simple task of proving that Wolf, over the twenty-year period between her *Moskauer Novelle* ('Moscow Novella') (1959) and *Kein Ort. Nirgends* (*No Place on Earth*) (1979), steadily came to reject this socialist realism in favour of what he refers to (interchangeably) as 'true literature' (p. 174), 'literature *per se*' (p. 155) and 'universally recognized literature' (p. 170), without ever making it clear what kind of alternative these nebulous terms might represent.

At the other end of the spectrum, the Dietz Verlag, the publishing house in East Berlin of the governing Socialist Unity Party (SED), produces studies of socialist realism in the GDR which depict it as a smoothly evolving concept, the product of a predominantly harmonious working relationship between German writers and critics since the 1930s. The collective authorship of the *Einführung in den sozialistischen Realismus* ('Introduction to Socialist Realism') of 1975[2] sees no

---

1. P. Lang, Frankfurt, Berne and New York, 1984. Subsequent page references are indicated in my text.
2. Collectively written by Erwin Pracht, Kurt Batt, Peter Feist, Heinz Plavius, Rolf Richter and Elisabeth Simons. This volume was a marked improvement on its predecessor of 1970, entitled *Sozialistischer Realismus: Positionen, Probleme, Perspektiven*, in its acceptance of much broader criteria and a comparative German dimension.

need to mention Stalin or Zhdanov, arguing that a German basis for socialist realism already existed in the Weimar Republic in the work of proletarian writers like Willi Bredel and Hans Marchwitza, but without discussing why this tradition has never been actively fostered in the GDR itself. It also claims Bertolt Brecht as the 'Klassiker des sozialistischen Realismus' (p. 64), while omitting to point out that most of his essays on the subject, which ought to have been seminal to the debate, could only be published after his death in 1956, and have really only had a major impact in the GDR since the late 1960s.[3] This emphasis on Brecht's achievements, and the corresponding playing down of the importance of Lukács's theory between the exile years and the 1960s, tells us more about the cultural-political priorities determined by Erich Honecker after he took office in 1971 than about the historical evolution of German socialist realism.

If, in contrast to both of these positions, we seek to place German socialist realism in an historical light which encompasses the fundamental disagreements of the 1930s about how it should develop and its actual course of development thereafter, then we need to differentiate between three broad conceptions:

(i) The Zhdanov model of Soviet socialist realism, as codified after the 1934 Congress, with its simplistic assumption of a direct relationship between the depiction of heroic endeavours, didactically underlined by a partisan narrator, and the reader's willingness to emulate them in the real world. It aspires to the social totality of the great epics of the past, while highlighting the industrial context of socialist revolution and encouraging the belief that 'typical' personalities can be dramatically transformed in the heat of the struggle.

(ii) The modified form of the classic German novel of education, the *Entwicklungsroman*, which Georg Lukács proposed as a model for German authors in exile, in the context of the Popular Front strategy of the mid-1930s, once the threat to creative independence and literary quality represented by a socialist realism codified in Zhdanov's terms had become apparent.[4] Even though Lukács might well

3. The complete *Schriften zur Literatur und Kunst* finally appeared in the GDR in two volumes in 1966. See W. Mittenzwei, *Der Realismus-Streit um Brecht: Grundriß der Brecht-Rezeption in der DDR 1945–1975*, Aufbau, Berlin and Weimar, 1978, esp. pp. 72–98.

4. For a more detailed account, see the introductory chapter to my *The East German Novel: Identity, Community, Continuity*, Bath University Press/St Martin's Press, Bath and New York, 1984, pp. 1–11. David Pike surprisingly overlooks this important distinction between Lukács and Soviet orthodoxy in his stimulating study *German Writers in Soviet Exile 1933–1945*, Chapel Hill, NC., 1982, pp. 259–306.

have regarded this as a transitional solution for authors as yet insufficiently mature to produce the Tolstoyan 'great proletarian work of art' which he projected as the ultimate goal of socialist realism, the focus it encouraged on the complex portrayal of individual experience was to provide a more substantial theoretical foundation for East German literature than the bureaucratic exhortation to conjure up 'epic totality' overnight. Specifically, this emphasis on exploiting the genre which forms Germany's distinctive contribution to the history of the European novel gave rise to J.R. Becher's *Abschied* (*Farewell*) (1940), a flawed, but nevertheless noteworthy early example of German socialist realism — a term which Lukács did not himself use in this context at the time, but which fell within his definition of socialist (in contrast to critical) realism in his important essay of 1956 in *Wider den mißverstandenen Realismus* (*The Meaning of Contemporary Realism*).[5]

(iii) The refusal of practising exile authors like Brecht and Seghers, who enjoyed greater independence (but were also extremely isolated) in their places of refuge outside the Soviet Union, to accept any definition of realism imposed from above and tied to a narrow canon of 'great works', whether in the European tradition of Balzac, Dickens and Tolstoy or the German heritage of the *Entwicklungsroman* since Goethe's *Wilhelm Meister*. Brecht's insistence on the transitory nature of all literary forms, their limitation to a specific stage in any society's socio-political development, led him to advocate for socialist realism an innovative 'breadth and diversity' of style and the close study of technical features like stream of consciousness, montage and multi-perspective narrative in the allegedly 'decadent' writing of Joyce, Döblin, Kafka and Dos Passos.[6] This allowed him, in a note of 1954, to summarise his understanding of socialist realism in the most open of terms, as if to underline the irrelevance of the rules upon which cultural politicians seemed so obsessively dependent: 'What socialist realism is should not simply be derived from

5. G. Lukács, 'Critical Realism and Socialist Realism', in idem, *The Meaning of Contemporary Realism*, trans. J. and N. Mander, Merlin, London, 1963, pp. 93–135. Even though much of this essay is devoted to the failure of conventional works of socialist realism to achieve literary distinctiveness, Lukács still insists on the idea of socialist realism as an elevation of bourgeois critical realism to a higher plane of political awareness, which, for him, also leads to increased qualitative potential. He accords special importance to the autobiographical novel of education (of which *Abschied* is an obvious example) in the lengthy period of transition towards mature socialist realism.

6. See Brecht's essays and notes of the late 1930s, notably 'Weite und Vielfalt der realistischen Schreibweise' and 'Volkstümlichkeit und Realismus', first published coherently some thirty years later, e.g. in the section 'Über den Realismus', in the *Gesammelte Werke*, vol. 19, Suhrkamp, Frankfurt, 1967, pp. 284–382.

available works or techniques of representation. The criterion should not be whether a work or a representation resembles other works or representations which are deemed to be socialist realism, but whether it is socialist and realistic'.[7] There was also a bitter irony in the way that Anna Seghers's novel of resistance to Nazism, *Das siebte Kreuz* (*The Seventh Cross*), first published in the USA in 1942 and incorporating dubiously modernistic techniques such as montage and multi-perspective, was to be hailed in the GDR as a classic long before these features were officially accepted as legitimate weapons in the armoury of a socialist realist.

When we come to review the actual development of East German literature in terms of these three competing approaches to German socialist realism — approaches elaborated, of necessity, in theoretical terms before the cultural conditions prevailing in a German socialist state could be even remotely envisaged — the untenability of the clichés of the ruthlessly imposed Soviet model and of the smoothly evolving collective concept quickly becomes apparent. Research carried out in recent years in both German states into the immediate postwar period has revealed a cultural vitality and breadth long obscured behind preconceptions of the extent of cold war repression.[8] During the lifetime of the Soviet Zone of Occupation (1945–9) the dominant voice was that of the Kulturbund (the Cultural Alliance for the Democratic Renewal of Germany) under the presidency of Becher. The Kulturbund revived the ideology of the Popular Front, setting out to unite left-wing authors returning from exile (most of whom opted, however tentatively, to settle in the Soviet Zone rather than in one of the Western Zones) behind the goal of a renaissance of Germany's national culture on the foundations of their classical literary heritage, as elaborated by Becher in tandem with Lukács during their Soviet exile. Furthermore, the Soviet Union's cultural administrators, such as Dymshits and Tulpanov, adopted a benevolent stance towards these endeavours, not least because the ultimate fate of Germany within the developing East–West power struggle in Europe remained unpredictable at

7. B. Brecht, 'Über sozialistischen Realismus', in ibid., pp. 547–9. All quotations from German sources in this essay are my translations.
8. Notable examples include S. Bock, *Literatur — Gesellschaft — Nation: Materielle und ideelle Rahmenbedingungen der frühen DDR-Literatur 1949–1956*, Metzler, Stuttgart, 1980; I. Münz-Koenen (ed.), *Literarisches Leben in der DDR 1945–1960*, Akademie, Berlin, 1979; and M. Jäger, *Kultur und Politik in der DDR: Ein historischer Abriß*, Wissenschaft & Politik, Cologne, 1982.

this stage. The first German Writers' Congress, held in East Berlin in October 1947, as ideological tensions began to mount, brought together writers from all four Zones of Occupation, and was marked by Becher's appeal to his fellow-authors to prevent literature being reduced to an ideological tool of government, by making it 'political in its own characteristic and autonomous way'. There was also a hint of pressures to come in the young Stephan Hermlin's warning that the call for what he termed 'progressive realism' was being interpreted too narrowly in terms of 'vulgar naturalism or neo-classicism', when it should have been synonymous with quality, diversity, and popular accessibility.[9]

It is no accident that the term socialist realism is almost completely avoided in the literary pronouncements of authors living in the Soviet Zone between 1945 and 1949. The sense that it was at that stage being understood only in the narrow Soviet sense of the 1934 conference, and thus as something alien to German socialist culture, arises from the protocol of the visit in 1948 of the first delegation of East German authors to the Soviet Union. Alexander Fadeyev, as spokesman for the Soviet Writers' Union, was politely asked to explain what socialist realism was and then, after offering the orthodox definition, had to cope with (still polite, but unmistakeable) expressions of doubt from Anna Seghers and others as to whether this style could be easily transferred to the German context. Furthermore, when Lukács reentered the German debate and employed the term (in an article of June 1949 in the Party newspaper *Neues Deutschland*) as the 'revisionism' campaign against him began to build up momentum, it was in the role he was advocating in the same article for literary critics generally: that of the 'clever tactician' mediating between the Party and authors, doing what was possible under increasingly difficult circumstances to uphold the criteria of literary quality evident in his realist tradition of great novels.[10]

It was therefore really only around the time of the establishment of the GDR that the concerted attempt of the SED to make authors put the Soviet principles of socialist realism into practice took place, and even then it was — as Stephan Bock has shown in his illuminating study of the period[11] — far less successful and more short-lived

---

9. *Zur Tradition der deutschen sozialistischen Literatur*, Aufbau, Berlin and Weimar, 1979, vol. 3, includes extensive excerpts from the First Writers' Congress, such as Becher, 'Vom Willen zum Frieden', pp. 504–21 (p. 507), and Hermlin, 'Wo bleibt die junge Dichtung ?', pp. 552–8 (p. 557).
10. Ibid., pp. 652–70, 717–20. For a detailed account of the 'revisionism debate', see Rodney Livingstone's contribution to this volume (Chapter 1 above).
11. See above, note 8.

than is generally believed. Of the novels produced with the desired speed and partisan orientation by authors prepared to accept Party commissions to tackle major industrial topics, only Eduard Claudius's *Menschen an unsrer Seite* ('Men at our Side') (1951) has survived, and by 1953 (the year of the Workers' Revolt of 17 June) a substantial public debate on the unacceptability of this trivialisation of literature was under way, featuring Brecht and younger critically minded authors such as Stefan Heym and Erich Loest. One of the editors of the journal of the newly formed Writers' Union, *Neue Deutsche Literatur*, described the bureaucratic urge to make Soviet socialist realism obligatory as 'just as absurd as it is damaging', in an article with a title conveniently derived from a slogan of Stalin's, 'Schreibt die Wahrheit!' ('Write the Truth'). The major reorientation needed meant, in Brecht's phrase, making socialist realism 'simultaneously a critical realism', entering into a serious debate about the persistence of attitudes forged in the Hitler era, and giving East German literature a broader German ('gesamtdeutsch') character.[12] This expression of dissent heralded an intellectual ferment which had elements in common with the more famous debate then taking place in the Soviet Union, even though it failed to generate a work to compare with Ehrenburg's *Ottopel' (Thaw)* (1954). At the Writers' Congress of January 1956 in East Berlin, which immediately preceded Khruschev's secret speech to the Twentieth Soviet Party Congress, the impressive show of solidarity against the bureaucratic control of literature in the GDR included contributions from all the main protagonists of the 1930s debates — Becher (as Minister of Culture since 1954), Seghers (as President of the Writers' Union since its creation in 1952), Lukács (the eminent guest speaker) and Brecht — with a clear emphasis on the priorities of a socialist *Nationalliteratur*.[13]

Within a few months, however, following the abortive efforts of the Harich Group to find a political channel for this cultural aspiration, the radical impetus had been entirely lost. With Brecht dead and both Becher and Lukács politically disqualified, the SED had a somewhat easier task to reimpose a narrow view of socialist realism, behind a rhetorical smokescreen of 'cultural revolution', on a largely inexperienced body of younger authors. As a result, the

12. G. Cwojdrak, 'Schreibt die Wahrheit!', *Neue Deutsche Literatur*, no. 8, 1953, pp. 23–30, and 'Über unsere Gegenwartsliteratur', *Neue Deutsche Literatur*, no. 1, 1953, pp. 157–65; Brecht, 'Über Kulturpolitik und Akademie der Künste', in idem, *Gesammelte Werke*, vol. 19, pp. 540–4.
13. All included in the two-volume *Protokoll*, Deutscher Schriftstellerverband, Berlin, 1956.

emergence of a distinctive East German literature was retarded for several years: outstanding talent was stifled (most notably in the field of lyric poetry, where Stephan Hermlin, Franz Fühmann and Johannes Bobrowski all underwent serious creative crises), persuaded to emigrate westwards (Uwe Johnson and others), or disorientated (to the extent that many of the new generation of authors, including Christa Wolf, Brigitte Reimann, Irmtraud Morgner and Günter de Bruyn, have since disowned their publications of these years). Anna Seghers fared little better: in a misguided departure from her literary production of the exile years, she completed the first volume of a neo-Tolstoyan epic with *Die Entscheidung* ('The Decision') (1959), attempting to realise the Lukácsian ideal of socialist realism through a panoramic portrayal of life in both parts of postwar Germany, but with predictably uninspiring results.

It was only after the political uncertainty about the permanence of the two German states was resolved, however crudely, for the foreseeable future with the construction of the Berlin Wall in August 1961, that some of the GDR's authors built up the resolve to redefine socialist realism for themselves. This resolve gave rise to a number of works, published in the period 1963–5, which represent the first lasting achievements of a home-grown East German literature. In our present context they are particularly interesting as an obvious compromise between bureaucratic expectations and authorial convictions, as the socialist realism of writers who had learnt the rules according to Lukács in the 1950s, but were now intent on adapting them to meet the needs of their own creative work. Christa Wolf, in *Der geteilte Himmel (Divided Heaven)* (1963), is an obvious case in point, making the theme of the divided nation, in the politically sensitive context of August 1961, the framework for her fictional action, but without the epic pretensions displayed by her mentor Anna Seghers in *Die Entscheidung*. She expresses her socialist partisanship through the narrator's moral solidarity with a readership assumed to have experienced the sealing of the GDR's frontiers as a deeply distressing event, instead of with the didactic omniscience of a Party mouthpiece. She goes on to offer a credibly dialectical view of the GDR's future progress depending on the elimination of Stalinist dogmatism, and dares to make the conventional villain of the piece, the faint-hearted intellectual who defects to the West, into a complex character typical of her own generation in many aspects of his disillusionment. But then, as if to restore the balance, she falls back on organic metaphors of growth to suggest the natural vitality of the socialist community and the inner strength of a decidedly positive heroine. This proved to be a remarkably successful compromise — the huge sales of *Der geteilte Himmel* in the GDR, the enthusiastic response of readers and the fact that it forced hitherto ultra-cautious literary critics into a vigorous public debate about its socialist realist pedigree,[14] all indicated that Wolf had found the key to popular accessibility and relevance, that elusive quality of *Volksverbundenheit* without which all the theorising about the new social function of this kind of literature appeared meaningless. And yet, once achieved, this sensitive balancing-act did not seem worth repeating, not just to Wolf, but to colleagues like de Bruyn, Fühmann and Heym, who quickly recognised that the function of this new socialist realism had to be more radical in its questioning of the status quo, and who found themselves as a result in profound conflict with Party authority at the end of 1965 (for broadly similar reasons of official retrenchment which brought Daniel' and Sinyavsky to international prominence as dissidents at the same time).

This renewed confrontation at first appeared to have stifled literary initiatives as effectively as the repressive aftermath of 1956 had done, but this time it only had the effect of driving them temporarily underground. A rapidly maturing generation of authors had learnt vital practical lessons about the untenability of the officially espoused formal criteria of realism and were in the process of making the decisive break with the notion of socialist realism as an inherently different style of writing from Western critical realism. Of the many factors which combined to accelerate this process of enlightenment, two should be highlighted here: frustration at the failure of the GDR to seize the opportunity created by the sealing of its Western frontiers in 1961 to make decisive progress towards the Marxist Utopia, by allowing greater scope for individual self-realisation; and a more complete awareness of the alternative aesthetic represented by Brecht's theoretical writings on realism, published in their entirety for the first time in the GDR in 1966. An indication of this process of change had been given by Stefan Heym in his essay of 1965, 'Die Langeweile von Minsk' ('The Boredom of Minsk'), which took its title from an anecdote recounting Brecht's view (of 1955) that the Soviet Union would only have a literature worth the name when a novel could begin with a sentence such as 'Minsk is one of the most boring towns in the world'. Heym went on to revive Brecht's open definition of socialist realism as synonymous with the uncompromising pursuit of the truth:

14. The debate is usefully documented in Reso (ed.), *'Der geteilte Himmel' und seine Kritiker*, Mitteldeutscher Verlag, Halle, 1965.

For Brecht demanded realism. If a town is boring, say so. If a man is a scoundrel, don't put a halo over his head. If life is not what newspaper editorials and travel bureaux claim it is: you are a novelist, dramatist, poet, and it is your duty to say what it is really like. For this, and this alone, is the meaning of the word *realism*. And socialist realism means portraying the truth with its inherent perspective, which, in the nature of things, can only be a socialist perspective.[15]

Brecht's view of literary form as a dynamic process of adaptation and experimentation, deriving from the conviction that 'new contents' require 'new forms', is the related point noted by Christa Wolf in her short essay of 1966, 'Brecht und andere' ('Brecht and others'), in which she describes his work as having given her confidence in the validity of her subjective perceptions as an author and the 'encouragement' she needed 'to find out for oneself'.[16]

This new self-confidence and readiness to challenge cultural-political orthodoxy, even if obscured from public view in the GDR and elsewhere until Honecker's liberalisation of the early 1970s had been translated into book publications, has marked the work of the GDR's best authors for some twenty years now. The watershed was Christa Wolf's *Nachdenken über Christa T.* (*The Quest for Christa T.*) (1968), one of the few significant works actually published between 1965 and Honecker's accession in 1971 (largely because of the huge popularity of *Der geteilte Himmel*, and the author's status until 1967 as a candidate for the Central Committee of the SED). It was significant, too, as the first novel about the contemporary GDR by an author still living there, which was both translated into English and taken seriously by critical opinion in the English-speaking world. *Christa T.*[17] mounts a frontal challenge to the conventional views of the positive hero(ine) and typicality. These are now seen by Wolf's narrator to be an ideologically inspired invention, a fiction which has little in common with the necessarily fragmented portrayal of everyday experience which she is committed to providing, even though she still nourishes the hope that the failure of a kindred spirit like Christa T. to find self-fulfilment in the GDR may be an exception arising from uniquely adverse historical circumstances:

15. 'Die Langeweile von Minsk', repr. in S. Heym, *Wege und Umwege: Streitbare Schriften aus fünf Jahrzehnten*, Bertelsmann, Munich, 1980, pp. 294–9.
16. C. Wolf, 'Brecht und andere', in *Lesen und Schreiben: Aufsätze und Betrachtungen*, Aufbau, Berlin and Weimar, 1972, pp. 62–5.
17. *The Quest for Christa T.*, Christopher Middleton's translation of *Nachdenken über Christa T.*, first published in 1970, has now reached a wide English-speaking audience through the paperback reprint (Virago, London, 1982).

Ah, if only I had the free choice of a nice clear-cut invention . . . It would never have occurred to me, I swear, to think of her [her protagonist Christa T.]. For she is, as an example, not at all exemplary, as a character not at all a model. I shall resist the suspicion that it would not be any different with any other real, living person, and I affirm my freedom and duty to invent. Just for once, this time only, I want to be allowed to discover, and to say, how things really were, in an unexemplary way and without regard for practical utility.[18]

The reception of *Nachdenken über Christa T.* in the GDR casts a revealing light on the way in which this determined creative adherence to newly-won perceptions and a newly-discovered aesthetic compelled a major cultural-political rethink on what constitutes socialist realism, in order to allow some semblance of coherence between theory and practice to be restored (retrospectively). In the year following its publication Wolf's novel was denounced as a betrayal of the principles of socialist realism: a concerted campaign around the time of the Writers' Congress in 1969 condemned it for its lack of partisanship, for the heroine's failure to qualify as a *Vorbild* (an example to others), for suggesting that alienation could exist in a socialist society, for 'erecting a pretty monument to individualism', and much else besides. Nevertheless, it was republished in 1973 and then praised, both in the *Einführung in den sozialistischen Realismus* of 1975 (mentioned above) and the first official *Geschichte der Literatur der DDR* ('History of GDR Literature') (1976), for its authenticity and its rigorous differentiation in the portrayal of the individual's relationship with society in the GDR.[19] Had an official rethink of this magnitude not occurred, then the history of socialist realism in the GDR might well have come to an abrupt halt around 1970, for *Christa T.* has provided the inspiration for most of the outstanding works of East German literature since then, which have also found the analysis of contradictions in a society failing to live up to the propagandists' image a more compelling task than the pursuit of the elusive worker-hero in an environment remote from most writers' experience.

A brief survey of the main achievements in the area of prose writing since *Nachdenken über Christa T.* will underline the extent to

18. I have supplied my own translation here, because Middleton's generally outstanding version does not, in this instance, bring out the full significance for the debate on socialist realism of the terms Wolf uses (Compare *Nachdenken über Christa T.*, p. 57 with *The Quest for Christa T.*, p. 45.)
19. See M. Behn (ed.), *Wirkungsgeschichte von Christa Wolfs 'Nachdenken über Christa T.'*, Athenäum, Königstein, 1978, pp. 52, 55, 70–2, 157–8, 175–8.

which this critical perspective has encouraged an impressive expansion of formal techniques. The 'subjective authenticity' (Wolf's term) of prose in which the dimension of the reflective narrator becomes more important than the artifices of character and plot has stimulated a succession of novels modelled on *Christa T.* (mainly by other female authors), acknowledging that the nature of identity under socialism is no less complex than in the pluralistic societies of Western capitalism. It has also pointed the way to documentary prose and autobiographical texts with an authority lacking in the ostensibly factual reportage and political memoir-writing of the 1950s and 1960s: Maxie Wander's collection of interviews with women, *Guten Morgen, du Schöne* ('Good Morning, my Love') (1977), which has revitalised the public debate on the barriers to female emancipation in a nominally egalitarian society, would have been unthinkable without the new understanding of 'typical' experience which works like *Christa T.* were determined to establish. The virtual disappearance of the distinction between the explicit autobiography of Franz Fühmann's *22 Tage oder die Hälfte des Lebens* (*22 Days or Half a Lifetime*) (1973) and Stephan Hermlin's *Abendlicht* ('Twilight') (1979) on the one hand, and autobiographical novels such as Wolf's *Kindheitsmuster* (*A Model Childhood*) (1976) and Hermann Kant's *Der Aufenthalt* ('Temporary Abode') (1977) on the other, is a further consequence of the swing of the pendulum away from coherent fictional worlds with only superficial resemblance to contemporary reality. This transformation of East German literature is most graphically demonstrated, however, by the growth of narratorial subjectivity into full-blown fantasy: the resurrection of a medieval poet to take satirical stock of the GDR in Irmtraud Morgner's montage novel, *Trobadora Beatriz* ('Beatrice the Female Troubadour') (1974); the visions of the inventor of an amazing air-balloon in F.R. Fries's *Das Luftschiff* ('The Airship') (1974); the metamorphoses of sexual identity conjured up in the anthology *Blitz aus heitrem Himmel* ('Bolt from the Blue') (again 1974); the post-nuclear war 'Brave New World' of Fühmann's *Saiäns-Fiktschen* ('Science Fiction') (1981), etc.

The cultural heritage used to legitimise these refreshingly original contributions to a previously rather colourless literature is still largely a German one: Jean Paul Richter, E.T.A. Hoffmann, Georg Büchner and Alfred Döblin are now major influences challenging the classical canon established by Lukács. A series of biographical fictions on German artists of the French Revolutionary era — notably Johannes Bobrowski's *Boehlendorff* (1965), Gerhard Wolf's *Der arme Hölderlin* ('Poor Hölderlin') (1972) and Christa Wolf's aforementioned portrayal of Kleist and Karoline von Günderrode, *Kein Ort. Nirgends* (1979) — complemented the new literature of fantasy by developing a more specific polemic against the orthodoxy based on Goethe and the tradition of the *Entwicklungsroman*. The recurrent theme of these ostensibly historical works — that of the revolutionary hopes for Germany aroused by the events of 1789 in France being thwarted by Napoleon's restoration of the virtual status quo a decade later — placed the sufferings of contemporary East German citizens like Wolf's Christa T. in the stark historical perspective of almost two centuries of what Lukács had called the 'German *Misere*'.[20]

The question of how this inventive and challenging literature of the 1970s relates to the development of socialist realism now requires closer scrutiny, and it is to the essays of the creative authors themselves that we first need to turn for orientation. In the face of the conformism displayed by most literary theorists in the GDR in the hour of greatest need after 1965, the writers (notably Wolf, Hermlin, Fühmann, Günter de Bruyn and Volker Braun) took over the role of defining where the realism of their work lay, and thereby provided the best available guide to the course of this debate. What stands out in their essays is the dearth of references to socialist realism as such: the incompatibility of their changed perception of what constitutes authenticity in literature, and the cultural-political line enforced (ironically, by Honecker himself) in 1965, seems to have led to a collective recognition that the term socialist realism should no longer be used to paper over the cracks between such diametrically opposed positions. At the same time, the authors endeavoured to uphold and refine the basic Brechtian conceptions of a broad 'non-Aristotelian' cultural heritage, of the synonymity of socialist and critical realism, and of 'new forms for new contents'.

The most programmatic of these essays is Christa Wolf's 'Lesen und Schreiben' ('Reading and Writing') (written in 1968, published in 1972), her theoretical counterpart to *Christa T.*, which elucidates her decisive break with the precepts of Soviet socialist realism in the middle 1960s in favour of a modified Brechtian position.[21] The 'crisis of the novel ' (p. 202) in the GDR has arisen from the realisation that 'the good old methods' (p. 176), 'the traditional plot composed of set-pieces' (p. 201), 'the old literary models with their plot modified' (p. 210) can no longer serve the needs of literary mimesis. For Wolf, the reality of socialist life no longer corresponds

---

20. See Chapter 5 of my study *The East German Novel*, pp. 177–226.
21. First published in the volume *Lesen und Schreiben*, pp. 176–224. Subsequent page references are indicated in my text.

to scientific laws, so the writer's task is now one involving tentative investigation, based on the limitations of subjective understanding, individual experience, and a fallible memory. 'Realism' (p. 206) can only arise from the infinite possibilities of what she calls (in acknowledgement of Brecht's example in the theatre) 'epic prose', in which the dimension of the narrator is extended in order to highlight the questionable nature of all fictional invention and to establish a dialogue with readers assumed to be his equals in this exploration of contemporary experience. This is, however, still a realism informed by a socialist vision of the future: there exists a 'deep correspondence between this style of writing and socialist society' (p. 209), the author is a 'normal, committed member of this society' working to realise his socialist vision, yet with a sober awareness of how severely the very future of mankind is threatened today (p. 218). This 'epic prose' is thus both 'revolutionary and realistic' (p. 224).

Wolf's arguments were then widely endorsed as literary debate was revived in the early years of the Honecker regime. The process of radical self-liberation from the bureaucratic understanding of socialist realism underlies the contribution of Volker Braun to the dynamic Writers' Congress of 1973, in which he forcefully rejects the unspoken assumption that writers should keep back 'reserves of realism' until the time is deemed right. It also led to Stefan Heym's statement of 1974 announcing the end of 'that socialist realism which was neither socialist nor realistic, but a cliché-concept breeding further clichés'.[22] Nevertheless, the recognition that progress will always depend on the individual author's readiness to extend cultural-political boundaries (rather than through joint reassessments) was not diminished by the literary achievements of the early Honecker years: Wolf offered a timely warning in 1975 against any temptation to assume that 'the struggle for realism in art will ever cease or be easy'.[23]

Even a cursory glance at official pronouncements on cultural policy in the years of liberalisation will show why East German writers still needed to display this kind of tenacity. Honecker's famous statement of December 1971 that there would henceforth be 'no taboos' as regards content and style for writers 'firmly rooted in socialism' might have suggested that he had been converted to a Brechtian view of socialist realism, but his subsequent speeches (like

22. V. Braun, 'Literatur und Geschichtsbewußtsein', in *Es genügt nicht die einfache Wahrheit: Notate*, Reclam, Leipzig, 1979, pp. 133–40; S. Heym, foreword to his anthology *Auskunft: Neue Prosa aus der DDR*, Rowohlt, Reinbek, 1977, pp. 7–9.
23. See C.Wolf, *Fortgesetzter Versuch: Aufsätze, Gespräche, Essays*, Reclam, Leipzig, 1979, pp. 135.

those of Kurt Hager, the Politburo's main cultural spokesman) invariably contained warnings against the 'realism without banks' (without reference to the originator of the phrase, Roger Garaudy) which might obscure the ideological irreconcilability of socialist realism and modernism. There was an ominous retreat into authoritarian rebuttals of excessive criticism of the GDR and all-too-familiar references to '*the* position of socialist realism', as defined by the Party, even before the 'Biermann crisis' erupted in 1976 and socialist realism again became a designation reserved for the truly partisan authors prepared to focus on the achievements of the working class, and used to distinguish them from their disaffected 'humanistic' colleagues.[24]

The fact that so many works of real merit were published under this disconcertingly fluctuating cultural policy may appear surprising. It is possible that the more oblique perspectives on the contemporary GDR offered by ostensibly historical or fantastic novels made them appear politically less threatening : the likelihood of publication was, however, much more uncertain in the case of works which had an unambiguously present-day setting and conventional narrative structures. The obvious examples are Stefan Heym's *Collin* (1979) and Erich Loest's *Es geht seinen Gang* ('Things take their Course') (1978). Both authors had come to prominence in the GDR in the 1950s, as creators of popular fiction which was regarded as compatible with socialist realism, and had not significantly developed their narrative styles since. Yet Heym's stocktaking of forty years' experience of socialism since the Spanish Civil War contained too many barely disguised historical facts and individual portraits even to be considered for publication. Loest's view of the typical citizen of the generation born together with the new State in 1949 was actually published, but the protracted conflict it provoked with authority caused him to leave the GDR and document his experiences as a case-study entitled *Der vierte Zensor* ('The Fourth Censor') (1984). Loest's frustrations remind us of how little the official definition of socialist realism had changed in practice in the middle 1970s. Even his relatively modest experimentation with narrative perspective, in presenting *Es geht seinen Gang* from the limited first-person viewpoint of his disillusioned protagonist Wülff, was seen by the chief-editor of the Mitteldeutscher Verlag as likely to confuse a readership still assumed to be in need of authoritative ideological

---

24. See E. Honecker, *Die Kulturpolitik unserer Partei wird erfolgreich verwirklicht*, Dietz, Berlin, 1982, pp. 36, 65–6, 176–7, 189, 223, 307; and K. Hager, *Beiträge zur Kulturpolitik*, Dietz, Berlin, 1981, pp. 67, 99–101.

guidance from the narrators of its novels.[25]

Loest and Heym were far from being alone in the 1970s in this experience of old-fashioned censorship behind the rhetoric of 'no taboos', but authors in the GDR generally began to benefit during the decade from a markedly more sympathetic literary criticism, which at last showed itself capable of mediating forcefully on their behalf. Kurt Batt, for example, as well as proving himself an astute critic of West German literature, was instrumental, following the fiasco of the official denunciation of Wolf's *Christa T.* in 1969, in establishing its profound importance as a model of literary realism. In his essay 'Realität und Phantasie' ('Reality and Fantasy') he stressed the new quality of authenticity to which *Christa T.* had given rise, and endorsed Wolf's view that realistic narrative today is only possible 'from socialist positions'[26] — an argument which has made it easier for the common ground between Wolf and, say, Heinrich Böll or Uwe Johnson to be seriously explored than in the days of the a priori assumption that the 'two German literatures' were irreconcilable. Dieter Schlenstedt's emphasis, in his *Wirkungsästhetische Analysen* . . . ('Analyses in the Aesthetics of Impact . . .') of 1979, on the communicative function of literature in a society of 'discriminating readers' presupposes a virtual revolution in the understanding of what this function is (i.e. initiating a dialogue on unresolved problems rather than providing a sermon on actual or imagined successes). He implies, through his avoidance of the phrase, that the concept of socialist realism is too tainted to serve any meaningful role in his account of the new collective process of communication and self-analysis ('kollektive Selbstverständigung').[27]

A further significant change of emphasis is the willingness of critics to view East German literature in its international context and to measure its achievements more objectively by comparative criteria. Hans Kaufmann's introductory essay to the volume of essays he edited concerning GDR literature of the 1970s, *Tendenzen und Beispiele* . . . ('Trends and Examples . . .') (1981), uses unfamiliar examples from recent South American literature (Márquez, Carpentier) and the controversial work of a Soviet author like Rasputin, in pursuing his aim of 'opening up GDR literature to wide-ranging points of reference'. 'Popular traditions, modernism

25. E. Loest, *Der vierte Zensor: Vom Entstehen und Sterben eines Romans in der DDR*, Wissenschaft & Politik, Cologne, 1984, pp. 19–20.
26. K. Batt, 'Realität und Phantasie', in *Widerspruch und Übereinkunft: Aufsätze zur Literatur*, Reclam, Leipzig, 1978, pp. 359–80 (p.374).
27. D. Schlenstedt, *Wirkungsästhetische Analysen: Poetologie und Prosa in der neueren DDR-Literatur*, Akademie, Berlin, 1979, pp. 37–45.

and political commitment' are fully compatible within his definition of 'socialist humanism', and he shows a new recognition of the global threats of the 1980s (emerging from the attitudes to ecology and nuclear weaponry of both superpowers) as factors which are bound to reduce to a snail's pace the speed of progress towards the Marxist Utopia, in the GDR as in any other socialist State.[28]

This international dimension is also becoming increasingly evident in East German literature itself in the 1980s. After evolving within a decidedly German cultural framework which, because of its relative isolation from the mainstream of European realism, may have made East German literature in turn less accessible to the non-German reader, its authors are now broadening their base. The common European heritage of Greek myth has become a major source of creative inspiration to authors such as Franz Fühmann, Irmtraud Morgner and Christa Wolf, offering archetypes of individuals torn apart by inner contradictions, who now appear entirely appropriate to their experience of the GDR in this bleak international context.[29] Wolf's *Kassandra* (1983),[30] for example, has had an equally profound impact in both German states through the moral force of its feminist critique of male-dominated militaristic society, a critique which has implications far beyond the ostensible context of the Greek–Trojan war. The stream of consciousness of her Cassandra, a first-person narrator taking stock of her life as she faces an inescapable violent death, has, for Wolf, the necessary complexity and subjectivity of all contemporary writing which aspires to realism, and she has no hesitation, in terms of the patronising worries about 'popular accessibility' which cultural politicians still express, in placing *Kassandra* before an East German readership familiar with 'the South Americans, Kafka, Proust, [and] Musil'.[31]

Another internationally recognised archetype of narrative realism, one which marks the emergence of modern class society in the eighteenth century, has been the no less surprising inspiration for Volker Braun's *Hinze-Kunze-Roman* ('Hinze and Kunze Novel') of 1985.

28. H. Kaufmann, 'Veränderte Literaturlandschaft', in idem (ed.), *Tendenzen und Beispiele: Zur DDR-Literatur in den siebziger Jahren*, Reclam, Leipzig, 1981, pp. 7–40 (esp. pp. 7–12).
29. Fühmann's essay of 1974, 'Das mythische Element in der Literatur', repr. in his *Essays, Gespräche, Aufsätze 1964–1981*, Hinstorff, Rostock, 1983, pp. 82–140, provides the theoretical access to this rich vein of new subject-matter.
30. An English translation by Jan van Heurck is available: *Cassandra. A Novel and Four Essays*, Virago, London, 1984.
31. In an interview of 1983, repr. in C. Wolf, *Die Dimension des Autors: Essays und Aufsätze, Reden und Gespräche 1959–1985*, Luchterhand, Darmstadt, 1987, pp. 929–40 (p. 938).

Diderot's *Jacques le fataliste* has provided the model of the interdependent master–servant relationship, elaborated as a characteristic of bourgeois society by writers as different as Brecht (in his *Puntila*, 1941) and Beckett (in *Waiting for Godot*, 1952, and *Endgame*, 1957). It now appears to have taken on a new relevance, almost simultaneously, for two major East European authors: the Czech exile, Milan Kundera, whose dramatic variant on Diderot was first published in French in 1981 as *Jacques et son maître*, and Braun, whose novel, including elements of montage from Diderot, was submitted for publication in the GDR in the same year. Kundera's unbounded admiration for Diderot arises from the latter's ability to achieve an authenticity which is the polar opposite to the 'illusion of realism' in the conventional novel,[32] while Braun's narrative involves a polemic against the clichés of bureaucratic socialist realism. The *Hinze-Kunze-Roman* culminates in the narrator's deliberations on the most appropriate style for the description of the State leadership's contingency plans to ensure its own survival in a nuclear bunker and abandon the rest of the population to its fate. This, the narrator concludes, 'demands a realism which gets on peoples' nerves, a more decisive, conspiratorial realism ('conspiratorial' in the sense that it means collectively considering facts otherwise withheld from the population).[33] Braun's satirical portrayal of today's GDR, focused on a sexually ruthless master of ministerial rank (Kunze) and his willingly subservient chauffeur (Hinze), who have no identity outside their chosen social roles and fail to develop as personalities within an equally directionless plot, has sparked off the most recent of the GDR's many debates on the limits of realism. Dieter Schlenstedt (in a detailed afterword to the novel, anticipating the difficulties to come) has defended Braun's provocative presentation of power relationships in the GDR as a Brechtian device, and has pointed to the survival of the Utopian socialist stimulus in the apotheosis of the third protagonist, Hinze's wife Lisa. His arguments have, however, been less than persuasive. The SED establishment's continuing inability to contain this degree of satire, narrative experimentation and purely long-term hope within its tortuously expanding notion of realism is reflected in Klaus Jarmatz's would-be sympathetic review in *Neue Deutsche Literatur*, preoccupied with theoretical aspects of 'how and whether' it 'takes realism a stage further', and unable to come to a clear-cut answer.[34]

32. M. Kundera, Introduction to *Jacques and his Master*, Methuen, London and Boston, 1986, p. 15.
33. V. Braun, *Hinze-Kunze-Roman*, Mitteldeutscher Verlag, Halle, 1985, p. 182.

Where, then, does this leave socialist realism in the GDR of the later 1980s? Its origins as a theoretical construct designed to underpin the status quo make it inevitable that the real cultural debate still relates to the limits of acceptable political criticism, even when the communicative function of literature is now acknowledged by the ideologues to be a far more subtle one than they had initially imagined. On the other hand, the desire to avoid a complete breakdown in understanding with cultural politicians has encouraged the GDR's avant-garde of internationally respected authors to continue discussing literature in terms of their own criteria, as committed socialists, of what constitutes realism. This has ensured, at least, that the official demarcation lines have considerably shifted since the 1960s in the direction of a Brechtian 'breadth and diversity'. While various reasons can be adduced to explain the failure of East German literature to produce an undisputed masterpiece of realistic fiction — the impenetrable complexities of divided Germany, the undermining of the whole notion of epic totality by the aesthetic of 'subjective authenticity', the losses to West Germany of many talented authors on the threshold of their creative maturity, and so on — its collective achievement since *Nachdenken über Christa T.* in giving credibility to the 1930s conception of a distinctively German socialist realism deserves wider recognition.

34. K. Jarmatz, 'Realismus mit Ecken und Kanten', *Neue Deutsche Literatur*, no. 2, 1986, pp. 132–9.

—5—

Socialist Realism and the West German Novel

AXEL GOODBODY

The rejection of socialist realism by West German writers and critics would seem to be both outright and general. Indeed the long-established non-mimetic, idealist German tradition remained so powerful after the Second World War that any form of realism was long viewed with suspicion. Initial support for a realist literature after 1945, either in the form of Wolfgang Weyrauch's 'total clearance' or Hans-Werner Richter's call, in *Der Ruf*, for a new realism 'with a humanist-socialist orientation', and early realist novels by Andersch, Plievier or Kästner, was succeeded in the early 1950s by works in which the problems of the day were deprived of historical and geographical specificity. The influence of French Existentialism coincided with a search for inner truth and preoccupation with a 'deeper' reality. Even politically engaged writers such as the members of the Gruppe 47 felt that the nineteenth-century realism on which socialist realism was based was no longer possible, since social processes had become impenetrable in a complex technology-dominated society in which there was no longer a clear antithesis between rich and poor.

In this anti-realist literary climate socialist realism was doubly unwelcome. Anti-Communist feeling arising from the cold war situation and fired on by the events of 1953 and 1956 compounded a general scepticism towards ideology and rejection of doctrinarianism resulting from the experience of Nazism and Stalinism. Official pronouncements in East Germany seemed to confirm the view that socialist realism was a kind of cultural propaganda demanding a subservience of writers to the State incompatible with their position of independence and nonconformity in the West.

In the debate on new forms of realism in the 1960s and 1970s socialist realism only gradually began to lose its negative image. Dieter Wellershoff, the initiator of a vigorous campaign for realist writing in the mid-1960s, described socialist realism in 1966 as

'ossified in pseudo-rational umbrella terms and ideological prejudices', and in 1970s as 'manipulatory light fiction supporting the
status quo'[1] and complained that realism in general suffered from
the proximity to socialist realism, with its superficial milieu and
crude psychology.[2] Jörg Drews used the association in 1975 to
dismiss all realism: he refers to a periodically reappearing wish in
certain literary circles for a return to 'the tried, seemingly so robust
realist styles . . . as decreed in the East by the socialist cultural
bureaucracy'.[3] As recently as 1987 Keith Bullivant uses the term
socialist realism in his study of the contemporary West German
novel[4] as a negative background against which more adequate forms
of modern realism are defined. He argues that the isolation of the
modern individual in a social and political reality largely outside his
awareness invalidates Lukács's principle of 'totality' and his demands that the writer appreciate the full nature of external reality
and present the underlying structures of society through individual
experience. Bullivant's view of socialist realism is essentially one of
rigidity of form and simplification of social processes. He associates
it with neglect of the inner life of the protagonist and naïve hope of
immediate and radical change in society brought about by individual conversion. Not surprisingly, the flowering of 'political realism'
in the prose of the 1970s is presented as an achievement of West
German literature, largely free of any debt to the tradition of
socialist realism and of links with contemporary East German
novels.[5]

The trivialisation of the principles of socialist realism underlying
such judgements springs from concentration on the more narrowly
dogmatic of Lukács's pronouncements and perhaps from a stereotype of the less successful East German industrial novels of the

1. D. Wellershoff, 'Fur einen neuen Roman',*Civis*, no. 10, 1966, p. 29; and *Merkur*,
   1970, p. 731. Both passages are here quoted from W. Powroslo, *Erkenntnis durch
   Literatur. Realismus in der westdeutschen Literaturtheorie der Gegenwart*, Kiepenheuer &
   Witsch, Cologne, 1976. All quotations from German sources in this essay are my
   translations.
2. D. Wellershoff, *Literatur und Veränderung: Versuche zu einer Metakritik der Literatur*,
   Kiepenheuer & Witsch, Cologne, 1969, pp. 85f.
3. J. Drews, 'Wider einen neuen Realismus', in P. Laemmle (ed.), *Realismus —
   welcher? Sechzehn Autoren auf der Suche nach einem literarischen Begriff*, Edition Text
   und Kritik, Munich, 1976, p. 151.
4. K. Bullivant, *Realism Today: Aspects of the Contemporary West German Novel*, Berg,
   Leamington Spa and New York, 1987.
5. See, however, Bullivant's acknowledgement of Christa Wolf's influence in the
   West (ibid. p. 55). Despite my disagreement with Bullivant's conception of
   socialist realism, I am indebted to this thoroughly researched account of realism
   in the West German novel.

1950s, characterised by schematic plot, unconvincingly positive heroes, conventionality and naïvety of world view. 'Totality' is reduced to a bureaucratic abolition of the writer's imagination, 'partisanship' to a didactically omniscient narrator and a closed ideology, 'popularity' to the exclusion of all modernist elements. Christa Wolf's radical questioning of Lukácsian theory in the late 1960s and early 1970s (for instance in *Lesen und Schreiben* ('Reading and Writing') 1972) must appear in this light as a clean break with socialist realism. Her views on the compatibility of realism with elements of modernist form, on the desirability of montage and interior monologue techniques, are, however, based on an alternative tradition of socialist realism with which the names of Brecht, Anna Seghers and Bloch are associated. Since aesthetic laws are not deducible from our knowledge of reality, we must experiment, Brecht argued. Furthermore, he insisted that the rightness of literary forms is limited to specific stages of socio-political development. The recent acceptance of such a broad definition of socialist realism in the GDR is reflected in the official East German history of West German literature (*Geschichte der Literatur der Bundesrepublik Deutschland*, 1983). Here perspectivising of narration, documentary, montage and stream of consciousness techniques in Andersch, Böll, Johnson, Koeppen, Lenz, Arno Schmidt and Walser are singled out for praise where they are used to depict society realistically, and are justified by reference to Brecht's definition of realism.[6]

From a less exclusively Lukácsian perspective, it becomes clear that the central principles of socialist realism have been of greater significance in the development of the West German novel than is generally recognised: the cleft between socialist realism and the critical realism of Böll or Walser is likely to be less profound than hitherto supposed. Both constitute a modern realism with roots in the nineteenth century, whose techniques were extended by Heinrich Mann and Döblin, Arnold Zweig, Remarque and Erich Kästner. Moreover, developments in the theory and practice of realism in both East and West Germany over the last twenty years reveal some surprising parallels.

The theoretical discussion triggered off in the East by the rediscovery of Brecht's and Seghers's views, and to which Braun, Fühmann, Hermlin and Kunert followed Christa Wolf in contributing in the 1970s, was matched by the intensive public debate in the West initiated by Dieter Wellershoff's call for a 'new realism' on the

6. H. J. Bernhard et al., *Geschichte der Literatur der Bundesrepublik Deutschland*, Volk und Wissen, Berlin, 1983, p. 145.

lines of the *nouveau roman* in 1965. The dramatic upsurge of interest in Marxist literary theory within the Student Movement and the Extra-Parliamentary Opposition (APO) in the late 1960s, reflected in publications such as Fritz Raddatz's *Marxismus und Literatur* (1969), Helga Gallas's *Marxistische Literaturtheorie* (1971) and Hans-Jürgen Schmitt's *Die Expressionismusdebatte* (1973), had a clearly traceable impact on statements by Martin Walser and Uwe Timm, the discussion on realism and partisanship in the Werkkreis Literatur der Arbeitswelt (literally: 'Craft Circle for Literature of the Working World'), and articles in the pages of such journals as *Kürbiskern* and *Literarische Hefte* in the early 1970s. The relative merits of Brecht's and Lukács's standpoints in the *Expressionismusdebatte* (the public debate on the Expressionists in the 1930s, which led to important statements on Marxist literary theory) were hotly disputed, and the success of Günter Wallraff's documentary works led to a rediscovery of proletarian-revolutionary prose forms, which was facilitated by reprints of texts from the 1920s and 1930s. In East and West alike authenticity and limits on the writer's ability to portray the totality of society were among the central issues.

In the practice of writing, too, there has been a degree of overlap between East and West. The erosion of the closed ideological framework in the GDR, the shift in the writer's position from one of affirmation and didacticism to criticism and a partnership of equals with the reader, and the treatment of conflicts between individual and society, have given rise to narrative structures comparable to those of critical realism. At the same time the emergence of the industrial novel in the 1960s and adaptations of the Lukácsian *Entwicklungsroman*, or novel of (political) development, in the 1970s in the West have explored areas familiar to the East German reader. And the integration of documentary and autobiographical elements in realist narrative has been an aim pursued almost simultaneously in both parts of Germany.

The significance of socialist realism for the West German novel may be illustrated by the common ground it shares with Heinrich Böll's critical realism, with Max von der Grün's social realism, and with the political realism practised by Uwe Timm and the writers of the *AutorenEdition* in the 1970s. The term critical realism was used by Lukács for bourgeois realist works essentially similar to his conception of socialist realism, but falling short of its level of critical awareness, whose strength lay in accuracy of description and social criticism rather than socio-economic analysis. In the context of postwar capitalist society a correct political standpoint was recognised as less important than a critically progressive one: in practice this meant nonconformity was acceptable where it coincided with democratic humanism and some appreciation of the historical and social roots of Nazism. Wolfgang Koeppen's *Der Tod in Rom* (*Death in Rome*) (1954), Martin Walser's *Ehen in Philippsburg* ('Marriages in Philippsburg') (1957) and *Halbzeit* ('Half-Time') (1960), and Heinrich Böll's *Billard um halbzehn* (*Billiards at Half Past Nine*) (1959) have been regarded as central works of West German critical realism. Böll, Koeppen, Martin Walser and other novelists such as Siegfried Lenz, Alfred Andersch, Hans Erich Nossack and Hans Werner Richter are valued by GDR and Soviet critics for revealing the erosion of basic human values in a society in pursuit of affluence. They share with socialist realism close observation of everyday life in specific historical circumstances and an at least partial presentation of historical social processes. In addition their works share a didactic element: the writer has a sense of social responsibility, he aims to explain the past and to influence the reader, hence to contribute to social change.

Lukács has expressed sympathy with Böll for the moral protest voiced in his characters' refusal to accept a condition of alienation and political manipulation in *Billard um halbzehn*. He contrasts Böll's historical analysis favourably with the dominant Western aesthetic of the Absurd and describes him as an ally in the great struggle to preserve and augment humanity in society.[7] The East German critic Kurt Batt devotes a major part of his article 'Die Exekution des Erzählers' ('The Execution of the Narrator')[8] — which deals with West German trends around 1970 away from works of fiction towards documentary literature, in a problematical search for authenticity — to digress on what he regards as Böll's praiseworthy counter-position in the novel *Gruppenbild mit Dame* (*Group Portrait with Lady*) (1971). Böll's commitment to humanity raises the novel above other examples of documentary montage and provides the totality of viewpoint which socialist realism demands: 'The narrative imagination, where it truly is this, encompasses a totality of deeply human pronouncements on life and historical experiences'. Though Batt does not use the terms, something akin to partisanship is recognised in Böll's view of the fundamental moral values of solidarity, kindness, trust and love as natural proletarian ones. Despite the limited extent to which the central character, Leni, is representative of her

7. G. Lukács, 'Lob des neunzehnten Jahrhunderts', in M. Reich-Ranicki (ed.), *In Sachen Böll: Ansichten und Einsichten*, dtv, Munich, 1971, pp. 250–6.
8. K. Batt, 'Die Exekution des Erzählers: Westdeutsche Romane um 1970', in idem, *Revolte Intern: Betrachtungen zur Literatur in der BRD*, Reclam, Leipzig, 1974, pp. 191–273.

generation, and her general passivity, she, her Russian husband Boris and her son Lew effectively function as positive heroes, in the sense that they are dream figures and 'personifications of projections of hope' in which the longings and frustrations of the author's informants are crystallised, and stand for an alternative, better way of life. Leni is a character with whom the reader is invited to identify, in which primitive Christianity and Utopian Communism are fused with Marcuse's *große Weigerung* ('great refusal') — the total rejection of the values of technologically advanced capitalism.[9] Despite the open form of the novel, Böll's faith in man's ability to change society for the better and his didactic aim speak, as Batt points out, from the action of the fictional author at the end of the novel, where he ceases merely to gather facts and views, and participates in bringing about the happy ending.

Böll's own statements on literature confirm the implication that his views are not incompatible with the basic principles underlying socialist realism. Though he does not use the word 'realism' in his Frankfurt lectures on poetics of 1964, the *Ästhetik des Humanen* he presents is implicitly a realist one which rejects formal experiment for its own sake. He calls for the development of forms and styles which serve the moral aim of preserving humanity. The way forward, he argues, lies closer to socialist realism than to the suicidal denial of the human and the social in the literature of the West: 'The part of the world called the East has despite all the crude, even forcibly administered attempts to create an aesthetic of the human and the social in vulgar coin, preserved in its readers a remarkable sensibility which makes it possible to see in the social sphere the cultural, the religious'.[10] Politicians in both East and West equally would like something like socialist realism in its administrative form, i.e. a 'positive' literature recognising achievement, propagating confidence and supporting those in power, he argues. By the nature of things politicians are outraged by literature and make foolish pronouncements on it.[11]

In his preface to the German edition of Solzhenitsyn's *Cancer Ward* (1969) Böll again expresses his respect for socialist realism. Though scorned in the West for decades, it has neither incapacitated nor emasculated writers in the East. The only aspect of it he rejects is the doctrinaire dogmatic optimism imposed on it, which, as he points out, is not without parallel in the calls for the presentation of an

9. See H. Marcuse, *One Dimensional Man*, Sphere, London, 1968, pp. 190–201.
10. H. Böll, *Essayistische Schriften und Reden 2 1964–1972*, ed. B. Balzer, Kiepenheuer & Witsch, Cologne, 1979, p. 46.
11. Ibid., pp. 90f.

ideal world directed at literature in the West. As a link between the old and a possible renewed socialist realism, *Cancer Ward* provides a model for the somewhat feeble attempts at a new realism in the West. Solzhenitsyn avoids oversimplified endowment of the world with meaning and observes and records from experience. His terse sobriety is superior not only to the compulsory optimism of traditional socialist realism, but equally to the intentions of the *nouveau roman*.[12]

Ideological scepticism and a conscious desire of the Gruppe 61 (whose full name was literally 'Group 61: Association for Artistic Examination of the World of Industry') to distance themselves from socialist realism are likely to have prompted Fritz Hüser, a founding member, to use the term 'social realism' for the writing of the group.[13] Similarities with socialist realism lay above all in the subject-matter of their novels, shorter prose and other literary works, which dealt with the world of industrial production and the everyday life of workers for practically the first time in the Federal Republic. The aims of the group are stated in a programme agreed on in 1964: 'Literary and artistic treatment of the sphere of industrial production today and its social problems. Intellectual analysis of the technological age. Links with the social literature of other countries. Critical study of earlier workers' literature and its history'.[14]

Though the group was conscious from the start of the need to present a contemporary working world characterised by co-determination, the forty-hour working week and relative affluence of the worker on the one hand, and by technological advances whose impact was beginning to be felt in new forms of isolation and alienation on the other, there were strong links with the workers' literature of the Weimar Republic. These were less, however, with the militant writing of the BPRS (League of Proletarian-Revolutionary Writers) than with local literary groups in the Ruhr area close to the SPD. In the opening speech at the first meeting of the Gruppe 61, Fritz Hüser, director of the Dortmund Archive for Workers' Literature and Social literature, referred to the association of 'Craftsmen of Haus Nyland', founded in 1912 and existing until the early 1920s, and to the 'Ruhrland-Circle', which met in Gelsenkirchen in 1926. The concept of social harmony which forms the basis of the work of members of these groups (Max Barthel, Karl Bröger, Gerrit Engelke

12. Ibid., pp. 329f., 364.
13. In his foreword to their most significant publication, F. Hüser, M. von der Grün and W. Promies (eds.), *Aus der Welt der Arbeit: Almanach der Gruppe 61 und ihrer Gäste*, Luchterhand, Neuwied and Berlin, 1966, p. 29.
14. Quoted from R. Dithmar, *Industrieliteratur*, 2nd edn, dtv, Munich, 1977, p. 169.

and Heinrich Lersch were among the better known) had a greater appeal in the economic climate of 1960 than the class antagonism of the BPRS. The SPD had agreed on its Godesberg Programme in 1959, by which it changed from a Workers' to a People's Party, and practised social integration in the cultural sphere, while the unions had been preaching social partnership since the founding of the Republic.

However, by 1966 it was recognised that Barthel, Bröger and Lersch could not be taken as models. The founding of the group had coincided with the end of the postwar economic reconstruction phase and a crisis in mining (1959–60) which predated the first recession of 1966–7. The changed situation provided the basis for a gradual re-emergence of a distinctive workers' culture and a rediscovery of the reality of exploitation, thus exposing the fiction of a classless society. Max von der Grün's treatment of specific malpractices of both employers and unions in his second novel *Irrlicht und Feuer* ('Will of the Wisp and Fire') (1963) led to litigation which ironically did much to assist in the breakthrough in reaching a wider public. The ensuing break with the unions, who had published much of the early work of the Gruppe 61, forced the group to seek outlets among book publishers. Market pressures became in part responsible for a growing stress on literary quality. Hüser and von der Grün regarded with scepticism the more militant earlier organisations of worker writers, the Worker Correspondent Movement in the 1920s, the BPRS and the Bitterfelder Weg (the movement initiated in the GDR in 1959 to bring writers into active involvement with industry and to encourage the literary efforts of workers). These were rejected for their fixation with class-struggle and their acceptance of a total subservience of literature to politics. Hüser stressed the need for new forms, 'to give literary shape to the changes in our society, the uncertainty and agonising unease of the worker, and to make the reader aware of these. Here neither the workers' literature of the Twenties and Thirties nor the attempts of the "writing workers" in the GDR can provide models'.[15] In fact the Gruppe 61 adopted a position close to Lukácsian socialist realism in demanding from its members 'individual ability to give literary shape' (the Lukácsian term *gestalten* is used) and 'signs of original form capable of development'. In its confrontation with the Werkkreis in the politicised climate at the end of the decade the central issues were similar to those debated in the BPRS journal *Die Linkskurve* (1931–2), when Lukács and Johannes R. Becher had opposed the

15. Hüser et al. (eds.), *Aus der Welt der Arbeit*, pp. 24f.

operative and documentary-based literary forms of Bredel and Ottwalt with demands for a descriptive realism closer to the bourgeois tradition, with rounded characters and organic development.

Measured by the yardstick of socialist realism, von der Grün's novels admittedly fall well short of the desirable. However, the working milieu in the Ruhr area is presented in realistic detail, and for the first time in West German literature the mechanisms of capitalism are viewed from the standpoint of the worker. Although there is no socio-economic analysis, the alienation of the worker is attributed to social causes. Through the various jobs which Jürgen Fohrmann takes up after pit-closure forces him to give up mining, *Irrlicht and Feuer* reveals different aspects of the confrontation between capital and workers, its intensification in the course of technological change and its impact on family life. The novel depicts the emergence of class-consciousness and human solidarity. However, the alternative to the circumstances described is never clearly defined, and there is an unmistakable element of resignation. Von der Grün's protagonists are anything but models or positive heroes, rather they are loners who indulge in irrational spontaneous action. Fohrmann remains disorientated even after he has recognised alienation as the source of his frustration. The almost exclusively first-person narration of the book limits the reader's perspective, although contradictions between Fohrmann's reflections and his actions point beyond the latter; and the political and social perspective is broadened somewhat by a constellation of other figures. Fohrmann reflects the actual absence of class-consciousness, political understanding and engagement of the West German worker at the time. The central message of *Irrlicht und Feuer* is directed at the workers themselves: the price of affluence, a loss of identity and self-determination. The workers' movement is shown as having bartered its political and moral aims for a share in the *Wirtschaftswunder* (Economic Miracle).

In a discussion with Erwin Strittmatter in 1964 von der Grün defended the absence of didactic clarity in his novels, asserting that it was the task of the writer not to give answers, but rather to recognise and express facts. In his later novels he continues to narrate without didactic pretension, identifying himself largely with the protagonists and only occasionally taking up a stance of perceptible detachment. Although the novel *Stellenweise Glatteis* ('Icy Patches') (1973) is based on an extensive research events are again seen through the central figure's eyes. Karl Maiwald becomes increasingly aware of corrupt workplace practices affecting him directly, and develops strategies for opposition on individual issues, but there is no coherent perspective of social change.

Von der Grün's refusal to simplify complex issues attracted criticism from both the GDR critics and the unions in the West, who would have preferred, as one of the writer's supporters phrased it, something more similar to socialist realism.[16] In an article entitled 'Ist so der deutsche Arbeiter?' ('Is the German worker really like this?') the union official Walter Köpping attacked von der Grün's characters for not working towards the liberation of their class, for their lack of political education and insight, and rejected his novels as unnecessarily pessimistic.[17]

None the less, von der Grün's novels were warmly received in the GDR and the Soviet Union: they were welcomed by critics, published in new editions and filmed for television, at a time when they attracted the attention of only the local press at home. Although members of the Gruppe 61 distanced themselves from socialist realism and from the Bitterfelder Weg, the fact that a sizeable article by the GDR critic Wolfgang Friedrich ('Bemerkungen zum literarischen Schaffen der Dortmunder Gruppe 61', 'Comments on the literary works of the Dortmund Group 61', which had appeared in *Weimarer Beiträge* the year before) was included in the anthology *Aus der Welt der Arbeit. . . .* ('From the Working World. . . .') (1966) suggests a degree of willingness to allow their work to be judged from a Marxist standpoint. Friedrich's verdict that the work of the group represents no more than a diagnosis of the social situation, accompanied by vague threats of rebellion, is tempered by praise of their achievement in recording alienation in its many different aspects. Moreover, von der Grün's protagonists are described as transcending the bounds of the manipulated consciousness of their fellow-workers.

In fact the consistent concern with readability and exciting plots in von der Grün's novels, largely responsible for their considerable success, may be seen in terms of the 'popularity' demanded by Marxist theory, and though the perspective for change is unclear, Grün has repeatedly expressed his intention to change society through his books in such terms as: 'First of all I want the worker not to vegetate so dully and lethargically'; 'I believe good literature is never without bias'; and 'I could not write were I not convinced that the future of mankind lay in socialism'.[18]

---

16. See Friedhelm Baukloh's review of *Irrlicht und Feuer*, *Frankfurter Hefte* 19, 1964, p. 531.
17. See S. Reinhardt (ed.), *Max von der Grün: Auskunft für Leser*, Luchterhand, Darmstadt and Neuwied, 1986, pp. 157–63.
18. See F. Schonauer, *Max von der Grün*, (Autorenbücher 13), Beck/ Edition Text und

Links with socialist realism are particularly strong in the work of another member of the group, Bruno Gluchowski, a former member of the BPRS. Gluchowski's contribution to *Aus der Welt der Arbeit*. . . . 'Die Wasserkanone' ('The Water Cannon') comes very close to socialist realism. This story, based on events which took place in Belgium in 1965, showing miners successfully resisting the closure of their pit by violent strike action, features positive heroes and heroic workers' solidarity, and was not surprisingly greeted by some critics as a dated story of class struggle and 'strike romanticism'.

If critical realism and the social realism of the Gruppe 61 may be regarded as significant movements in the 1950s and 1960s, interfacing with socialist realism, this is certainly true of the political realism practised in the 1970s in its most specific form by Uwe Timm and Gerd Fuchs. At a time when the Lukácsian form of the *Entwicklungsroman* had been practically abandoned in the GDR, it experienced a revival in the West in the works of writers with socialist sympathies, who set out to portray the conversion and development of representative individuals from petty-bourgeois individualism to collective consciousness and solidarity with the working class. In an article entitled 'Zwischen Unterhaltung und Aufklärung' ('Between Entertainment and Instruction'' Uwe Timm stresses the need to integrate elements of the popular novel, but at the same time to provide a stimulus for specific work towards change.[19] Milieu, local colour, exciting plots and romance are central to these attempts at a didactic popular literature, which were to show the attainment of personal fulfilment as 'a result of change. The programme of the *AutorenEdition*, in which Uwe Timm and other writers acted as publishers' editors within the Bertelsmann publishing house, reads: 'The *AutorenEdition* directs itself towards a large circle of readers. Only novels, tales and short stories by German writers are to be published. The social problems are to be portrayed graphically and entertainingly. A realist style is aimed at'.[20]

In Timm's first novel, *Heißer Sommer* ('Hot Summer') (1974), Ullrich Krause's development from passivity to action, solidarity and an understanding of politics is presented as a model for the reader. Narrated in the third person, the novel seeks to capture the totality of social experience by following Krause's participation in

---

Kritik, Munich, 1978, pp. 78, 141, 147.

19. The article is to be found in *Kürbiskern* (1972), no. 1, pp. 79–90. See also K. Bullivant, 'Politischer Realismus heute?', in K. Pestalozzi (ed.), *Kontroversen, alte und neue. Akten des VII. Kongresses zur internationalen Vereinigung für germanistische Sprach- und Literaturwissenschaft*, vol 10, Niemeyer, Tübingen, 1986, p. 180.

20. Quoted from Laemmle (ed.), *Realismus — welcher?*, p. 115.

the various phases of the student revolt. Fuchs's novel *Beringer und die lange Wut* ('Beringer and Long Anger') (1973) portrays a comparable process of rejection of anarchist revolt by a young intellectual, and eventual identification with the proletariat and the Communist Party. The novels of the pro-Communist protest-singer and writer Franz Josef Degenhardt fit in to the same broad category. At the same time Martin Walser, now at his closest to the Communist Party, adopts a related form in *Die Gallistl'sche Krankheit* ('Gallistl's Disease') (1972). This is the first-person diagnosis of the symptoms of a disease which derives from the competitiveness of life in capitalist society and other alienating factors. The somewhat unconvincing ending of the book shows the crisis of the individual in the process of being overcome with the help of Communist friends.

Max von der Grün's novels, in particular *Stellenweise Glatteis* (mentioned above), may be seen as comparably open-minded adaptations of the socialist *Entwicklungsroman*. A positive Utopia is sketched out, but there is no suggestion that this can be achieved simply, with as much space being devoted to the doubts and fears of the protagonist as to his criticism and hopes. Further examples of the novel of political development are to be found in the Werkkreis. Josef Ippers' *Am Kanthaken* ('By the Billhook') (1974), the story of a roving dock worker who marries and settles down, depicts in an unusual twist the narrator's development from individualism to political consciousness, while the central character, Franz Ritter, illustrates the obstacles in the way of growth in class-consciousness, by withdrawing from participation in a spontaneous strike from fear of losing his position as foreman. Margot Schroeder's more fundamentally unconventional *Ich stehe meine Frau* ('I'm Fighting Like a Woman') (1975) traces the parallel emergence of political consciousness, self-knowledge and self-confidence as the result of a young woman's action. Although the central figure is far from exemplary and the end is left largely open, solidarity is shown to be necessary for both individual self-realisation and political progress.

The integration of modernist features such as documentary elements, reportage and autobiography in the realist novel constitutes one of the most significant parallels between the development of realism in East and West in the last twenty years. The pre-1931 BPRS tradition, as constituted by the not unsophisticated novels of Bredel, Gotsche, Grünberg, Marchwitza, Ottwalt and others, which had developed out of reportage and autobiography before the debate in *Die Linkskurve* became dominated by the traditionalist concept of realism and Popular Front cultural policy, was not revived in the early years of the GDR. Nor did the brief phase of the Bitterfelder

Weg between 1959 and 1963, despite its adaptation of reportage forms central to the Worker Correspondent Movement of the 1920s (such as the 'Work-Team Diary' or *Brigadetagebuch*), lead to any lasting change in the essentially Lukácsian expectations levelled at literary form. Until the late 1960s documentary literature was regarded as 'compilation without evaluation', failing to point out the historical significance of individual events and show society as changeable, and lacking scope for artistic mastery. Through her novel *Nachdenken über Christa T (The Quest for Christa T.)* (1968) and her pronouncements on realism Christa Wolf initiated a trend towards the inclusion of facts, biographical material and diary entries in realist narrative. This shift from ideal to social reality inevitably led to a gradual relaxation of the demand for 'rounded epic form' and a new understanding of 'epic totality'.

The politicisation of West German culture in the 1960s led also to a demand for socially engaged literature which favoured documentary forms. Unease with avant-garde experimentation for its own sake and hitherto practised forms of inwardness, metaphysical parable and the grotesque accompanied a crisis of the traditional narrative stemming from doubts as to the authenticity and social relevance of the (bourgeois) author's imagination. The documentary drama which emerged in the early 1960s was followed by prose works such as Erika Runge's *Bottroper Protokolle*, ('Bottrop Protocols') (1968), consisting of the tape-recorded statements of members of a community affected by pit-closures in the 1966 recession. In his foreword to the book, Martin Walser, one of the prime movers in this 'literature of non-writers' ('Literatur der Nicht-Autoren', Reinhard Baumgart), states:

> It is ridiculous to expect of writers living as freelance writers in bourgeois society that they could imitate by means of some sham spiritual grace and so-called creative talent the existence of workers in an artificial product, or hope to express it in words. All literature is bourgeois in our society. Even when it strikes its most anti-bourgeois gestures.[21]

Subsequent works promoted by Walser such as Wolfgang Werner's *Vom Waisenhaus ins Zuchthaus* ('From Orphanage to Prison') (1969) were however severely limited in their authenticity by clichéd language and their authors' unreflected adoption of literary convention.

More successful both aesthetically and in terms of their reception were the journalistic reporting-style works of Günter Wallraff. In *Dreizehn unerwünschte Reportagen* ('Thirteen Undesirable Reports')

21. Erika Runge, *Bottroper Protokolle*, Suhrkamp, Frankfurt, 1968, p. 9.

(1969) and *Neue Reportagen* ('New Reports') (1972), he arranged his material in a montage technique which was much admired. His use of experiences, historical reflection, analysis and dialogue went far beyond neutral reportage. His partisanship was already reflected in the personal experience he presented, which had been carefully organised in advance so as to give a representative cross-section of working and living conditions. Despite the depicted alienation of the worker, he brings elements of solidarity to light and the way he finds out the truth deprives circumstances of their seeming unchangeableness. Further examples of varying documentary methods are exemplified in the works of F.C. Delius, von der Grün's portraits of German and foreign workers based on authentic statements *Menschen in Deutschland (BRD): 7 Porträts* ('People in Germany (FRG): 7 Portraits'), 1973, and *Leben im gelobten Land* ('Life in the Promised Land') (1975), and in a whole series of documentary works from the Werkkreis.

The aims of the Werkkreis were defined at a meeting in Wuppertal in 1971 as revealing the social causes of human and technical problems at work and changing social conditions in the interest of the worker. Whereas kinship with the Weimar Worker Correspondent Movement and the BPRS was explicitly recognised, parallels with the Bitterfelder Weg remained unexplored. This was doubtless in part due to restraints imposed by the unions, whose support and cooperation the Werkkreis, in contrast to the Gruppe 61, was determined to retain.[22] None the less, there were significant parallels with the GDR movement, in the central aim of stimulating class-consciousness and furthering the workers' movement, in the appeal to workers to write and thereby become more politically conscious, and in the collective production methods practised.

To begin with the Werkkreis pursued a policy of modelling its writing closely on Wallraff's reportages. Two competitions run in 1969 to 1970 to attract members and to encourage workers to write specified that submissions be in 'unliterary language'. However it soon became clear that copying Wallraff without significant advances in content or form led to monotony. From the start, in fact, more traditional realist writing was practised side by side with documentary and reportage. Whereas Erasmus Schöfer championed reportage, Carlo Bredthauer defended the realist principle of 'giving literary shape to the whole of life', and Lukácsian elements are traceable in such novels as Ippers' *Am Kanthaken* (mentioned above),

---

22. See G. Heyder, 'Gewerkschaftsgeld für den Weg nach Bitterfeld?', *Die Quelle* 24, no. 3, 1973, pp. 136–8.

in which the adherence to third-person narration by an older, more experienced fellow-worker leads to an element of inadvertent voyeurism in the erotic scenes.

The early years of the group's existence saw internal disputes on form remarkably similar to those in *Die Linkskurve*. Neither militant agitatory forms nor the essentially post-revolutionary stabilising form of Lukácsian socialist realism seemed to provide suitable models in the clearly non-revolutionary political and social circumstances. *Realistisch Schreiben* ('Writing Realistically'), the record of a seminar held in 1972,[23] reveals discussion of Brecht's definitions of 'Realism' and 'Partisanship' (pp. 60f) and their appositeness when applied to Margot Schroeder's *Ich stehe meine Frau* (referred to earlier). While socialist realism is nowhere mentioned, a balance is struck between Brecht's 'breadth and diversity' and Lukácsian principles. At a regional seminar in Essen, Wallraff's reportage form had been studied and the Brecht–Lukácsian debate discussed: a decision was reached that choice of form should depend on the target group and context of use. Although Wallraff was to be taken as a model for 'shaped documentation' (case-studies in which social regularities are made explicit by inserting verse and songs, contrasting passages from other sources, etc.), provision was also made for stories, novels and straight reportage, sketches, agitatory poetry and song where appropriate. This standpoint was confirmed at the main seminar, where a policy of diversity following the example of the BPRS was agreed on, in which documentation, reportage and the novel (in which the perspective for change could better be presented) were all welcomed as fulfilling different purposes and complementing each other.

The central discussion of realist method (pp. 61–4) arrived at the following conclusions: economic, political and social structures were to be shown from the worker's standpoint. The credibility of the text depended on typical, and not exceptional circumstances being shown. Conditions were to be shown as changeable, and strategies for liberation from exploitation at work, in the family and in society, portrayed with realist imagination, must be 'politically correct', i.e. neither unrealistic nor Utopian. (Although politically unaffiliated, the Werkkreis in practice took up an ideological position between the SPD and DKP.) The future perspective of a socialist society, in which the individual can achieve self-realisation under truly demo-

---

23. *Realistisch Schreiben: Springener Protokolle und Materialien*, Werkkreis Literatur der Arbeitswelt, 2nd edn, Werkkreis, Erkenschwick, 1972. Subsequent page references are indicated in my text.

cratic circumstances, was essential.

Modernist elements were integrated most successfully in the framework of the popular novel in two works published in 1975. Formal flexibility (stream of consciousness, monologues, recollected dialogues) and frank recognition of tensions between the individual and the collective help Margot Schroeder's *Ich stehe meine Frau* to avoid the simplifying tendency of the *Entwicklungsroman*. No claim is made to demonstrate the total social complex, and no easy solutions are offered. By montage of documentary evidence within a vivid conventional narrative Hermann Spix's *Elephteria oder die Reise ins Paradies* ('Elephteria or the Trip to Paradise') (1975) places personal experience in a context of empirical research. This case-study of the human problems arising from working conditions touches on important contemporary issues such as the treatment of foreign workers, the exploitation of women, the role of the unions and the impact of work conditions on leisure.

Outside the Werkkreis, the early 1970s saw the publication of a number of realist novels by Böll, Johnson, Grass and others blending conventional narrative with documentary elements. Kurt Batt's favourable assessment of the form of Böll's *Gruppenbild mit Dame* has already been referred to. Here socio-political comment is presented in a way scarcely attainable in the conventional realist novel. The varying perspectives presented on the central figure Leni Pfeiffer contain often confusing and contradictory testimony, forcing the reader to face up to the complexity of reality. In place of an essentially omniscient narrator and firm authorial stance, Böll introduces an ostensibly neutral researcher, from whose detached stance, however, he ironically distances himself, even before the surrender of neutrality at the end of the novel. A similar quasi-documentary method is again used to great effect in *Die verlorene Ehre der Katharina Blum* (*The Lost Honour of Katharina Blum*) (1974).

Parallels in the development of realism in East and West Germany in the 1970s go beyond the integration of documentary elements to include subjectivity and a critical analysis of alienation. Christa Wolf's conception of 'subjective authenticity' gives greater recognition to the role of the writer in perceiving reality than had previously been conceded within socialist realism. Wolf insisted on the right to discover reality, a process calculated to disturb and activate the reader. Among the formal consequences of her approach to reality by way of the sensibility, experience and memories of individual characters are the replacement of the omniscient narrator by one whose explorative reflections are more important than the plot, unexemplary and problematic protagonists, absence of individual development and replacement of linear chronology by an inter-cutting of past and present. The acceptance of the writer's limited insight meant that reconstruction of social totality must inevitably be subjective and subject-centred, restrictions more than compensated for by the gain in authenticity.

Wolf's actual influence in the West is probably clearest in the publications of the *AutorenEdition* writers, who seek to link general insight into society with subjective perception and individual experience.[24] However, there has been a broader congruence. In the wake of the Student Movement, which tended to neglect personal aspects of emancipation in favour of social and group processes, it became increasingly recognised in the West that the Utopian dimension central to any realism going beyond mere naturalist reproduction of reality must include individual fulfilment. There followed a new emphasis on emotional life, subjective needs and personal relationships. Subjectivity acquired a critical and potentially subversive role in the realist literature of the 1970s in both East and West.

Whereas 'inwardness' (Innerlichkeit), one of the catchwords of the 1970s, meaning a resigned withdrawal from social issues in order to concentrate on psychological processes, naturally had little to do with the principles of socialist realism, the 'new subjectivity' (neue Subjektivität) practised by Karin Struck, Peter Schneider and others examined the social roots of neurotic introspection and loss of orientation, a crisis of the individual originating in the alienation, isolation and existentialist fears endangered by the structures of capitalist industrialised society. The subjective narrative stance of Margot Schroeder's *Ich stehe meine Frau* provided an important extension to the literary form of the Werkkreis novels. A degree of objective judgement is still possible here by means of the narrator's self-irony and detachment. Von der Grün's subject-centred presentation of issues also deserves mention in this context. In *Stellenweise Glatteis* Maiwald realises that success is only possible in collective action, but far from becoming an activist, he remains uncertain and confused. His inability to draw appropriate conclusions from the situation takes account of obstacles to growth in political insight among German workers and is not intended as a model to the reader. Von der Grün described it as his duty to present events subjectively, 'through the eyes of those involved, those done out of

24. See U. Timm, 'Die realistische Literatur und ihr gesellschaftliches Subjekt', in U. Timm and G. Fuchs (eds.). *Kontext 1. Literatur und Wirklichkeit*, AutorenEdition, Munich, 1976, pp. 134–40.

their rights, the suppressed and exploited. Claims to objectivity are nothing more than sidestepping into vagueness, which has as is well known reduced literature to folly'.[25]

Martin Walser's statements on literature in the late 1960s and early 1970s reveal views not unsimilar to those formulated at the same time by Christa Wolf. Walser had written rather vaguely of a 'Realismus X' in the mid-1960s as aiming to increase the reader's recognition of reality, and to raise consciousness of social processes as the determinants of our actions (*Imitation oder Realismus*, 'Imitation or Realism', 1964). He comes closer to both communism and socialist realism in *Wie und wovon handelt Literatur?* ('How does Literature Present Things and What is it About?') (1969). However, Lukács is implicitly rejected in favour of Brecht: literature cannot be the handmaiden of politics, there can be no artistic clothing of previously recognised abstract mechanisms, no packaging of political thought. The ability to recognise and depict historical processes can never become rigid or schematic.[26] In a DKP seminar on literature in 1974 Walser expressed the autonomy of the writer, the function of creative writing as discovery of things, as opposed to purveyance of truths, in terms which could have been used by Christa Wolf.

> For a realist, 'partisanship' can only result from experiment, and not from the intention: now I shall be partisan. . . . For me writing is a way of life and a form of experimentation which I cannot do without, and I believe if this work is necessary for me, then I can draw others into it too. . . . That is what I mean by partisanship, not an intent, but something which results from work.[27]

As we have seen, the distinction between critical and socialist realism becomes less significant after about 1965. The general acceptance of a broader, Brechtian definition of socialist realism in the East as a result of the pioneering work of writers such as Christa Wolf is reflected in a new, open-minded discussion of Western critical realism by critics such as Kurt Batt and Ursula Reinhold. Brecht had dissociated realism from any particular style or form,

25. M. von der Grün, 'Parteilichkeit der Literatur', *Deutsche Volkszeitung* 19, no. 41, 7 Oct. 1971, p. 14. Quoted from Bernhard et al., *Geschichte der Literatur der Bundesrepublik Deutschland*, p. 543.
26. M. Walser, *Wie und wovon handelt Literatur? Aufsätze und Reden*, Suhrkamp, Frankfurt, 1973, pp. 130–2.
27. Quoted from U. Reinhold, 'Realismus in der Diskussion: Anmerkungen zum Problemkreis Literatur und Wirklichkeit im literarischen Kontext der BRD', *Weimarer Beiträge* 25, no. 2, 1979, p. 47.

reducing it to its epistemological and Utopian dimension. The official East German history of West German literature (see note 6 above), published in 1983, praises non-Marxist writers who have introduced or practised new realist techniques: the absence of a plot linking the characters in a novel, associative links, the absence of an ordering narrator, and a combination of social criticism with the study of alienation, which can have far-reaching consequences. The terms in which Keith Bullivant describes political realism are not so very different from the basic principles Ursula Reinhold demands: that the author comprehend reality at least in part, Utopian belief in progress, and a conviction that creative writing can contribute to an amelioration of the human condition.

To the extent which parallel developments in East and West German realism are attributable to an exchange of ideas, this has by no means exclusively consisted of Western influence on the GDR novel, as is shown by the revival and adaptation of the *Entwicklungs-roman* by Timm, Fuchs, and Schneider. The volume *Realismus — welcher?* ('Realism — of What Kind?') which combines contributions from two conferences on realism held in 1974 with other related articles, contains a statement of realist theory by Uwe Timm en-titled 'Realismus und Utopie' ('Realism and Utopia') in which principles very similar to those practised in GDR novels of the 1970s are put forward.[28] Realism, Timm argues, must present reality as comprehensible and capable of change. Political realism is more than a mere naturalist depiction of existing conditions, it must show perspectives pointing beyond the present. It differs from nineteenth-century realism in presenting characters who are not only critical of society, but also attempt to change it. Its essence is a progression deriving from the dialectic contradiction between alie-nation in the present and our consciousness of a Utopian alternative.

Timm demands of realism a concrete historical dimension and portrayal of man not as an isolated individual, but as a social being acting in solidarity with others. This does not imply simplification or narrow-minded insistence on a positive dimension, but rather a faithful record of contradictions in society. At the centre of realist literature stand rounded, life-like individual characters who undergo a development process in their consciousness, feelings and actions. Timm defends presentation of individual 'heroes', pursuing political aims in the struggle against uncollective individualism. In his stress

28. Laemmle (ed.), *Realismus — welcher?*, pp. 139–50. The final section of the book (pp. 137–183) is devoted to the public debate between Uwe Timm and Jörg Drews.

on narrative fable, his insistence on presentation of a Utopian development of society typified in the fate of individual characters, Timm is close to Lukács. 'The writer's productive imagination can outline and depict *lives*, that is individual history, within a literary world. (History is as it were organised in the work of literature.)'[29] Like Christa Wolf, however, he stresses that literature fulfils special functions which make it more than a mere illustration of political theory, through conveying emotional, rational and ethical experiences and insights absent in contemporary reality.

The revival of the realist novel in the Federal Republic and the diversification of style in East German socialist realism in the 1970s reflect a degree of convergence between the two German literatures, in the position of the writer, in content and in form. Conscious reassessment of socialist realism in the West, however, has naturally been slow in view of the political and cultural prejudices involved. It has been easier for Western writers to appreciate the potential of Russian than of East German socialist realism. In an open letter to Yury Trifonov Martin Walser recognised his own concept of realism as realised in the modern Russian novel. Trifonov's novels are not the 'infamous socialist realism', but rather a realism which narrates seemingly insignificant events, from which a vivid history of everyday life is built up. Their precision is made possible by experience of the characters' suffering. Here there are no automated heroes programmed by the party, but, rather humanity, in the shape of characters whose suffering is caringly described and which motivates the reader.[30]

Almost ten years earlier Heinrich Böll had written in similarly glowing terms of Solzhenitsyn's novels. *The First Circle* (1968) had passed through socialist realism, overcome it, renewed it, restored it to the level of world literature. Its fusion of daring, experimental form with the spirit of Tolstoy, Dostoyevsky and Gogol rendered it a revelation for a helplessly floundering Western literature. Böll predicted: 'The world development of art and literature will probably be inverted: the West will tire of playing with "formalism" and will seek a new realism. . . . The East will have to get all the "formalist" experimentation behind it, . . . and will then return to its great and wonderfully lengthy tradition of realism'.[31]

---

29. Ibid., pp. 147f.
30. M. Walser, 'Wie geht es Ihnen, Jurij Trifonow?', in idem, *Wer ist ein Schriftsteller? Aufsätze und Reden*, Suhrkamp, Frankfurt, 1979, p. 25.
31. Böll, *Essayistische Schriften und Reden 2*, pp. 330, 367, 471ff.

—6—

Socialist Realism without a Socialist Revolution: The French Experience

J.E. FLOWER

Socialist realism appears in France during two relatively self-contained periods and relates quite precisely in each instance to a certain political climate. The first is the 1930s; the second extends for about twenty years from the late 1940s. It should be added that for the former not only the political climate but certain literary developments also played a major contributory role in its evolution and it is with these that we should begin.[1]

For at least sixty years there had been an increasing concern amongst certain writers — and novelists in particular — for the representation of working-class people in imaginative writing. In 1864 in the 'Preface' to *Germinie Lacerteux* the Goncourt brothers had remarked: 'We were curious to know. . . whether, in a country without social hierarchy and a recognised aristocracy, the misery of the poor and wretched would provoke as much interest, emotion and pity as the misery of the great and wealthy'. Zola had ambitions to write 'a novel that would take the working-class world for its setting'[2] and he claimed when it first appeared in 1877 that *L'Assommoir (Drunkard)* did indeed have 'the stench of the people'.[3] From this time on attention was increasingly given to the working class. Charles-Louis Philippe, Barbusse, Lucien Bourgeois, Henri Poulaille with his attempt to create 'proletarian literature', a literature produced by genuine working-class writers, or Léon Lemonnier and André Thérive with their 'populists', bourgeois observers of working-class conditions, all made their contributions. Differences

1. For a fuller discussion of these developments see my *Literature and the Left in France*, Macmillan, London, 1983 and Methuen, London and New York, 1985, chaps. 1–4. See also the various surveys by M. Ragon, for example *Histoire de la littérature prolétarienne en France*, Albin Michel, Paris, 1974.
2. Letter to Lacroix quoted in *Emile Zola: Les Rougon-Macquart*, vol. 1, ed. H. Mitterand, Bibliothèque de la Pléiade, Paris, 1961, p. 1, 539. All quotations from French sources in this essay are my translations unless otherwise indicated.
3. Ibid., p. 374.

between them are considerable, not only in the selection of relevant material but in their treatment of it. This is a problem on which Barbusse focuses his attention in the chapter 'Les Gros Mots' ('The Big Words') in *Le Feu* (*Under Fire*) (1916). Poulaille was consistently critical of any use made of the working class in literature for political ends and was hostile to all forms of condescension (displayed, for example, by the populists) on the part of the writer. For him authenticity was essential.

For the emergence of socialist realism, however, a third factor was vital — namely contacts with the Soviet Union. These were maintained both through a series of reports and articles in journals and newspapers such as *L'Humanité*, *Clarté* and *Monde* and through visits — by Raymond Lefebvre in 1920, Barbusse and Francis Jourdain in 1927, Aragon and Sadoul in 1930, for example. During the 1920s in the Soviet Union an increasingly hard line was taken regarding working-class literature,[4] an issue which came to a head at the Conference for the International Union of Revolutionary Writers (RAPP) at Kharkov in November 1930. The transactions of this conference appeared the following year in a special issue of the *Literature of World Revolution* which, published in Moscow, was customarily translated into English, French and German and disseminated accordingly. Criticism of literary activities in France was acute. France was in a state of decadence and corruption, a fact directly reflected in its literature: 'France is so far behind that it is impossible to say that at the present moment there is the slightest sign of revolutionary, proletarian literature'. Bourgeois literature was characterised by adventure stories and eroticism; populism was a 'specifically reactionary literature'; proletarian literature as envisaged by Poulaille exhibited 'fascist tendencies'; the group around Barbusse (a founder member of RAPP!) and *Monde* 'has fallen, from its very first issues, into the web of false bourgeois values'[5] and even the Surrealists were going to have to purge themselves of what an article in an earlier issue of the *Literature of World Revolution* (No. 3, 1931), had termed 'Freudian and idealist conceptions', if they were to make any real progress.[6] In such a context, it was argued, a new school of politically motivated proletarian writers was needed:

4. See in particular G. Struve, *Twenty-five years of Soviet Russian Literature (1914–1943)*, Routledge & Kegan Paul Ltd, London, 1964.
5. All of these quotations are from an anonymous article 'Résolution sur les questions de la littérature prolétarienne et révolutionnaire en France', Special issue of *Littérature de la Révolution Mondiale*, no. 3, 1931, pp. 87–94. The writer is probably A. Selivanovsky.
6. A. Selivanovsky, 'La littérature prolétarienne de Monsieur Poulaille', *Littérature de la Révolution Mondiale*, no. 3, 1931, p. 86.

The proletarian artist cannot remain as a passive observer of the real world; he is more than anything else someone who practises revolution; every one of his productions contributes to the liberating class struggle. It is his task to understand in the deepest and most objective way possible that real world about him in order for him to be able to influence it and transform it in a revolutionary manner.[7]

The definition of proletarian literature had already been examined in the previous issue:

Not only does proletarian literature take stock of the real world, it is a powerful element in the revolutionary transformation of this world. This it achieves by isolating a sense of purpose in a mass of contradictions, by underlining those trends which point to a future and thereby shape the thoughts and emotions of working-class people, and by pointing to clear values through the logical development of its metaphors.[8]

Now the same idea is repeated: 'We see this literature discovering new forms — different from those of the bourgeois literary tradition — responding directly to its message. It will go beyond the old genres and create new ones'.[9] In such statements as these, three points in particular should be noted: the emphasis on the writer as enlightener; the illustrative and instructive qualities of such writing; and the exemplary progressive dynamic of the language in which it is all described — 'sense of purpose', 'point to the future', 'logical development', 'revolutionary practice', 'go beyond old genres' and so on.

Such statements are representative of a climate in which attitudes to literature in the Soviet Union were extreme and as such largely reflect a period of strict ideological orthodoxy. In France membership of the French Communist Party (PCF) reached its lowest point in 1932 with 28,000, only half that of 1928. The dangers were evident and the time for a degree of liberalisation had come. In April 1932 in the Soviet Union the RAPP was dissolved, and replaced by the Union of Soviet Writers which, it was claimed, would remove centralising authoritarian control over literature. The review, *Literature of World Revolution* was replaced in 1933 by *International Literature* (a less provocative title) whose first issue contained what amounted to a manifesto by Vladimir Kirpotin of the new formula for literature — socialist realism.

At first there appears to be a marked degree of liberalisation and

7. [Selivanovsky?], 'Résolution sur les questions', p. 90.
8. [Selivanovsky?], 'La littérature prolétarienne', p. 89.
9. [Selivanovsky?], 'Résolution sur les questions', p. 89.

apparent awareness of the danger of schematisation inherent in any strictly centralised system: 'Artistic creation is complex and varied. The directives of socialist realism cannot be transformed into schematic tricks of the trade. Different artists will achieve it in different ways'. But it is not long before such latitude is seen to have its limits:

> When we talk about socialist realism we have in mind that which in art represents the objective world, not only in its superficial or even essential details but in its fundamental circumstances and characteristics. We have in mind everything which represents life in all its truth with both its negative and positive aspects, with the victorious element of the forces of the socialist revolution. We have in mind the anti-capitalist nature of our works which nurture in our readers the will to struggle for a better future for mankind.[10]

For the French intellectual Left the publication of this article was interestingly timed. Already in 1931 Maurice Thorez had drawn attention to the dangers of ideological isolation and had indicated cultural activities of various kinds as being one way of reforging links with the mass of working-class people. In March 1932 the Association des Ecrivains et Artistes révolutionnaires (AEAR) was formed with Paul Vaillant-Couturier (who was to become editor of the French version of *International Literature*) as secretary. On 22 and 29 March the group's manifesto appeared in *L'Humanité*, its tone strongly reminiscent of Kharkov: 'First of all to encourage around us the growth of proletarian literature and art: to stress to people of the working class the need and the urgency for a proletarian art and literature in France: to denounce all the subterfuges and manoeuverings of the bourgeoisie in this respect'.

By July 1933, however, a change could be noted. AEAR produced its own review *Commune* ('a militant journal') which was to play a vital role in filtering and shaping much left-wing thinking about literature during the 1930s. Its editorial team was made up of Vaillant-Couturier, Guéhenno, Barbusse and Rolland, with Nizan and Aragon as secretaries. It is difficult to imagine the coexistence of such a range of political positions as are represented by these people occuring three years earlier!

Despite such a varied group, however, it is clear that many of *Commune*'s statements were inspired by ideological directives emanating from Moscow and are less liberal or liberalising than they may at first appear to be. One example of such 'interference' is the 'Lettre à l'AEAR' by Bena Illès, Ludkewicz and Nizan, published

---

10. V. Kirpotin, 'La littérature soviétique au XVIème anniversaire de la Révolution d'octobre', *La Littérature Internationale*, no. 1, 1933, pp. 120–8.

in the third issue of *International Literature* in 1934. After a survey of the first two years of the AEAR's activities and policy of recruitment the authors return to the question of ideological direction: 'new recruits must gain the impression that the AEAR is an organisation where they can breathe freely, where they do not feel that they are confronted by a vain dogmatism, but discussion must at no point appear inadequate'. Those in the AEAR should concentrate on 'the question of literary creation and literary forms within the revolutionary movement'.

In the May–June issue of the same year, *Commune* published a seminal article on socialist realism — 'Le Réalisme socialiste. Méthode fondamentale de la littérature soviétique' ('Socialist realism. The basic method for Soviet literature') — by Yadin and Fadeyev. Once again we find an emphasis on the non-reductive, non-schematising quality of socialist realism, but, significantly, it is presented as a form of literature that has developed naturally within a post-revolutionary culture: 'Socialist realism is not a dogma, nor a collection of laws placing limits around artistic creation, reducing a rich variety of exploration and forms to literary rules. On the contrary socialist realism is the natural expression of new socialist relationships and of a revolutionary concept of the world'. The essential difference between this form of realism and traditional historical realism — a photographic technique stripped of social and didactic significance — is that it will depict the advance and benefits of socialism both by its content (*fond*) and by its means of expression (*forme*). This new literature 'can reveal the historical movement inherent in reality and how the future already exists in the present'. At the same time socialism will become 'the very essence of the work incarnated in its images'. A similar somewhat imprecise claim is also made in the guidelines prepared for the August conference to be held in Moscow by the Union of Soviet Writers and published in the same issue of *Commune* (May/June 1934): 'Socialist realism ensures that the artist has an exceptional opportunity to display his creative initiative, to select genres, forms, different methods'.

At the conference, attended by Aragon, Malraux, Bloch, Pozner and Nizan, the major speeches were given by Gorky, Radek, Bukharin and Zhdanov who was later to become Stalin's minister of culture. Each in turn emphasised the paucity and weakness of bourgeois literature which failed to offer the writer an opportunity 'to participate directly in the construction of a new life'.[11] A fresh

11. The transactions of the congress first appeared in English as *Problems of Soviet Literature*, ed. H. G. Scott, Lawrence, London, 1935. This quotation is taken from

literature must be created which would point the way forward and which would be accessible to working-class people. Certainly there were lessons to be learned from the past. Revolutionary romanticism in particular is to be admired, as are all writers (Shakespeare, Goethe, Schiller, Hugo for example) whose work reflects a bourgeois society struggling to emerge from an oppressive feudal system. For Bukharin even a lyrical portrayal of an individual is acceptable since it underlines not simply that individual's position in society, but offers a particular demonstration of a general movement towards the wakening of a collective conscience.

In September 1934 *Commune* published extracts from the speeches by Radek and Bukharin with an accompanying statement of strong approval: 'Following the example set by Soviet writers the AEAR must forge strong links with the working-class masses, not simply through the nature of the works produced by its members but by the fact that it will help provide for artists and writers from those masses the opportunities denied by the domination of the bourgeoisie'.

Yet there were reservations, expressed in particular by Malraux, Bloch and Gide (who had been invited but had declined at the last minute). Malraux was interviewed by Aragon for *L'Humanité* in September, and in October his conference speech 'L'Art est une conquête' ('Art is a Victory') was published by *Commune*: Bloch's contribution in Moscow appeared in the September issue of *Europe*: Gide spoke at a public meeting in October at the Palais de la Mutualité in Paris. As David Caute has observed, the publicity given to these non-party writers was important, for it lent support to the image of a new liberal attitude within the Party.[12] However, all three issued warnings of substance. Cleverly playing on Stalin's phrase of writers being engineers of the soul, Malraux remarked to Aragon in *L'Humanité* (September 1934): 'If writers are the "engineers of the human soul" we should not forget that the highest task of an engineer is to invent. Art is not passive; it is a conquering force'; Bloch, in spite of his admiration for the Soviet Union, argued for diversity in writing and pointed to the danger of 'mass ideas'; Gide, typically, was the most cautious of all: 'I consider all literature to be in danger once the writer sees himself obliged to obey any directives'.[13] In addition Bloch and Rolland expressed concern

---

the facsimile reprint, *Soviet Writers' Congress 1934: The Debate on Socialist Realism and Modernism in the Soviet Union*, Lawrence & Wishart, London, 1977, p. 67.

12. D. Caute, *Communism and the French Intellectuals : 1914–1960*, André Deutsch, London, 1964.

13. Gide's talk, 'Littérature et Révolution', was published by *Commune*, November 1934, pp. 161–5.

about the appropriate register of language for this 'new' literature and about the problems of communicating with the working-class people at whom it was principally aimed: 'In nine cases out of ten the revolutionary writer owes his formation to the humanities and to the teaching of the *lycée*. His problem is to free himself from knowingly complicit systems with their implied metaphors and allusions, without falling into a disgusting affectation of "popular style" '.[14] Such a change could only occur in a country which had already undergone social and political revolution, a view which echoed an argument made in earlier years by Victor Serge and Jean Fréville and which Léon Moussinac repeated with some pertinence in his article 'Réalisme socialiste' ('Socialist realism') (*Europe*, June 1936, pp. 183–90): 'Socialist realism presents particular problems for those of us who are writers in a country where the revolution has yet to be achieved, since it requires the renewal both of the subject-matter and of the form of the novel or play or poem'.

This cautionary attitude best represents the general reception given to socialist realism in France at this time. Even someone like Henri Lefebvre, whose left-wing ideology was in no way in doubt, recognised the impossibility of imposing a formula. All that was certain was that realism in literature should reflect the ever-present and ever-shifting conflicts and tensions inherent in human existence: 'Realism gradually aligns itself with socialism not because it borrows themes from a particular doctrine but because socialism has its roots in human reality and is a practical way of trying to solve problems. Such a realism is inherently didactic because it shows awareness of the deep movements and conflicts within life'.[15]

Only Aragon in a series of talks given in 1935 and published that year as *Pour un réalisme socialiste* ('Towards a Socialist Realism') attempted in any substantial way to formulate definitions based on Soviet models. Aragon uses his own position and his formative meeting with Mayakovsky to illustrate what he considers to be the general and irrevocable shift experienced by society as a whole and which, he argues, it is the writer's duty to reflect. The argument is by now a familiar one as is his emphasis on content rather than expression. Only in the vaguest terms does Aragon claim that contact with peasants and soldiers has, in the case of one unnamed Soviet writer, created 'a language of the future, understandable for

---

14. J. -R. Bloch, 'L'Ecrivain et le prolétariat', *Commune*, May 1945, pp. 1062–5 (p.1064). R. Rolland, 'Du rôle de l'écrivain dans la société aujourd'hui', ibid., pp. 929–36.
15. H. Lefebvre, 'Essai sur les rapports de la critique et du roman', *Commune*, August 1937, p. 1482.

all with no reduction in its stylistic qualities'.[16] This belief in the natural evolution of an appropriate style was given some support by Nizan who, in a tribute to Eugène Dabit in *L'Humanité* (6 September 1936), suggested that the writer's task was to 'have the spirit of revolution infuse art without destroying it'. But there is little more. Real questions about style and form remain unanswered and the whole debate was clouded in any case by others concerned with the related but distinct issues of proletarian and populist literature. It would not be for another ten years and during a harsher political climate that the question of socialist realism would be raised again — this time with rather more force and success.

Undoubtedly the most important factor in the creation of this climate in the late 1940s was the enhanced reputation of the PCF after the Occupation and Resistance — no matter what De Gaulle had managed to do to dispel the idea that the communists had been the most active amongst the first real resisters. This reputation was reflected in a membership in 1946–47 of about 800,000 and, despite being outmanoeuvered politically, the PCF remained influential in creating a particular moral and intellectual climate to which many young intellectuals were drawn and in which some found personal fulfilment. The account Edgar Morin gives of his own experience was not unusual: 'I was one of those adolescents for whom becoming a communist meant at the same time becoming a man. Joining the Party was all mixed up in me with initiation, the risk of death, of setting out on a real life'.[17]

Initially the principal vehicle for the transmission of ideas concerning art and literature was the paper *Les Lettres françaises*. In an 'editorial' statement made by Elsa Triolet, 23 June 1947, it was claimed that as a public figure the writer had a responsibility: he was 'someone who is both part of and in advance of an event, who describes it and comments upon it, works it out and illuminates it both socially and poetically'. On 25 August 1949 the label socialist realism reappeared in an article by one of its new apologists Pierre Daix ('Une littérature de parti'('A Party Literature'), pp. 52–9): 'socialist realism is the aesthetic expression of this political force', namely, Communism. The momentum steadily increased. The Left preached the view that not only did art and literature reflect the socio-political reality of its time but that it should do so in a way that ensured a correct interpretation of that reality. In a very broad sense this was a view shared by many: as the opening editorial statement

16. L. Aragon, *Pour un réalisme socialiste*, Denoël & Steele, Paris, 1935, p. 29.
17. E. Morin, *Autocritique*, Seuil, Paris, 1970, p. 51.

of *Les Temps modernes* claimed in October 1945: 'The writer is part of his time'. Camus and Sartre in particular saw the need for a committed writing, but they remained resolutely opposed to the imposition of rules and limits intended to encourage the emergence from imaginative writing of a specific and preordained truth. Such control could lead only to sterility.

> To have the unity of the world of the novel match that of the real world can only be done if there is an a priori judgement which eliminates from the latter anything that does not suit the doctrine. So-called socialist realism is bound by the very logic of its nihilism to bring the advantages of the didactic novel and of propaganda together.[18]

The militant Left remained untroubled by such reservations, however. An orthodoxy whose source was Moscow was championed quite uncritically; Stalin, his minister of culture Zhdanov and, in France, Maurice Thorez became cult figures; Laurent Casanova and Jean Kanapa (scornfully dismissed by Sartre) became the PCF's leading intellectual spokesmen; Aragon assumed the role of a guru. Volumes of essays such as Casanova's *Le Parti communiste, les intellectuels et la nation* ('The Communist Party, Intellectuals and the Nation') (1949), *Responsabilités de l'intellectuel communiste* ('Responsibilities of the Communist Intellectual') (1949) and, later Kanapa's *Situation de l'intellectuel* ('Situation of the Intellectual') (1957), and reviews such as the *Cahiers du Communisme, Pensé, Europe* and, above all, *La Nouvelle Critique* were vehicles for a massive dissemination of Party propaganda on all subjects.

Although unquestionably much more militant in tone, a great deal of what appeared recalled the kinds of statement made in the 1930s. The climate was set, notably, by the translation and publication in 1948 of three talks given by Zhdanov on literature, art and music which quickly acquired, and retained for a decade or so, the status of dogma.[19] Their thesis is once again predictable. All forms of bourgeois art like the general culture from which they spring are necessarily decadent, self-indulgent, individualist and the preserve of a small elite. What is necessary for the rejuvenation of all art forms is for them to be infused with a sense of purposeful historical development based on patriotism and socialism and directed at the

18. A. Camus, 'L'Homme révolté', in idem, *Essais*, Bibliothèque de la Pléiade, Paris, 1977, p. 673. See S. de Beauvoir, 'Littérature et Métaphysique', *Les Temps modernes*, April 1946, p. 1154: 'The novel is only to be justified if it communicates something in a way that is not otherwise possible'.
19. A. A. Zhdanov, *Sur la littérature, la philosophie et la musique*, Editions de la Nouvelle Critique, Paris, 1948.

people. In literature, socialist realism with the writer as guide is the only answer — a view propagated at regular intervals by the faithful. Thus Aragon can repeat in 1949 statements from a lecture given in 1937 and published in *Europe* in March 1938: 'before all else realism is the novelist's way of looking at things which in turn reflects his view of the world as a whole' and 'the perfecting of progressive ideas in France'.[20] Jean Larnac in his article 'De la critique Marxiste et du réalisme socialiste' ('On Marxist Criticism and Socialist Realism') (*Pensée*, No. 30, 1950) observes: 'the socialist writer must be aware of man's progress, of his striving for a better way of life, of his revolutionary development. At the same time as being meticulous as a historian he must also show himself to be a moralist'. In 1952 André Stil, who was awarded the Prix Staline for his *Au Château d'eau*, ('The Water Tower') (1951) the first volume in his trilogy *Le Premier Choc* ('The First Blow') (1951–3) wrote in one of the speeches gathered together as *Vers le réalisme socialiste* ('Towards Socialist Realism'): 'quality is not simply a matter of form, but first and foremost of subject-matter . . . formal quality is not only a question of work and application : it reflects both the subject-matter directly and the artist's reaction to it'.[21] Five years later Pierre Daix made the same point as Larnac, only a little more firmly: 'Socialist realism . . . implies a new social awareness on the part of the writer, his links with and responsibility to the revolutionary movement. In the strict sense of the word it is a way which demonstrates knowledge, action and work'.[22]

It must be acknowledged, however, that there were at the same time a few signs of a more pronounced concern than in the 1930s for *forme* and for its relationship to *contenu*. Equally an awareness was expressed for the problem of accessibility and the dangers of schematisation. And yet, perhaps not surprisingly, *precise* recommendations as to how these difficulties might be avoided were no more forthcoming than they had been twenty years earlier. The conviction that 'correct' content would somehow produce an appropriate form still prevailed and at worst resulted in statements that could appear circular. For example: 'we know that form is easier to find and to realise if the subject-matter leaves no room for doubt'[23] or 'a typical

20. L. Aragon, 'Réalisme socialiste et réalisme français', *La Nouvelle Critique*, May 1949, pp. 27–39.
21. A. Stil, *Vers le réalisme socialiste*, Editions de la Nouvelle Critique, Paris, 1952, p. 89.
22. P. Daix, 'Lettre à Maurice Nadeau sur les intellectuels et le communisme', *La Nouvelle Critique*, April 1957, p. 69.
23. F. Billoux, 'Premiers enseignements de la Bataille du Livre', *La Nouvelle Critique*, June 1951, p. 102.

subject, expressed in a form which is not typical and hence appropriate, would not be a typical subject-matter'.[24]

Yet a degree of concern existed and by the mid-1960s the thawing of the political and hence cultural climate would become much more evident. In June 1964 *La Nouvelle Critique* published an issue entitled 'Esthétique et littérature' ('Aesthetics and Literature') in which an introductory article by André Gisselbrecht contained statements which only a few years earlier would have been almost if not completely heretical: 'from an artistic point of view the most acute socialist awareness is not necessarily superior to bourgeois agonising. There is no single rising and continuous line in art which goes from the least to the most refined moral and ideological perception'. Bourgeois writing hitherto regarded as static and decadent can now be admitted as making a contribution to social progress since it reflects a world which must be exposed and destroyed. Furthermore, two additional factors begin to exert an influence by the mid-1960s. The first is that writers can no longer be expected to produce works according to specific directives however deep their own ideological convictions may be. The second acknowledges that when attempts are made to evaluate a literary work, the kind of normative criticism favoured by proponents of socialist realism is severely limited. When Claude Prévost writes about that most introverted and individualist of novelists, Franz Kafka, in *La Nouvelle Critique* (February 1965), he admits that 'people have neither *understood* nor really yet *explained* the secret of his art' and suggests that attention should be paid primarily to *form* and not to content. A year later in March 1966 at a meeting of the Central Committee of the PCF at Argenteuil, Roger Garaudy also significantly observed: 'to reduce a work of art to its ideological ingredients, is not only to lose sight of its specificity, but also not to take into account its relative autonomy and the unequal development of society and art'. And he continued: 'Realism therefore is an attitude towards reality and not a method. Method at any time depends on man's ability to control nature, on technical standards and social relationships. It is the duty of the artist to discover the most appropriate form of expression whether in literature or the plastic arts'.[25]

Even André Stil to whom the Prix Staline had given a certain authoritative status — and who was later to have a different authority as a member of the Prix Goncourt panel! — would admit in 1979 that literature could not be subject to externally imposed

24. P. Daix, 'La culture soviétique et nos propres problèmes', *La Nouvelle Critique*, March 1954, p. 278.
25. R. Garaudy, *Cahiers du Communisme*, May–June 1966, pp. 17–19.

directives. Nor indeed could or should it exist *solely* as a vehicle for political ideas. Its success must depend on its capacity to absorb such ideas without detriment to its artistic qualities: 'Politics in the novel is like sugar in water. If the sugar has not melted in a glass of sweetened water then it has not been properly prepared'.[26]

This, broadly, was the position reached by all those who in the 1950s had been stridently intransigent. Admittedly there would be a new direction. *Forme* could and indeed should itself become *contenu* and new poetic or structuralist readings of texts would now lead to the kind of conclusion envisaged earlier but by different and more complex means. In essence, however, the French revival of socialist realism had come to a close by the mid-1960s. Of the two periods when it was fashionable the latter was certainly the more productive. Stil himself, Roger Vailland, Pierre Courtade, Pierre Daix, André Wurmser and others all contributed substantially to a corpus of imaginative writing nicely illustrative of the theories which most of them propounded or at least accepted.[27] Beyond its relatively easily defined historical parameters, however, socialist realism does offer a number of problems of a theoretical nature. Some of these, notably structural in kind, have been examined by Susan Suleiman in her book *Authoritarian Fictions: the Ideological Novel as a Literary Genre*.[28] Equally instructive for an evaluation of socialist realist works would be such matters as common sources of imagery, registers of language, the use of authorial voice, the role given to hero (Stalin) figures, the use and accuracy of historical material, and critical and public reception.[29] Nor is there any reason to limit such investigations to a single genre or national literature. In fact the possible perspectives are rather more complex than some of the authoritative statements about socialist realism might lead us to suspect.[30]

26. A. Stil, *L'Optimisme librement consenti*, Stock, Paris, 1979, p. 133.
27. In several cases — for example *La Place rouge* (1961) by Pierre Courtade or Roger Vailland's *325,000 francs* (1956) — the imaginative work goes beyond the limits imposed by any theory, just as Aragon's *Les Cloches de Bâle* had done in 1934. It is interesting to note that during this most militant period Aragon is at his least productive.
28. S. Suleiman, *Authoritarian Fictions : The Ideological Novel as a Literary Genre*, Columbia University Press, New York, 1983. This was originally published in France as *Le roman à thèse ou l'autorité fictive*, PUF, Paris, 1983.
29. Although not necessarily directed at socialist realism some approaches of a theoretical kind can be found in, for example, H. Mitterand, *Le Discours du roman*, PUF, Paris, 1980, or P. Hamon, *Texte et idéologie*, PUF, Paris, 1984.
30. Since the completion of this essay, my attention has been drawn to R. Robin, *Le Réalisme socialiste*, Payot, Paris, 1986. Robin's study is concerned primarily with developments in the Soviet Union but is also rich in suggestions for the reading (*lecture*) of socialist realist texts.

PART III

Textual Analysis

—7—

Persona as Propaganda: Neruda and the Spanish Civil War

ROBIN WARNER

The issue of propaganda is central to the socialist realist debate, since it directly concerns the utilitarian conception of art as well as the question of its ideological content. Any attempt, however, to analyse the propaganda dimension in literary production must contend with problems of definition. The concept itself tends to slide up and down a scale of meaning which refers to justified beliefs and helpful information at one end and lies, exaggerations and distortions at the other, according to one's viewpoint. The ideological sympathies of the commentator can have as much importance as narrowly aesthetic criteria in determining approaches and judgements.

Such problems are particularly acute in the context of the war in Spain (1936–9), a conflict marked by a degree of tendentiousness and relativism that prompted one contemporary observer to claim he witnessed 'history being written not in terms of what happened but of what ought to have happened according to various "party lines"', and another to complain that 'truth and lies were inextricably entangled . . . the deceivers were also deceived'.[1] Against such a background, the relations between propagandistic writing and socialist realist theory were further obscured, as I hope to show, by Popular Front policies which favoured a blurring of revolutionary perspectives.

In a previous discussion of Pablo Neruda's response to the Spanish conflict I endeavoured to bring a fixed point of reference to the pervasive relativism of the propaganda question by identifying some themes and formulas which supported specific political objectives.[2]

1. G. Orwell, 'Looking back on the Spanish War', in *Homage to Catalonia*, Penguin, Harmondsworth, 1975, p. 234. J. Symons, quoted in B. Bolloten, *The Spanish Revolution*, University of North Carolina Press, Chapel Hill N.C., 1979, p. xxvi.
2. R. Warner, 'The Politics of Pablo Neruda's *España en el corazón*', in J. England (ed.), *Hispanic Studies in Honour of Frank Pierce*, Department of Hispanic Studies,

A possibly more rewarding although inevitably more speculative approach is to focus on the poetry's internal structure, on the deeper levels at which ideological elements are embedded, with particular attention to the poet's consciousness of his role as propagandist. We should bear in mind, of course, that to thematise poetic practice may well constitute in itself an effective form of propaganda. In order to analyse Neruda's *España en el corazón* ('Spain at Heart')[3] from such a perspective it is essential to situate the work against the background of the poetics of commitment prevalent among writers in the Republican Zone, especially those with whom the Chilean poet was in close contact.

Neruda took up consular duties in Spain in 1934, the year of the Asturias insurrection and an increasing polarisation of politics in general. His immediate circle of friends included the poet Rafael Alberti and his wife, María Teresa León, both Communists, who edited the avowedly revolutionary literary journal *Octubre*, and who were among the foreign delegates at the First Soviet Writers' Congress (August 1934), where the method of socialist realism was officially promulgated. Exposure to such influences may possibly be reflected in Neruda's shift toward an anti-aestheticist concept of poetry in this period, but the catalyst for his change to a poetry of open political commitment was provided, as it was for many other writers in Spain at this time, by the outbreak of war.

The events of July 1936 and their aftermath instigated a keen desire among many writers and intellectuals to render practical assistance in what was perceived as a revolutionary struggle. Indeed, some of them scrupulously insisted on alternating editorial, administrative or propaganda activities with service at the front.[4] Such militants vehemently repudiated the charge that to gear their writing to a political programme was to accept limitations on creative scope and quality. The arguments put forward in response to the charge of propagandistic reductionism broadly reflect the debate about political commitment among European writers and

---

University of Sheffield, Sheffield, 1980, pp. 169–80.

3. *España en el corazón* (1936–7), the fourth section of Neruda's *Tercera residencia* in his 'Complete Works', was published as a separate collection in Chile in 1937 and Spain in 1938. (An English translation by Donald D. Walsh of *Tercera residencia* is also available: *Residence on Earth*, Souvenir Press, London, 1976.) My translation of the title aims at conveying a certain ambiguity in the original; similarly, my English versions of passages from the poems are oriented to the sense rather than to aesthetic considerations. All quotations from Spanish sources in this essay are my own translations unless otherwise indicated.

4. The changes in editorship of the journal *Hora de España* (1937–8), for instance, reflected such periods of active service.

intellectuals in the 1930s in that they stress that every writer is a social being whose creative activity ineluctably expresses collective aspirations, and that, far from being restrictive, the values which inform Marxist-oriented propaganda are truly liberating because they are directed toward an extension of personality and consciousness; in the succinct formula of one (non-Communist) young writer: 'Fascism imprisons and Communism sets free'.[5] The tendency, followed by the more radical writers, to challenge the assumptions on which claims for artistic freedom are based by linking them to bourgeois individualism and its degeneration into aesthetic mystique also reveals awareness of a characteristic line of argument in the pronouncements of, say, Zhdanov and Radek. Such an approach, for instance, is evident in an article which appeared in the first weeks of the war and in a journal (aimed at popular militias rather than intellectuals) in which Neruda's first openly committed poem was shortly to appear:[6]

> The time has come for intellectuals to listen to that voice [of the people] and make it intelligible, actual and unforgettable; the time has come to renounce treacherous and hypocritical bourgeois freedom and serve the cause of real human freedom instead, which can only be done by ruthlessly exposing the useless relics of a past which is reluctant to give way and by accepting and illuminating the truth that is revealed only to a people that has risen to its feet.[7]

The broad doctrinal basis of such exhortations is a familiar one. What distinguishes the outlook of Spanish writers is a concept of reality which is conditioned not so much by theories of class-consciousness as by direct participation in a situation of armed struggle, together with a tendency to emphasize passionate engagement with day-to-day experience rather than ideological correctness: 'We are in favour of socialist realism in art if we understand by reality not a cold external appearance, something death-like, but a living source of appearances and suggestions. What counts is the passion the artist brings to the reality of the world, a world conceived in all its weight and rich fantasy'.[8]

5. A. Sánchez Barbudo, 'La adhesión de los intelectuales a la causa popular' ('The Intellectuals Join the People's Cause'), *Hora de España*, no. 7, 1937, p. 73.
6. The poem, 'Canto a las madres de los milicianos muertos' ('Song for the Mothers of Slain Militiamen'), appeared anonymously in *El Mono Azul* ('Blue Overalls'), no. 5, 1936.
7. M. Zambrano, 'La libertad del intelectual' ('The Freedom of the Intellectual'), *El Mono Azul*, no. 3, 1936.
8. Sánchez Barbudo, 'La adhesión . . .', p. 74.

But it is also a world at war. Close involvement with the practical issues of the conflict, while making it easier to reject accusations of enslavement to theoretical programmes, does introduce the suspicion that artistic integrity might be sacrificed to the exigencies of the war-effort. A positive evaluation of propaganda thus becomes necessary, one which dismisses not only the idealist conception of writing but also the simple obverse notion, since 'to defend propaganda as an absolute value seems as demagogic and senseless to us as it would be, for example, to defend art for art's sake or bravery for bravery's sake'.[9]

The arguments in favour of propaganda, while unmistakably left-wing in outlook, do appear to rest on ethical claims which can be considered legitimate in the context of a struggle which, in broad terms, pitted the mass of the people against the military apparatus of privilege. It is a depressing feature, however, of the ideological schisms in Republican Spain, that it is precisely in appeals to broad democratic values and to passionate human involvement rather than rigorous analysis that the influence of factional interests — those of the Communist Party — can be detected. To appreciate the paradox involved here it is necessary to understand the policy dilemma of the Communists during the Spanish War, a dilemma which obliged them to promote the values of bourgeois democracy while continuing to voice vaguely revolutionary slogans. As a recent analysis explains: 'Soviet policy on Spain was constrained by Stalin's search for Western allies against Hitler. This meant guaranteeing that the Spanish Republic remained a bourgeois democratic parliamentary regime. In any case, the Spanish communists were convinced that Spain was obliged by an iron historical destiny to pass through a bourgeois stage on its road to socialism'.[10] The logic of such a view gave rise to a number of policy themes. A central one was the presentation of the war effort as an imperative which overrode all ideological scruples; while the conflict itself was characterised as a struggle for national independence, the defence of a legitimate popular democracy against foreign aggression, rather than an internal struggle for class hegemony. 'The people must rise to prevent our country being trampled under the bloody hooves of the foreign robbers', exhorted a Communist pamphlet as early as

---

9. 'Collective Statement' of the Spanish Delegation to the Second International Congress of Writers for the Defence of Culture (Valencia and Madrid, 1937). The statement was read by A. Serrano Plaja. See: *Hora de España*, no. 8, 1937, p. 91.

10. P. Preston, *The Spanish Civil War*, Weidenfeld & Nicolson, London, 1986, p. 129.

August 1936.[11] Another important motif (which acquired increased emphasis with the Communist decision to work toward incorporating independent militias into a centrally controlled People's Army) was that of unity and discipline: a unity defined as transcending differences of class and political outlook, and a discipline which meant accepting orders or policies without question, 'a revolutionary war-discipline of iron'.[12] The presentation of issues such as revolution and social justice is, understandably, confused; the Collective Statement of the Spanish delegation at the Second International Congress of Writers for the Defence of Culture (Valencia 1937) actually claims that 'just by winning the war — nothing more and nothing less — the most positive and formidable revolution will have taken effect in the world'.[13] The heroic popular initiatives of July 1936 are indeed described as a revolution, but one which must now be consolidated in an orderly fashion (that is, deferred) under the Popular Front Government.

The process by which such formulations found their way into the work of sympathetic writers was not necessarily straightforward. Rather than directives or overt pressures, it would be more helpful to posit a Communist-led ideological consensus whose mechanisms included a network of reliable agents in sensitive positions.[14] The dissemination and acceptance of the Communist viewpoint was made easier by the prestige which accrued to the Party after its decisive role in the defence of Madrid, as well as its assiduous courting of intellectuals and opinion-formers in general. It was the Communist Fifth Regiment, for instance, which, amid the chaos of the Government's hasty departure for Valencia in November 1936, took care to organise the evacuation of senior intellectuals from the threatened capital; and while prestigious positions in the Alliance of Anti-Fascist Intellectuals tended to be filled by independent figures such as the liberal Catholic José Bergamín, administrative control

---

11. D. Ibarruri, *Union of All Spaniards* (Report to the Plenary of the Spanish Communist Party (PCE), Barcelona, May, 1938), p. 25. The text, in English, includes the 1936 Manifesto.
12. See the Resolutions of the March 1937 Plenary of the PCE., in: M. C. García Nieto, and J. M. Donezar, *La Guerra de España*, Guadiana, Madrid, 1974, pp. 175–84.
13. See *Hora de España*, no. 8, 1937, pp. 93–4.
14. Bolloten, in *The Spanish Revolution* makes detailed allegations of behind-the-scenes Communist machinations. It is also worth noting that, in spite of frequent Cabinet changes, the Ministry of Education (heavily concerned with cultural activities) remained in the hands of the Communist J. Hernández for most of the war. A list of ministries and incumbents during the war can be found in García Nieto and Donezar, *La Guerra*, pp. 469–76.

lay in the hands of Communists such as Rafael Alberti and his wife María Teresa León. It was Bergamín, rather than someone open to the charge of political bias, who acted as spokesman for all Republican writers in vilifying André Gide's recently published *Retour de l'U.R.S.S.* (*Back from the USSR*) (1936), while continuing to affirm that 'we are all committed to freedom of thought and criticism'.[15]

The problem of the often blurred distinction between consensus and coercion, freedom of expression and expression of pre-defined freedom, is brought into revealing if contrasting focus in the reminiscences of three editors of the independent journal *Hora de España*. Rafael Dieste refers more than once to unhelpful directives from 'our political advisers',[16] whereas Antonio Sánchez Barbudo recalls that 'our firm intention was to be genuinely liberal, and since our policy coincided with that of the Popular Front, we could defend ourselves perfectly well against the attacks of those who said the journal had to be more militant, more proletarian, more revolutionary, etc.'[17] A more cynical view is taken by Juan Gil-Albert: 'Behind the scenes the inevitable party-political disputes led to us being accused of one thing and another, and thus some considered us aesthetes, while others called us communists, although the Communists themselves, if they took sides, labelled us Trotskyists, a term which served in those days to designate anything uncommitted ['vago'] heteredox and reprehensible'.[18]

It should by now be clear that an adequate account of propaganda and commitment among Republican writers cannot be given on an abstract theoretical level alone, and that the antagonisms and contradictions involved in Popular Front policies can have important effects on outlook and self-definition. In the particular instance of Pablo Neruda we should remember that his political sympathies were not, in any case, of a general nature: 'Although I received my membership card of the Communist Party later, in Chile, I believe I defined myself, in my own eyes, as a Communist, during the Spanish War'.[19] *España en el corazon* certainly presents a view of the conflict that follows the broad outlines of Communist policy. The work repeatedly emphasises faith, patriotism, sacrifice, discipline and

15. See M. Koltzov, *Diario de la guerra española*, trans. J. Fernandez Sánchez, Akal, Madrid, 1978, p. 473.
16. R. Dieste, *Testimonios y homenajes*, ed. M. Aznar, Laia, Barcelona, 1983. See, for example, p. 77.
17. See M. Roumette, '*Hora de España, Revista Mensual*', in M. Hanrez (ed.), *Los escritores y la guerra de España*, Monte Avila, Barcelona, 1977, p. 237.
18. J. Gil-Albert, *Memorabilia*, Tusquets, Barcelona, 1975, p. 214.
19. P. Neruda, *Confieso que he vivido* ('I Confess I Have Lived'), Seix Barral, Barcelona, 1974, p. 191.

unity in an inspiringly human struggle for freedom against an enemy who is sinisterly alien. Such themes, moreover, are to be found in the work of Alberti, Emilio Prados, Arturo Serrano Plaja and Miguel Hernández (to mention only some better-known names among the younger radical poets) and are sometimes present in the war poetry of older and ideologically more independent figures such as Antonio Machado and León Felipe. Nor was the propaganda value of such verse marginal; the innumerable ballads written by established poets and ordinary soldiers and workers alike produced a cultural climate in which poetry in general was regarded as an important means of mass-communication, reaching a wide audience through the radio and the press as well as readings at the front.[20] Thus there is a tendency for orality of style to be matched by an emphasis on communicative efficacy, that is, in socialist realist terms, a style of poetry which ordinary workers and soldiers can understand and respond to . Such an approach has important repercussions on the level of persona, the mode of self-presentation adopted by the poet.

It is a paradox of much left-wing verse that although the idiosyncratic 'I' as source of the lyrical utterance is replaced by a speaker aiming at solidarity with others, the result is often an increase in self-conscious postures. Making assertions about the poet's function can be a convenient way of repudiating bourgeois illusions about the nature of artistic production. Similarly, the poet's relationship with members of the wider community can be effectively concretised by illocutionary statements (avowals, exhortations, confessions, etc.) in the first person. Thus, in *España en el corazón*, Neruda consistently employs a formula which could be represented as 'I witnessed, I feel, I speak'. The poem which recalls the arrival of the first International Brigade units in Madrid provides a good example of this technique:

> Comrades,
> then
> I saw you,
> and my eyes even now are full of pride
> because I saw you through the misty morning arriving
> on the pure brow of Castile . . .[21]

The effect of this type of avowal is to suggest an identity of

20. S. Salaün, in *La poesía de la guerra de España*, Castilia, Madrid, 1985, goes so far as to claim that 'the cultural phenomenon found in verse its privileged instrument, since a whole nation effectively communed through its means' (pp. 11–12).

21. P. Neruda, *Obras completas*, I, Losada, Buenos Aires, 1967, p. 282. Subsequent page reference throughout the text of my essay are to this volume.

affective viewpoint. Neruda presents himself as just one pair of eyes, one uplifted heart ('these eyes I have, this heart that sees') in the crowds lining the streets to welcome the volunteers in Madrid's hour of need. A similar perspective informs the poem addressed to the mothers of dead militiamen; in traditional elegaic manner, the poet professes an identical grief:

> And just as in your hearts, mothers,
> in my heart there is so much mourning, so much death
> that it is like a forest
> drenched in the blood that killed their smiles. (p. 278)

The attachment between mothers and sons, Neruda suggests, is analogous to the bonds of solidarity uniting poet and combatants:

> I do not forget your afflictions, I know your sons,
> and if I am proud of their deaths,
> I am also proud of their lives. (p. 278)

Such declarations of empathy are important for establishing the anti-individualistic basis of the poet's outlook in a vivid, non-abstract way. The speaking 'I' can also be defined in terms of the collective 'we' by a more traditional claim to the status of official orator, solemnifying and commemorating events of great public importance.

> Brothers, from now on let
> your purity, your strength, your solemn history
> be known to the child and the man, to the woman and
>   the old man,
> let it reach all those who live without hope . . . (p. 282)

The consciousness of such a role pervades Neruda's celebration of the crucial and costly Jarama victory to the extent that he formally confesses his talents inadequate to the task of recording such heroism:

> Jarama, to speak of your regions
> of splendour and dominance, my mouth is not
> enough and my hand is pale. (p. 283)

In 'Paisaje después de una batalla' ('Landscape after a Battle'), such a profession of modesty as a means of enhancing the gravity of the poem's topic takes the form of ritual, of stooping to the ground in an act of commemorative reverence:

> Let my knees hold it buried
> deeper than this fugitive territory
> let my eyelids grasp it till they name and pierce,
> let my blood hold this taste of shadow
> lest there be any forgetting. (p. 290)

The poetic conceit underlying such gestures — the convention that the supreme importance of certain human qualities or public events puts them beyond the poet's expressive powers — is well-established in the Western lyrical tradition, but Neruda is able to introduce new resonances. Behind the general reference to the insignificance of the individual when measured against the scale of a heroic communal enterprise lies a more specific abnegation: the disciplined subordination of personal pretensions to the demands of the war. In presenting himself as a humble artificer of words, moreover, Neruda allots himself a social role, a 'trade' no more or less exceptional than any other in the collective struggle. Poems such as 'oda solar al ejército del pueblo' ('Solar Ode to the People's Army') or 'Los gremios en el frente' ('The Unions at the Front'), with their emphasis on the collaboration of manual and professional workers of all kinds in the war-effort, clearly illustrate the importance for Neruda (and for the Popular Front) of this aspect of solidarity. Self-conscious denials of privileged difference became something of a cliché among intellectuals — especially poets — during the Spanish War. Serrano Plaja's 'Estos son los oficios' ('These are the Trades') is a typical example:

> I want, I ask, I beg for words well worn
> by use and time, like mattocks . . .
> I want a voice of rope and hands of bread
> to join me to work and kisses
> and to the smell of well-earned weariness.[22]

The poets draw attention to their own feelings and personal situation for the precise purpose of raising to an explicit level their sense of attunement to the needs, aspirations and emotions of the millions of men and women engaged in a common cause. Frequently it is the stubbornly heroic resistance of the people of Madrid, Alberti's 'Capital de la gloria' ('Capital of Glory'), which exemp-

22. A. Serrano Plaja, *El hombre y el trabajo* ('Men and Work'), Ediciones Hora de España, Barcelona, 1938, p. 22.

lifies and inspires such solidarity. Neruda's sympathy is consistently directed to the ordinary people of the beleagured city, whose heroes are not doctrinally conventional proletarians or party-members, but simply 'you who live, John, / today you who look, Peter, conceive, sleep, eat' (pp. 293–4). Although the geographical location of Neruda's 'Canto sobre unas ruinas' ('Song over some Ruins') is not specified, the poem's approach is identical to that of Alberti's 'Madrid-Otono' ('Madrid-Autumn'), where the havoc visited on the lives of ordinary citizens is conveyed by pathetic descriptions of exposed, scattered and broken domestic artefacts. There is a widespread tendency, among the poets, to apostrophise the city whose steely resolve[23] bolsters their own commitment. When Neruda begins 'Madrid 1937' with a solemn incantation,

> At this hour I remember everything and everyone,
> fibrously, deeply in
> the regions which — sound and plumage —
> beating a little, exist
> beyond the earth but on the earth. (p. 292)

he is honouring a living legend of courage and tenacity, the days when 'with shotguns and stones, Madrid, freshly wounded, / you defended yourself' (p. 275). He is also recalling his personal participation in an experience memorably evoked by Emilio Prados, in a ballad which tautens to its limit the thread linking lyrical subjectivity to civic involvement:

> Castle of my reason
> and frontiers of my dream,
> my city is under siege,
> among cannons I move.
> Where do you begin, Madrid,
> or are you, Madrid, my body? [24]

The poem which most fully articulates Neruda's feelings about Spain in general and Madrid in particular, and which most thoroughly exploits the dimension of persona in terms of a dialectical

23. 'The steel of Madrid' was a frequently-evoked motif and was used as the title of a prose epic by J. Herrera Petere (*El acero de Madrid*, Editorial Nuestro Pueblo, Barcelona, 1938), as well as for the name of militia organisations. An allusion to a local source of curative spring-water is possibly involved.
24. E. Prados, 'Ciudad sitiada' ('Besieged City'), in *Romancero de la guerra de España*, Ministerio de Instrucción Pública, Madrid, 1936, p. 65.

relationship between private experience and a sense of collective identity, is 'Explico algunas cosas' ('I Explain a Few Things') (pp. 275–7), the *ars poetica* of his commitment to the Spanish cause. From the outset,

> You will ask: And where are the lilacs?
> And the metaphysics covered in poppies?
> And the rain which often used to beat
> on his words filling them
> with holes and birds?

the poet casts himself as an apostate from the modernist orthodoxy of Western poetry and from an intellectual caste detached from the great mass of the people. The plural 'you' whose reproachful questions Neruda sets out to answer represent the broad Hispanic intellectual community as much as uncomprehending fellow-Chileans.[25] The poet's self-dissociation from their point of view is announced by a reference to himself in the third person ('his words') and confirmed by a switch to the first person and to pointedly prosaic language for his offer of a full explanation: 'I am going to tell you about everything that is happening to me'.[26]

Neruda follows up with apparently artless pieces of information: 'I lived in a suburb/of Madrid, with bells,/with clocks, with trees', and even includes a literal explanation of why the building in which he had lived was called 'the house of flowers': 'because all over it/geraniums burst into flower: it was/a lovely house'. Such details serve to introduce an age-old poetic theme: remembrance of a time of happiness from the perspective of present grief. Neruda, however, gives the motif a communal as well as a private dimension.

> It was all
> loud cries, piquant merchandise,
> agglomerations of palpitating bread . . .
> olive oil flowed on to spoons,

25. Even the specific reference to Chile at the close of the poem uses the third person, '*his* native country' rather than 'my' or 'our'. It is also worth noting that, in this collection as a whole, the term 'patria' (fatherland) invariably denotes Spain.
26. The force of this statement can usefully be contrasted with the opening lines of 'No hay olvido' ('There is no forgetting'), the penultimate poem in *Tercera residencia*. An initial hypothetical question, 'If you ask me in what place I have been' is followed by the enigmatic 'I must say: it befalls', a statement which introduces a characteristically esoteric recital of existential preoccupations, of the type Neruda, in 'Explico...', is warning his readers *not* to expect. See Neruda, *Obras completas*, I, p. 251.

a deep throbbing
of feet and hands filled the streets,
metres, litres, the sharp essence
of life.

It is worth noting that such evocations of former (that is, pre-1936) prosperity and joy in life can be found in the work of other writers. Neruda's fond recollection of Argüelles is comparable, for instance, to the depiction of pre-war Málaga in Emilio Prados's 'Tres cantos en el destierro' ('Three Songs of Exile'):

City, I have known the glow of your neighbourhoods;
the quivering flame of your ample markets;
the sound of your voices by the taste of wine,
the daily drama of your round plazas.[27]

The aim, of course, as well as to idealise the Republican era, is to keep in view a necessarily postponed Utopia, a vision which serves to justify the material and ideological sacrifices which have to be made for the sake of winning the war. The fact that the future is thus presented as reinstatement of the past reveals much about the reformist bias of Popular Front policies, a bias, it might be noted, which hardly favours the perspective of building a Communist society urged upon socialist writers outside Spain.

The particular point Neruda is making in 'Explico algunas cosas' is that what has happened and is still happening, the difference between *then* and *now*, legitimises the change that has taken place in his way of writing. Whereas *then* it was possible to lead a peaceful private life and indulge in esoteric poetry, *now* a poet must be first and foremost an active participant in the collective struggle against the forces of murderous barbarism, the 'bandits' who

came through the skies to kill children
and in the streets the blood of children
ran simply, like children's blood.

The powerful simplicity of these lines, with their characteristic renunciation of artifice (the poet seems to consider using the device of simile only to reject it, as if the reality were too horrendous to admit comparison), represents only one facet of a thoroughgoing critique directed against the sort of cultural consensus that gives

27. E. Prados, 'Tres cantos en el destierro', *Hora de España*, no. 10, 1937, p. 91. It should also be kept in mind that Prados is providing an idealised contrast to the plight of the city on falling into Nationalist hands in 1937.

priority to narrow aesthetic considerations or to a subject-centred paradigm of creative writing. Neruda speaks from personal experience, since his home was in a zone of Madrid which became a battleground in November 1936,[28] but his own reactions are valid precisely because they are shared by the many thousands whose homes and domestic happiness have been destroyed:

> Treacherous
> generals:
> look at my dead house,
> look at Spain shattered.

The temporal antithesis past/present is matched in 'Explico algunas cosas' by a socio-spatial binomy, house/street, which refers to the replacement of tranquility and privacy by violent emotions and public events; yet a third conceptual contrast is provided by the opposed notions Spain (homeland of the heart) and Chile (country of birth). The three themes are superimposed in the poem's conclusion, where the original query is answered by a twice-repeated exhortation:

> You will ask why his poetry
> does not tell us about dreams, about leaves,
> about the great volcanoes of his country of birth?
> Come and see the blood in the streets,
> Come and see
> the blood in the streets,
> come and see the blood
> in the streets!

Logically, this is neither an answer nor a reasoned explanation. But the fact that the poem was originally entitled 'Es así' ('It is so'), the traditional dogmatic reply to ingenuous questions, suggests that it was conceived as a criticism of pedantic 'reasons'.[29] Neruda is dismissing concern for geotropic definitions of patriotism or privileged notions of culture as absurdly and shockingly irrelevant.

Since 'Explico . . .' rejects inspirational individualism it is natural

---

28. 'Explico . . .' may well have been inspired by Neruda's visit to his ransacked apartment when the Writers' Congress of 1937 held its final sessions in Madrid. Intriguingly, for the topic under discussion, Neruda was particularly upset by the disappearance of his collection of Oriental masks. (See Neruda, *Confieso*, p. 197.)

29. See *El Mono Azul*, no. 22 (1937).

for Neruda to invoke the support of committed colleagues. Fittingly, the apellation is associated with the motif of loss and irrevocable change in outlook:

> Raúl, do you remember?
> Do you remember, Rafael? Federico, do you remember
> under the ground,
> do you remember my house with its balconies where
> the June light drowned flowers in your mouth?
> Brother! brother!

The mention of Rafael Alberti needs no comment; that of Raul González Tuñón, an Argentinian poet resident in Madrid, where he published a collection inspired by the Asturias insurrection of 1934, serves to emphasise the internationalist perspective of 'Explico . . .'. Federico García Lorca, on the other hand, although a close friend of Neruda, had been more moderate in his political stance. His death, however, had made his name a rallying-cry for radical intellectuals, both in Spain and abroad, as the most tragic — and most famous — victim of the barbaric enemy's hatred for life-affirming cultural values. In the eyes of his fellow poets Lorca had been executed precisely *because* he was a poet, and to allude to his death was to link personal feelings of loss with the theme of political commitment as both choice and necessity.

Although commentary can be no more than speculative at this point, the possibility of a fourth exemplary poetic presence in 'Explico . . .' cannot be entirely discounted: that of Antonio Machado. Neruda's switch of patriotic allegiance from his birthplace to Spain reflects, no doubt, a rejection of bourgeois nationalism appropriate to his new ideological sympathies. But in defining homeland in terms of deep emotional identification Neruda is following a path already marked out by the veteran and enormously respected Machado. More than a quarter of a century earlier the movement in Machado's work toward a more exoteric and civically conscious poetry had been explicitly associated with a transfer of affective centredness from his native Andalusia to Castile. In more than one poem of *España en el corazón* Neruda links his special feelings for Spain with an evocation of the high central meseta, 'plain and eagles' nest' (p. 279); indeed, in 'Explico . . .', he recalls that from his house

> . . . you could see
> the dry face of Castile
> like an ocean of leather.

But even here we must remain alert to propaganda resonances. Neruda's projection of an emotional aura on to the Castilian landscape might be suspected of corresponding to the Communists' tendency to ascribe privileged importance to Madrid and the Central Front, where their influence was strongest.

I have attempted to show that in spite of — and even through — its apparent simplicity, 'Explico...' is a complexly structured poem; sufficiently so, in fact, to refute the claim that propagandistic writing is necessarily superficial or of limited artistic scope. The problem remains, however, of matters such as truthfulness and creative integrity. There is little point in appealing to the notion of interior fictional persona as distinct from Neruda the individual; the 'I' of these poems stresses his concrete, personal involvement in objective historical experiences, and it is precisely the denial of artistic 'distance' that constitutes one of the most telling ideological arguments.

Given Neruda's political sympathies and those of the circles in which he moved, it was natural that his approach to committed poetry should be broadly compatible with the concept of 'revolutionary romanticism' identified by Bukharin in 1934 as a component of socialist realism which was of particular relevance to poetry.[30] On the other hand, the political situation in the Republican Zone and the general Communist concern to consolidate anti-Fascist alliances encouraged an active tolerance of certain liberal-democratic values, including the notional creative autonomy of the artist. The poetic persona of *España en el corazón*, moreover, is located at the intersection of private and collective viewpoints, the domain where artistic consciousness and civic concern must recognise and come to terms with each other. In the last resort, rather than to convey a particular ideological message, the mask is worn to reconcile claims to sincerity as an artist with those of the believer in a political cause.

30. See N. Bukharin, 'Poetry, Poetics and the Problems of Poetry in the U.S.S.R.' in *Soviet Writers' Congress 1934: The Debate on Socialist Realism and Modernism in the Soviet Union*, Lawrence & Wishart, London, 1977 (facsimile repr. of *Problems of Soviet Literature*, ed. H. G. Scott, Lawrence, London, 1935), pp. 185–258. Revolutionary romanticism, of course, can be taken to refer to the optimistic orientation to the future held to be essential for socialist realist art — an interpretation adopted by Zhdanov at the same Congress (see pp. 21–2). Bukharin, however, is equally interested in the notion that 'within poetic unity there coexist intellectual, emotional and volitional elements, forming a single, indivisible whole' (p. 252). Subjective emotional experience is thus, for him, an integral aspect of socialist poetics. Bukharin's comment that 'the feeling of a collective bond between people is one of the principal traits of socialism, and the poetised form of this feeling must inevitably be reflected in the distinguishing stylistic traits of socialist realism' (p. 255) seems to have some bearing on the approach adopted by Neruda.

—8—

Paul Nizan and Socialist Realism: The Example of *Le Cheval de Troie*

MICHAEL SCRIVEN

The effect of a red rag on a bull is well known.[1] The effect of a socialist realist text on a Western liberal critic is less well publicised but frequently similar. There is a tendency to see red at every page. Whatever merits a particular text might have are overlooked in the raging pursuit of an ideology that must at all costs be met head on and combated. The critic chooses to remain blind to the textual specificity of a given novel in order to retain the strength and credibility of comprehensive ideological positions. Throughout, the implicit aim is to denigrate and patronise. The socialist realist novel, in short, is frequently dismissed in a rather condescending manner as devoid not only of ideological freedom of expression but also of technical competence.

The socialist realist pedigree of Nizan's second novel, *Le Cheval de Troie* (*Trojan Horse*) (1935) has consequently done little to enhance its reputation. Perceptions of this novel not only as a 'classic example of Zhdanovite socialist realism',[2] but also as a 'particularly "pure" version of the structure of confrontation in the *roman à thèse*',[3] are doubtless reassuring to critics seeking to restrict the novel within established ideological and technical boundaries, but are ultimately an impoverishment of the problematical textual specificity of the novel itself.

This lack-lustre critical performance is compounded by the significant omission of *Le Cheval de Troie* from Sartre's otherwise gener-

---

1. The editors wish to thank Macmillan Press for permission to reproduce this extract from M. Scriven, *Paul Nizan: Communist Novelist*, Macmillan, London, 1988.
2. A. Cohen-Solal, and H. Nizan, *Paul Nizan : communiste impossible*, Grasset, Paris, 1980, p. 187. All quotations from French sources in this essay are my translations.
3. S. Suleiman, *Authoritarian Fictions : The Ideological Novel as a Literary Genre*, Columbia University Press, New York, 1983, p. 103.

ally positive assessments of Nizan's work. Sartre is in fact curiously tight-lipped regarding this particular novel. His eloquence when speaking of other aspects of Nizan's literary production stands in marked contrast to a decided unwillingness even to mention *Le Cheval de Troie*, an unwillingness that can only be interpreted as tacit criticism. Such reticence could be explained in political or technical terms, given Sartre's opposition to socialist realist literature.[4] More likely, however, is a purely personal explanation. Sartre was convinced that the character of Lange, an abstract, solitary individual obsessed by thoughts of death and ultimately aligning himself with Fascism, was based on himself.[5] Thus the discretion with which Sartre treats *Le Cheval de Troie* is probably motivated more by personal than by ideological or literary reasons.

Ultimately, however, hostile, condescending and even discreetly critical value-judgements merely function as an ideological screen, an obstacle impeding understanding. In order to assess the legitimacy of categorising *Le Cheval de Troie* as an unproblematical exemplification of Zhdanovite socialist realism, it is necessary to probe the specific ideological and formal structure of this novel by focusing on the relationship between its historical moment of production and the textual dynamics of the narrative itself.

Despite Nizan's consistent defence of the theory and practice of Soviet socialist realism, despite his genuine belief in the lessons to be learnt from the Soviet socialist realist experiment by writers in France, a belief highlighted in the remarks that he made in 1935 in support of Aragon's prosletysing text *Pour un réalisme socialiste* ('Towards a Socialist Realism'),[6] Nizan's own literary production reaches beyond the boundaries of Zhdanovite socialist realist fiction. Nizan's writing practice, although undeniably heavily influenced by Soviet socialist realist models, has an inner logic and originality of its own, an unusual blend of political activism and metaphysical angst, which calls for imaginative critical evaluation rather than restrictive classification.

Lodged at the heart of Nizan's fictional enterprise are two competing discourses struggling in narrative combat. In his novels Nizan speaks with a forked tongue. He uses two different languages, two different voices within each narrative site, one political and historical, the other literary and metaphysical:

4. J. -P. Sartre, *Situations II, Qu'est-ce que la littérature?*, Gallimard, Paris, 1948, pp. 277–89.
5. S. de Beauvoir, *La Force de l'âge*, Gallimard, Paris, 1960, p. 272. Nizan is alleged to have told Sartre that the model for Lange was Brice-Parain.
6. P. Nizan, '*Pour un réalisme socialiste* par Aragon', *L'Humanité*, 12 Aug. 1935.

Language 1:   Communist discourse — Historical authority
LENIN

Language 2:   Existential discourse — Metaphysical *angst*
DOSTOEVSKY

At one level, Nizan's novels proclaim certainty, truth, authority. This is the voice of Communism relaying to the reader unfaltering ideological orthodoxy, pushing the reader constantly towards greater political, social and historical awareness. It is the voice of Nizan speaking the language of Lenin.

At another level, Nizan's novels betray uncertainty, disorientation, doubt. This is the voice of existentialism transmitting to the reader a sense of metaphysical alienation and despair arising from the contemplation of death. It is the voice of Nizan speaking the language of Dostoevsky.

From a strictly Communist perspective, the secondary existential discourse could be dismissed as 'petty-bourgeois' and 'alienated' since it overflows the boundaries of orthodox Communist ideology and points to an alternative vision. However, to classify this secondary discourse in a pejorative sense is to remain blind to the dynamic configuration of Nizan's narrative technique.

The object of the following analysis is not to carry out a Stalinist witch hunt of the text in order to pillory a deviant, existential, petty-bourgeois discourse ensconced illegitimately at the centre of Nizan's literary production. Rather it is to demonstrate that the success of Nizan's writing technique is ultimately dependent on the interaction of two different but in the final analysis mutually dependent discourses.

These are at times indistinguishably fused, at times distinctly separate. Separate or fused, they contradict and complement each other simultaneously. Their precise disposition, organisation and arrangement constitutes the basic fabric of Nizan's fictional technique. Irrespective of the content of each of Nizan's novels, whether it is a tale of apprenticeship (*Antoine Bloyé*, 1933, and *La Conspiration* ('The Conspiracy'), 1938), or of confrontation (*Le Cheval de Troie*), the formal articulation of the content is achieved by means of these two competing narrative modes. The bedrock of Nizan's work as a novelist can therefore be defined as the evolution of two interactive discourses.

Le Cheval de Troie was published in 1935. It was written partly in the Soviet Union in 1934 in the aftermath of the Soviet Writers'

Congress,[7] and partly in France in 1935 amidst growing Popular Front optimism engendered initially by the events of February 1934, when Communists, socialists and trade unionists, conscious of the need to create a strong anti-Fascist coalition of the Left, had clashed with the police in a series of violent street confrontations. Its moment of production therefore coincides with a highly significant transition phase politically, ideologically and culturally. *Le Cheval de Troie* is in this sense a unique text since it reflects in mediated form Nizan's attempts not merely to formulate a technical response to the exigencies of socialist realist doctrine as articulated in the 1934 Congress, but also to formulate a political and ideological response to the transformed historical climate that was to culminate in the governments of the Popular Front.

It is important to stress the *transitional* nature of this moment of production. Since the ideological objective of the novel is to pinpoint the year 1934 as an historical watershed, a moment when political consciousness was transformed, there are of necessity two perspectives encoded in the narrative: a past perspective of Communist Party isolationism and working-class docility and defeatism prior to the events of 1934, and a future perspective of Popular Front cooperation and working-class social awareness and militancy subsequent to the events of 1934. Although the novel is divided into two distinct parts corresponding in terms of the narration of events with a past perspective of despair and a future perspective of hope, the text overall testifies to a sustained tension between a sectarian and a Popular Front ideological stance, a tension reflecting this transitional moment between two phases in the political development of the French Communist Party.

Despite a residual sectarianism manifesting itself in this narrative ideological tension, *Le Cheval de Troie* unquestionably constitutes a radical departure from Nizan's previous writing practice, and graphically illustrates his conviction that 'nobody in 1935 is capable of writing the sequel to the books of 1933'.[8] There are major differences politically, historically and technically between his first novel, *Antoine Bloyé*, published in 1933, and *Le Cheval de Troie*, published in 1935.

7. Nizan spent twelve months in the Soviet Union. He arrived in January 1934 and departed in January 1935. Apart from a trip to Central Asia, he was for the most part resident in Moscow working at the Marx–Engels Institute. During the Soviet Writers' Congress held in August of that year, Nizan was given responsibility for welcoming foreign 'fellow-travelling' writers and artists. In particular, he spent much time in the company of André Malraux, a kindred spirit endowed with a similarly heightened sense of metaphysical anguish.
8. P. Nizan, '*Les Violents* par Ramon Fernandez', *Monde*, 1 Aug. 1935.

The political development could not be more visibly apparent. The lessons of the negative exemplary narrative, *Antoine Bloyé*, recording the story of a father alienated in the deathly existence of the petty bourgeoisie, have been learnt and put into practice by his son Pierre Bloyé, a militant Communist Party member who is elevated to the status of narrator in *Le Cheval de Troie*. The centre of gravity has consequently shifted decisively from the analysis of petty-bourgeois alienation to the description of Communist Party militancy. A negative tale of apprenticeship within an oppressive class has been transformed into a positive tale of confrontation with the same oppressive class.

It is the change in historical perspective, however, which is the most profound development and which has the most far-reaching consequences for the tone, structure and content of the novel itself. Unlike *Antoine Bloyé*, a 'balance-sheet' novel aimed at drawing up an account of a closed historical period, *Le Cheval de Troie* is manifestly 'problem-centred', that is to say, set in the confusing flux of contemporary events at a moment when the full implications of the events themselves are far from clear. The fact that Nizan was attempting to disclose the significance of the events of February 1934 *in their immediate aftermath* cannot be overemphasised. He was, in other words, writing history as it was being made. The risks for the political novelist are self-evident.

The epic tone of the narrative, clearly signalled in the title of the novel itself, a title eventually preferred to the more immediately evocative but less morally uplifting 'Le Jour de la colère' ('Day of Wrath') is consequently not the product of casual imitation of Soviet socialist realist models. It is a narrative tone that coincides precisely with the sense of moral and political regeneration that the events of February had appeared to have engendered, and which seemed to be sweeping the country before it in a Popular Front crusade.

The fundamental shift of historical perspective accomplished in *Le Cheval de Troie* has implications beyond mere narrative tone, however. The focusing of attention on the contemporary struggle in its unfolding produces a marked attenuation of the voice of omniscient historical narration legislating a definitive Marxist interpretation of events, the legislating voice itself becoming part of the process of history in the making. This is an important point since it highlights the significance of the material presence of the Communist Party in this particular novel. Unlike *Antoine Bloyé*, where the depoliticised consciousness of the central character, and the material absence of the Communist Party itself, created an ideological space in the novel which was ceaselessly filled by the voice of an omniscient Communist narrator, a disembodied discourse at a distance from the concrete social relations depicted in the text, the ideological presence of Communism in *Le Cheval de Troie* is guaranteed by the physical presence of Communist militants. The thoughts, emotions, words and deeds of the Party activists become the natural expression of Communist ideology organically linked to the theme and structure of the narrative. The ideological content of the novel is therefore predominantly communicated to the reader by the social actors themselves.

The transformed historical perspective in *Le Cheval de Troie* also produces a movement away from the examination of individual characters as exemplifications of the life style of a particular class, towards the description of class-conflict at a moment of political and social realignment. Specifically, whereas *Antoine Bloyé* was centred on the situation of one individual progressively ensnared in the serial relations of the petty bourgeoisie, *Le Cheval de Troie* seeks to capture the defining characteristics of a Communist group at a moment of intense political activity. In *Antoine Bloyé* the focus was the *analysis* of a given life, in *Le Cheval de Troie* the focus becomes the *description* of a conflictual political event.

This development is reflected in the epigraphs that Nizan selects for the two novels. For *Antoine Bloyé* an extract from Marx's *German Ideology*, locating the root cause of bourgeois alienation and proletarian oppression in the work process itself, gives pre-eminence to a Marxist discourse aimed at disclosing the underlying causes of class conflict. For *Le Cheval de Troie*, by contrast, an extract from a worker's letter addressed to the editorial committee of *Iskra*, Lenin's revolutionary newspaper, requesting assistance in the search to understand the processes of living and dying within the class struggle, gives pre-eminence to a Communist discourse aimed at describing the problems and actions of men and women directly implicated in class conflict.

The centre of the novel is consequently no longer the distant voice of history dispassionately recording the alienation and death lodged at the heart of an oppressive class. It becomes the ideologically charged description of the social, moral and emotional predicament of the members of two opposed classes at a moment of political confrontation. The challenge issued by one class to another constitutes an act of social and moral regeneration. The challenge itself forms the narrative centre of *Le Cheval de Troie*.

History

The events recorded in *Le Cheval de Troie* take place in June 1934 in the town of Villefranche.[9] The novel begins one Sunday afternoon amidst the relaxed and peaceful atmosphere of a country setting just outside the town, and ends the following Sunday afternoon amidst an atmosphere of violence and polarised class-conflict inside the town itself. The stark contrast between the opening scene depicting docile workers slumbering in the bosom of nature, and the concluding scenes depicting militant workers struggling in the heart of the city is pointedly symbolic. The journey in text, time and space, from initial to final chapter, from one Sunday to the next, from country to town, is a journey of deepening political and social awareness.

The division of the novel into two distinct parts, the first recording the gradual build-up of events during an entire week beginning in the peace and calm of an initial Sunday afternoon, the second recording the explosive street-fighting of the subsequent Sunday afternoon, is a structural reflection of this awakening working-class consciousness. In the first part the various social actors are presented to the reader within their own specific living and working environments. Each distinctly separate group of social actors is situated within an all-encompassing economic, political and cultural hierarchy which regulates the town. In the second part, the stultifyingly predictable social existence of the town is shattered. The town's principal actors are involved in a dramatic and dynamic performance of class-conflict set in the public square, suitably and ironically named 'La place du théâtre'. Years of pent-up resentment and anger explode violently in the June sunlight. In a festival of confrontation, the injustice and oppression of the town's political and social hierarchies are publicly denounced.

The extent to which this fictionalised movement from social and political stasis described in Part 1 to dynamic fusion and growing working-class consciousness described in Part 2 reflects an ideological movement from sectarianism to Popular Frontism can be gauged by an assessment of the evolution of the Communist discourse within the narrative itself.

9. Villefranche is almost certainly a fictionalised version of the towns of Bourg and Vienne which Nizan knew well following his year of grass-roots political activity in Bourg in 1931–2. Nizan's total understanding of the political, social and cultural dynamics of this town is articulated in an analytical piece 'Présentation d'une ville', which was published in *La Littérature Internationale*, no. 4, 1934, pp. 3–36 and which doubtless served as the basis of the descriptions of the town and its inhabitants in *Le Cheval de Troie*.

A sectarian discourse is clearly visible in the opening pages of the novel. The initial scene of relaxation in the countryside serves several purposes. To begin with, not only does it function as a peaceful counterpoint to the subsequent violence, it also acts as an effective means of presenting the Communist group to the reader. In this introductory ceremony the Communist militants are described at a moment of respite when they are briefly withdrawn from the front-line of an endless political battle. The image of the group projected in this opening sequence is that of an isolated sect, surrounded on all sides by powerful political enemies, and locked in a desperate life and death struggle against the forces of darkness:

> They were men and women who lived all their lives in a world of anxiety and struggle. They were familiar with factories, workshops, the police. They lived in a world which was divided and torn apart, a world resembling the background of those pictures by painters of the Middle Ages, separated into celestial and infernal divisions, a conflict between heaven and hell. They were at war with their town, with their own lives, in a struggle which had not yet been lit up by heroic explosions and where there had been only isolated deaths; but it was a battle in which they had little protection, in which the blows aimed against them usually found their mark. For them, hunger, homelessness, prison, the destruction of love, incurable diseases, were not monstrous fables but merely misfortunes which they had escaped for the time being. The future appeared to them as an awesome and pitiless snare.[10]

What is striking in this passage is not only the extent to which this fundamentally Manichaean image of the Communist group as besieged and isolated coincides with the reality of a sectarian French Communist Party during the late 1920s, but also the extent to which it plays down the possibility of epic events at this juncture in the narrative. On this initial Sunday afternoon in June 1934 there is as yet no premonition of the imminent political explosion that is about to detonate Villefranche. The Communist group is described simply as committed to pursuing its bitter struggle, with little hope of major success in the foreseeable future.

It is significant, in fact, that the concluding pages of the opening chapter focus on the setbacks and failures of the past as recollected by individual members of the Communist group. The conversations between the militants, centred as they are on the development of the labour movement since the outbreak of the First World War, enable historical assessments to emerge organically from the fictional situation itself. Although buoyed by distant memories of anarchist rebel-

10. P. Nizan, *Le Cheval de Troie*, Gallimard, Paris, 1935, p. 17.

lion in 1910 and 1911, there is no attempt at self-delusion. It is recognised that after 1920 the working class entered a historical phase of division and disenchantment. The only beacon of hope on the horizon was the possibility that the political consciousness of the labour movement might be reactivated by the growing world economic crisis.

The tragic Communist discourse in which the voice of sectarianism takes stock of the oppressed and isolated existence of the working class in general and the Communist group in particular is, none the less, progressively abandoned in the course of the narrative and replaced by a more optimistic, occasionally euphoric discourse climaxing in the concluding explosive confrontation.

A significant moment of transition occurs at the point at which the threat of Fascism is introduced. Mid-way through the first half of the novel the enemy is clearly signalled. Posters announcing a Fascist meeting to be held the following Sunday inject into the text the catalyst of working-class solidarity. The Communist narrator reacts immediately, shifting the emphasis from division and defeatism to the imminent struggle against Fascism.

> Things were beginning to stir in France.
> On Sundays, in town squares which had known centuries of tranquillity, squares which had occasionally not even observed the passing shadows of revolutions, of wars and of invasions, where the inhabitants had for generations not experienced a quickening of their heart-beat, hostile groups were confronting one another. The French had for a long time lived in their own isolated little world; Europe was seething around this rock of France, and all the while the French continued to look upon Germany, Italy, Spain, all their neighbours, with the detached gaze of spectators. . . Then suddenly, on these same squares, stones were being hurled, horses were galloping, trucheons were crashing down on heads, and guns were being fired. In every town secret meetings were being held, hatred and anger were growing more intense. People were getting to know hunger and privation at first hand. Despair was assuming an explosive potency. It was a period which called to mind the beginning of the religious wars, when the barns of Protestants went up in flames and men took to the highways to fight.[11]

The epic tone of this passage in which the forthcoming conflict is likened to a religious war, stands in marked contrast to the tone of the opening pages of the novel where emphasis was placed on a more mundane struggle for existence. None the less, despite a clear recognition that the advent of Fascism has fundamentally trans-

11. Ibid., pp. 68–9.

formed the political and social situation, attention at this stage is focused primarily on the brutal emergence of conflict and violence in the political sphere, rather than on Popular Front opposition to Fascism itself. It is significant, in fact, that there is no overall coordination of political strategy in the first half of the novel. Each political party acts independently, holding separate meetings to devise individual responses to the Fascist threat. Although a Popular Front strategy is doubtless implied, it comes into existence only at the moment of the counter-demonstration itself when Communists, socialists, radicals, trade unionists and the unemployed unite spontaneously to form a coherent and unified group facing a common enemy.

The sense of burgeoning political consciousness conveyed in the novel occasionally borders on the apocalyptic. Segments of the narrative which project a violent and courageous political stance based on heroism in the face of death are doubtless the product of a residual anarchism in Nizan's personality, so clearly visible in the early and violently iconoclastic text, *Aden Arabie* (1931).

The presence of such violent epic discourse within *Le Cheval de Troie* can also be explained organically, however, as an expression of the anarchist tendencies of the working-class characters portrayed in the novel. So deep-rooted, in fact, are the anarchist traditions in this region that the workers of Villefranche are described as bearing a resemblance on occasions to 'sectarian, orthodox Protestants', capable of experiencing fervently religious emotions at the thought of a general strike.[12] In this sense, the violently ethical discourse which functions primarily as a direct appeal to the reader to support the anti-Fascist struggle, does none the less arise naturally from the fictional situation itself.

Although the appeal to support the anti-Fascist struggle is clearly located at the political centre of the novel, the emergence of the Fascist threat is paradoxically presented not only as a moment of impending catastrophe, but also as a moment of political opportunity. Above all, the Communist discourse presents Fascism as the catalysing agent which unmasks the democratic pretensions of bourgeois society, forces the working class into political self-consciousness, and in the process rejuvenates a previously isolated Communist Party.

The presentation of Fascism within the narrative is, in other words, ideologically motivated. *Le Cheval de Troie* is not a democratic, anti-Fascist text. It is a strategic narrative which aims at analysing

12. Ibid., pp. 89–90.

the Fascist phenomenon from a Marxist perspective in order to re-situate the French Communist Party at the centre of the political arena.

The strategic nature of the presentation of Fascism is clearly visible in the bourgeois dinner party sequence located towards the end of the first half of the novel. Leaving aside the highly idiosyncratic contribution of Lange, the dialogue between these representatives of bourgeois law and order is a narrative pretext designed primarily to disclose the underlying economic contradictions of Fascism threatening the continued stability of bourgeois democracy. The industrialist, Provost-Livet, informs both the dinner party guests and the reader in an implacably cynical voice that despite his personal ideological attraction to Fascism, economically it is a dangerous and misguided ideology. Once the demagogic economic promises of Fascism have proved to be illusory, he asserts, the consequent social disorder unleashed will become uncontrollable and the only remaining solution will be war.

This dialogue illuminates the fact that Fascism simultaneously threatens the social stability of the bourgeoisie and activates the political rebellion of the working class. It is consequently not Fascism as such which is the subject of this novel. It is rather the twin effects that Fascism itself produces: on the one hand, the disruption of the bourgeois State, on the other, the politicisation of the proletariat. The second half of the novel, although centred on an anti-Fascist counter-demonstration, is in reality a festival of liberation in which a Fascist meeting is exploited as a means of exploding the law and order of the bourgeoisie and of celebrating the political activism of the working class.

It is quite clear at the end of the novel that the significance of the events themselves lies not primarily with the struggle against Fascism but rather with the rebirth of working-class political consciousness: 'The political significance of the day was perhaps simply that thousands of men had at long last given vent to their anger. Resistance and militancy, fundamental values of the working class, had once again entered into their lives with a certainty and clarity which exalted them'.[13] Fascism is opposed in the novel, but the overriding teleology of the novel is to designate the working class as politically active after a long period of docility. Significantly, Fascism disappears from the conclusion of the novel which is dominated by images of the political reawakening of the labour movement.

The transitional phase in which the novel appeared is conse-

13. Ibid., p. 189.

quently reflected in the progressive development of the Communist discourse in the narrative. Throughout, there is a sustained tension between a sectarian and a Popular Front strategy. Initially sectarian and defensive, the narrative adopts a progressively more combative stance with the emergence of Fascism, climaxing in the Popular Front fusion of the anti-Fascist counter-demonstration. However, Fascism recedes into the distance in the conclusion where attention is focused on the rebirth of working-class political consciousness and militancy. At the same time the entire narrative is coloured by a persistent anarchist tone, echoing Nizan's early iconoclasm, the political culture of the workers portrayed, and the anti-authoritarian, undisciplined quality of the counter-demonstration itself.

From a purely political and historical perspective, therefore, *Le Cheval de Troie* resists classification as an archetypal exemplificaton of Zhdanovite socialist realism. A secondary, existential discourse adds a further dimension to such resistance.

Existence

Death is an inescapable presence in *Le Cheval de Troie*. It is not an external, supernatural phenomenon that descends upon the world unexpectedly. Rather it is a deadly poison which enters the pores of life at birth, relentlessly corrodes the body fabric of the living, and is secreted only at the moment of dying. This ceaseless flow of death in life's bloodstream forms the metaphysical centre of *Le Cheval de Troie*.

Death refuses to recognise class boundaries. The revolution does not banish the fears that death instils in the minds of men and women. Nizan's bitter realisation that even the Soviet revolutionary State ultimately did not protect its citizens from an anguished confrontation with death is never far from the surface of the narrative of *Le Cheval de Troie*. Unlike *Antoine Bloyé*, where death was for the most part presented as the defining characteristic of the existence of an oppressive class, in this second novel men and women on both sides of the class-divide are equally tormented by death, although in different ways.

The clear-cut distinction between a deathly bourgeois existence and a dynamic Communist existence is none the less retained in *Le Cheval in Troie*. An explicit comparison is made between the burgeoning, life-giving existence of the Communist militants on the one hand, and the dead, oppressive life style of the bourgeois teaching profession on the other. Bloyé's professional colleagues are described as frightened, ghostly figures, desperately seeking ways of masking the emptiness of their lives and the inevitability of their death. Their existence is dismissed as a cowardly pretence, a life sentence in which genuine human relations have been abandoned in a sadistic teaching enviroment dominated by mindless, self-deluding petty-bourgeois careerism.

The links between death and the bourgeoisie, the central theme of *Antoine Bloyé*, are analysed in a more deeply metaphysical vein, however, in *Le Cheval de Troie*. The character of Lange, exploited in the narrative to symbolise the deathly void at the heart of bourgeois existence, graphically exemplifies the intricate interweaving between the metaphysical and the political in the novel.

Lange is presented as an extreme example of petty-bourgeois alienation, a man who inhabits a ghostly, shadowy world, and whose thoughts centre morbidly on death and the production of a book describing the desolation of a solitary individual exploring the death-filled landscape of an urban environment. In the description of Lange's nocturnal prowling in the town there is a haunting intensity which reaches beyond the limitations of stereotypical socialist realist literature. Lange, Roquentin and Sartre become merged in the deathly twilight existence of Villefranche.

The highly metaphysical presence of Lange is, however, not gratuitous to the political message. As well as offering a hallucinatory example of the aberrations of petty-bourgeois alienation in an extreme form, the character of Lange also functions as an integral part of the comprehensive ideological thesis that emerges from the novel. In the dinner party sequence Lange's metaphysical anguish appears naive compared to the cynical economic views of the industrialist Provost-Livet. Yet the strategic objective of the dialogue itself is to highlight the imminent bankruptcy of the bourgeoisie not only politically and economically (Provost-Livet), but also spiritually and ethically (Lange). The alienated voice of Lange communicates to the reader the desolate conclusion that the only surviving values in bourgeois society are the values of death. Lange projects the deathly spiritual void at the heart of bourgeois society and in the process completes a picture of total bourgeois degeneration.

The figure of Lange consequently poses the more general problem of the regeneration of spiritual and ethical values in a society defined by death. Lange's final response, aligning himself with Fascism at the moment of the street confrontation, is aimed not merely at highlighting the need to progress beyond sterile intellectual masturbation and engage in political action. It is also pointedly symbolic of the need articulated generally in the novel to search for a response to a wider ethical problem. Although the narrative of *Le Cheval de Troie* makes it abundantly clear that Lange's response is misguided, and that the solution is to be found on the other side of the class-divide in the ranks of the Communist militants, none the less, the importance of this character resides primarily in his expression of the death, decay and disintegration of the entire value-system of bourgeois society. Metaphysics in this instance lends effective support to politics.

It is symbolic that whereas the descriptions of the bourgeoisie evoke images of death that are linked primarily to the sterile and anaesthetised process of *living*, the descriptions of the working class evoke images of death that are centred primarily on the heroic and painful moment of *dying*. Beyond the general exploitation of the death theme to symbolise the oppressive living and working environment of the Communist militants, the process and the act of dying are together exploited to project a specific ideological message.

Two deaths in the narrative, those of Catherine and Paul, are effectively orchestrated to serve the ideological objectives of the novel itself. Catherine dies totally alone, bleeding to death after an abortion. Paul dies in the company of Communist comrades, hit by a stray bullet during the street-fighting. The reader is given little insight into the personality of either of these characters. The strained marital relationship between Albert and Catherine is briefly sketched but the overriding objective is to explain the tensions and emotional problems of private life as the inevitable product of a society which makes back-street abortions necessary. Paul remains a totally anonymous figure, an unknown militant who comes to symbolise the essential qualities of the political struggle itself.

Catherine dies almost without a struggle, at the precise moment when the militant crisis of working-class protest are ringing through the streets of Villefranche. She dies of a haemorrhage, her life-blood streaming from her as she secretes her own death. This harrowing episode which interrupts the narrative flow of the street-fighting, is strategically placed. The reader, confronted by the sickening description of a young woman dying in a pool of blood, unaided, helpless, too weak to resist, is forced to reflect not only on the injustice of one particular death, but also on the inescapable presence of death in life. For a brief moment, the narrative subsumes the dominant political thesis beneath broader metaphysical concerns, before pointing a finger of accusation at the society of unequal chances which makes such a death possible.

This process of fusion between the political and the metaphysical is prominent in the narrative exploitation of the death of Paul. Compared to the meticulous description of the moment of Catherine's death, Paul's is but briefly described. Yet this death in the heat of the street battle prompts the articulation of the underlying political/metaphysical message of the novel.

Dying alone and at a distance from the struggle, Catherine's is a pointless, insignificant death which merely highlights the waste of an entire existence. Hers can only be a negative exemplary tale. Dying for the Party in the midst of the struggle, by contrast, Paul's is a heroic, exemplary death. It comes to symbolise a victory not only over political enemies but also over death itself : 'Either lead a fearful life of anguish, or risk death in order to conquer life itself', notes Bloyé towards the end of the novel,[14] highlighting a fundamental choice to be made between defensive, angst-ridden acquiescence and militant, risk-taking combat. Such a conclusion not only brings to the fore the twin struggles against death and the bourgeoisie, it also signals a synthesis between two discourses, existential and Communist, within the narrative itself.

The existential discourse encoded in the narrative, although enmeshed inextricably in Communist ideology, does, none the less, occasionally strike a different chord. Segments of the narrative drift tantalisingly close to metaphysical speculation devoid of ideological ballast. Certain passages depicting Lange's metaphysical angst and certain aspects of the description of Catherine's death cannot be entirely subsumed within the Communist framework. Likewise, the concluding pages of the novel contain elements which attach an importance to the metaphysical oppression of death which transcends orthodox Communist ideology:

> For years at a time we do not think about death. We simply have sudden brief intimations of its existence in the midst of our lives, although there are people who think of it more often than most : they are born like that. Death passes nearby, a cloud poisoning the earth upon which its shadow falls, and our spirit is caught by fear. Then we recover, and begin again to live as though we were immortal; we continue to play the game of cheating death, we take medicines and follow diets or indulge in passionate pursuits. But still it appears again. However much we try, we cannot forget the army of men who die each second, the vast cavalcade of funerals proceeding towards all the cemeteries of the earth. We need only see the mangled body of a cat lying on the shiny surface of a road to realise that death may come and that our hearts may stop.[15]

14. Ibid., p. 211.
15. Ibid., p. 205.

The principal foe here is death, not political oppression. The paradox of *Le Cheval de Troie* is revealed in these lines. This text, which is the most visibly politicised of Nizan's novels, is *at the same time* the most deeply metaphysical. Politics and metaphysics collide in a kaleidoscopic confrontation.

Ideology and Form

The formal structure of *Le Cheval de Troie* reflects the comprehensive political, metaphysical and cultural position that Nizan had reached during 1934 and 1935. His political perception had been transformed by the events of February 1934. His cultural views had been influenced by the Soviet Writers' Congress of the same year. His sense of metaphysical alienation had been heightened not only by his realisation that death remained a formidable presence even in the revolutionary Soviet state, but doubtless also by his close contact with André Malraux in the Soviet Union. *Le Cheval de Troie* is consequently a formal synthesis of thoroughgoing ideological development which represents a marked progression from *Antoine Boylé*.

The ideological view that emerges from *Le Cheval de Troie* is inherently more problematical than the view that is presented in *Antoine Bloyé*. Whereas in *Antoine Bloyé* the implication of the narrative was that avoidance of a deathly existence could be achieved by breaking with an oppressive bourgeois class and entering the dynamic, living existence of the working class, in *Le Cheval de Troie* it is apparent that death is a metaphysical presence which even encroaches upon the lives of the Communist Party militants. The consequence of this all-pervading presence of death in *Le Cheval de Troie* is a fusion between the collective effort of all the Communist militants to struggle against the oppression of a deathly class enemy, and the individual effort of each Communist militant to struggle against the oppressive presence of death itself. This revised ideological view inevitably has implications for the formal structure of the novel itself.

Most strikingly, the material presence of the Party in *Le Cheval de Troie* facilitates the organic emergence of Communist ideology from within the text. The uneasy presence of abstract segments of narrative in *Antoine Bloyé*, where an omniscient Communist narrator legislates the significance of historical developments, is replaced by the voices of the Communist militants themselves expressing their own political convictions in the context of their living environment. Occasionally, such dialogue sequences are not entirely convincing. Specific utterances do not ring true, sounding more like the unmediated slogans of the Party than the ideas of the individuals voicing them. Yet for the most part, this technical device is skilfully handled and enables the effective integration of Communist ideology into the narrative.

The structural division of the narrative is also ideologically significant. The first half of the text, a series of separate tableaux depicting the hierarchical divisions and class-distinctions in the town, constitutes an analytical phase in which the social actors are introduced, and the reader is allowed time to reflect upon the established economic and political order. The second half of the text, by contrast, depicting the violent confrontation and fusion of the various social groups in conflict, conjures up vivid images of political struggle, and propels the reader relentlessly towards the concluding synthesis of the narrative.

The individual characters soon fade from the reader's mind. What remains is the memory of a powerfully evoked scene of political confrontation which reinforces through its emotional intensity the comparisons previously made between two classes, two life styles and two social and political orders. This enduring memory of class-division, class-conflict and class-consciousness is the ultimate proof of the ideological potency of this novel.

This potency is also greatly enhanced by a more effective use of images evoking natural settings and the passage of time. Unlike *Antoine Bloyé*, where the naturalising effect of such images tends to subvert the historical dimension of the novel, images of time and nature in *Le Cheval de Troie* work to the ideological advantage of the text.

The time-scale is limited to one week. The reader's thoughts are consequently focused on immediate practical action, not on the irretrievable passage of time as in *Antoine Bloyé*. The reader's attention, in other words, is not diverted from the passage of *historical* time by a lament on the passage of time *in general*. Images of nature are also exploited in a more effective, contrastive fashion. Whereas in *Antoine Bloyé* images of natural settings tend to mask the realities of urban existence, in *Le Cheval de Troie* nature is presented as the image of a counter-culture to the town, a refuge from oppression, a place to breathe freely. This contrastive technique ultimately reinforces the ideological message of the novel aimed at disclosing the oppressiveness of working-class living conditions in the town.

Ultimately, however, the most important aspect of the narrative technique is the merging of the Communist and existential discourses within the very substance of the text, a merging which reflects the intimate relationship that Nizan perceived at this stage in his ideological development between the political struggle against the oppression of a hated class and the metaphysical struggle against the oppression of death itself. It is precisely the extra dimension given to this text by the existential discourse woven into the fabric of the narrative that enables the effective insinuation of ideology into the reader's mind.

This strategic merging of Communist and existential discourses not only releases *Le Cheval de Troie* from the authoritarian grip of Zhdanovite socialist realism, it is also the crucial factor explaining Nizan's success in achieving a fine balance between artistic means and ideological ends. More than fifty years after its publication, *Le Cheval de Troie* remains a powerfully evocative and mobilising image of a group in fusion, a vivid illustration of the leap from acquiescence and seriality to rebellion and authenticity.

PART IV

Revitalisation

—9—

Art, Politics and *Glasnost'*: The Eighth Soviet Writers' Congress and Soviet Literature 1986–7

DAVID C. GILLESPIE

Given that relatively little time has elapsed since the Writers' Congress of June 1986, this essay is intended as an interim report which tries to gather together the various strands that can be detected in the run-up to the Congress, during the Congress itself, and in its aftermath.[1] It will consequently be divided into three parts: firstly, some background information will be required on the role played by the Writers' Congress in Soviet literary life, and here contemporary economic and political developments will be touched on in order to highlight the changes taking place in society as a whole. Secondly, the Eighth Writers' Congress with particular reference to statements made on the theory and practice of socialist realism and its relevance to the contemporary literary process will form the central part of this paper.[2] Thirdly, and finally, I will look at some of the developments that have taken place since the Congress, and point to some general tendencies in Soviet literary life in 1986–7.

The Congress itself: what is it? The Congress of the Union of Writers of the USSR is the sounding-board of the Writers' Union which was set up in April 1932 by a decree of the Party's Central Committee. Nominally the Writers' Union is controlled by its Congress, but real power lies with the First Secretary of the Board of the Union of Writers and with its Secretariat. This has been demonstrated in recent years with the hounding of errant writers such as Vladimov,

1. I am indebted to Dr M. Dewhirst, Mr M. Basker and Mr R. Porter for the help and advice they provided in the preparation of this paper.
2. For further discussion of the Writers' Congress, see S. Cosgrove, 'Thoughts on the Eighth Writers' Congress', *Detente*, 7, Autumn 1986, pp. 16–18.

Voynovich and Aksyonov by powerful literary bureaucrats and Secretaries such as Feliks Kuznetsov and Boris Pankin, and their apparent power to withold publication of the works of these and other writers.

The First Writers' Congress took place in 1934, and over the past fifty-odd years it has consistently been linked with national political developments or Party pronouncements. The First Writers' Congress met to approve the doctrine of socialist realism as the 'basic method' of Soviet literature and criticism and in effect drew up what Geoffrey Hosking calls the 'charter which appears to subordinate literature to explicitly extra-literary goals'.[3] Although the intention was to hold a Writers' Congress every four years, in fact there was only one Congress in Stalin's lifetime. The Second Congress took place only twenty years later, in 1954, following the death of Stalin in 1953 and the ensuing but short-lived 'thaw' of 1953–4 in which writers played a major part. The Third Writers' Congress was in 1959, and was used by Khrushchev to reconcile writers with the Party's policies following the literary and intellectual ferment of the second 'thaw' of 1956, and to urge them to solve their problems by their own efforts rather than seek direct intervention by the Party. (In effect, the Pasternak affair in 1957–8 had demonstrated already that literary bureaucrats had the power and the will to put their own house in order, following the publication of *Doktor Zhivago* in Italy. The hounding of Pasternak by the then First Secretary of the Writers' Union, Aleksey Surkov, culminated in Pasternak's expulsion and renunciation under pressure of the Nobel Prize for Literature.) The Fourth Writers' Congress was held in 1967, and, being in honour of the fiftieth anniversary of the October Revolution, was seen as an occasion for celebration and self-congratulation on an unprecedented scale. However, it was also closely linked with the rise of literary and political dissidence in the 1960s, as it followed the arrest and trial of Sinyavsky and Daniel' in 1966 for publishing their works under pseudonyms in the West. It was also at this time that Solzhenitsyn found himself publicly pitted against the Writers' Union and the Party, and he used the occasion to send an open letter to the Congress delegates demanding an end to censorship. This was the first Congress of Soviet Writers to be held under Brezhnev, and was meant to consolidate the artistic freeze-up taking hold of the country from 1966 onwards.

Since 1971, when the Fifth Writers' Congress was held, the

3. Hosking, *Beyond Socialist Realism: Soviet Fiction since 'Ivan Denisovich'*, Granada, London, 1980, p. 1.

Congress has taken place every five years, and follows the All-Union Party Congress of the same year, also now held every five years. It thus becomes obvious that literature and literary policy in the Soviet Union are closely tied to the country's social, economic and political developments, and are required to respond accordingly to any shifts that might occur, such as those now taking place under Gorbachev.

The Party's hold on the Congress is strong: in 1976 only eighty or so of the 542 delegates were not Party members. Furthermore, the Writers' Union is subordinated to both Government and Party bodies: in the former instance, to the USSR Ministry of Culture and, more importantly, to the CPSU Central Committee Departments of Culture and Propaganda, the latter headed since summer 1985 by Alexander Yakovlev, Gorbachev's adviser on ideology and foreign policy. Yakovlev was recently brought into the Politburo and in late 1987 was reported as being third in the Politburo hierarchy. He first attracted attention in 1972, when he was working in the Central Committee Department for Propaganda, and attacked the idealisation of some aspects of the Russian pre-Revolutionary past and right-wing Russian nationalist sentiment in the works of some 'village prose' writers and critics publishing in the nationalist journal *Molodaya gvardiya*. In the same article, called 'Protiv antiistorizma' ('Against Anti-Historicism'), he also called on writers to stress the importance in their works of Marxist-Leninist ideology.[4]

There exists an All-Union Writers' Union, but in addition each of the fifteen Union Republics has its own Union of Writers. There are also important branches in Moscow and Leningrad, the former well-known for developing autonomous tendencies in the troubled year 1956. It was, indeed, as a response to the publication in 1956 by the Moscow Writers' Organisation of the second volume of works by Moscow authors entitled *Literaturnaya Moskva*, ('Literary Moscow') many of which were critical of not only Stalin's 'personality cult' but also the Party, that the Russian Writers' Union was set up, to supervise and control the activities of the large urban Writers Union branches in the Russian Soviet Federal Socialist Republic (RSFSR).

The Writers' Union and its branches are nominally controlled by the All-Union Congress. Like the Party itself, the Union is run according to the principles of democratic centralism, which means that the rank-and-file membership take part in discussions of policy,

4. A. Yakovlev, 'Protiv antiistorizma', *Literaturnaya gazeta*, 15 November 1972, p. 5. Yakovlev's article is discussed in N. N. Shneidman, 'Soviet Prose in the 1970s: Evolution or Stagnation?', *Canadian Slavonic Papers*, 20, 1, March 1978, pp. 63–77 (p. 71).

but must obey the resolutions and decrees handed down to them from the higher levels of the Union apparatus, the highest of which is the All-Union Congress.

Furthermore, the Party and literary officials clearly expect the Writers' Congress to be merely a showcase of the political unity of writers and Party, where delegates are told what is expected of them in the future, where ideologically exemplary works written since the last Congress are held up for praise as examples to be emulated by others, and where the occasional flawed work can be criticised or a writer censured. The doctrine of socialist realism is upheld by literary bureaucrats, and writers are exhorted to express the principles of *ideynost'* (ideological orthodoxy), *partiynost'* (adherence to the Party line) and *narodnost'* (having broad popular appeal), to pursue *tipichnost'* ('typicality') in a changing environment, and to present to the reading public the 'positive hero' who embodies the best and most progressive features of the time. Furthermore, works by Soviet writers must be imbued with the spirit of proletarian class-consciousness (*klassovost'*). However, the Congress in the past has been used by writers and delegates to air differences, criticise officials, and to seek a better *modus vivendi* with the ruling ideology (in particular in 1954 and 1967, the latter occasion when Solzhenitsyn sent a letter to several hundred Congress delegates urging the abolition of censorship and calling on the Writers' Union to be more active and effective in defending its members against 'slander and unjust fabrication').[5]

Because literature, as has been said, is so closely tied to politics and ideology in the Soviet Union, and to the changes in the political temperature, it is not out of place here to discuss, however briefly, the changes going on in the political and social life of the Soviet Union in the mid-to-late 1980s.

Undoubtedly a new literary 'thaw' is going on, what has been dubbed here in the West as 'Gorbachev's literary spring'. However, it seems prudent to suppose that Gorbachev does not necessarily see a greater measure of artistic freedom as a desirable aim in itself. He is no 'culture vulture', although his wife may be. It is more likely that he is enlisting writers to support his programme of *perestroyka*, economic and social reorganisation. As he himself said at a meeting on June 19 with writers who were deputies of the USSR Supreme Soviet:

5. Solzhenitsyn's open letter to the Fourth Soviet Writers' Congress, in Labedz (ed.) *Solzhenitsyn: A Documentary Record*, Penguin, Harmondsworth, 1970, p. 67.

It is natural that today, when the hard struggle of war and peace is going on, when efforts to renew all spheres of life in Soviet society are being developed, the writer's word and the artist's voice are of particular importance and have particular impact. Writers can play a significant part in effecting psychological and moral restructuring ['perestroyka'] and in the struggle with negative phenomena. With this in mind it is clear that the artistic investigation of the present demands a way of thinking that is both bold and untouched by triteness, as well as an understanding of the profound phenomena and processes of life. We now urgently need works which depict to a high artistic standard the conflicts and actual clashes of interest in society today, works which convey the intensity of the struggle to achieve our appointed tasks, works which would instill confidence in the ultimate victory of the ideas and plans of the XXVII Congress of the CPSU and which would affirm genuine human values.[6]

Gorbachev is also reported as having has a 'closed' meeting with writers in July 1986, after the Writers' Congress, and remarks attributed to him have been published subsequently in the West. Speaking frankly about the immense problems in society to be overcome, the General Secretary goes on to outline the tasks of writers:

The Central Committee needs support. You cannot imagine how much we need the support of such a group as writers. . . . This restructuring is progressing with great difficulty. We have no political opposition. How then can we establish control over ourselves? Only through criticism and self-criticism. Most important of all is openness. There can be no society without openness. In this respect too we're learning. We are restructuring everything, from the General Secretary to the grass-roots communists. There can be no democratic rule without openness. At the same time, however, democracy without a framework is anarchy. Therefore it won't be easy.[7]

In fact, mobilising literature for social and political ends is a tradition respected by successive Soviet leaders. Gorbachev's ends, outlined in his words just quoted (if, indeed, they belong to him), include the desire for more of the rank-and-file to be involved in decision-making (*demokratizatsiya*), a policy of bringing to public attention abuses and shortcomings on a much greater scale than in the past, and publishing works and ideas previously proscribed (*glasnost'*), and the 'acceleration' (*uskoreniye*) of economic development, including improving the nation's standard of living in a short

---

6. *Literaturnaya gazeta*, 25 June 1986, p. 1. All quotations from Russian sources in this essay are my own translations.
7. *Detente*, 8, Winter 1987, p. 11.

period of time. The long-term aim is to effect far-reaching economic and social 'restructuring' (*perestroyka*), which, if we believe reports coming from the Soviet Union, would significantly alter the economic and political system established under Stalin and create greater freedom and choice for the individual. *Glasnost'* is not equivalent to 'freedom' as such, as it is a policy imposed from above, not a movement from below. Its purpose is to change the way people have been accustomed to think and behave, to effect 'psychological and moral restructuring' in order to overcome Russia's traditional resistance to change. There is no doubt, moreover, that since last year's Party Congress the most dramatic and visible achievements of *perestroyka* have taken place in the fields of literature and literary policy.

Before looking at the All-Union Congress, we should spend some time on the Republican Writers' Congresses which followed the Party Congress in February and preceded the All-Union Writers' Congress in June, as the discussions involved give useful indications of the tensions and concerns among Soviet writers following the Party Congress and the adoption by the political leadership of the 'new road'.

Some of these Republican Writer's Congresses, as reported in *Literaturnaya gazeta*, organ of the USSR Writers' Union, contained sharp speeches and acrimonious attacks. Indeed, it seems that the call for *glasnost'* has given many writers an opportunity to settle old scores in public. For example, the former head of the Kirghiz Writers' Union was severely criticised by some delegates at the republic's Writers' Congress for 'persecuting' talented young writers, and for 'protectionism' and 'bribe-taking'. Delegates also noted that there was an 'unhealthy atmosphere' within the Kirghiz Writers' Union itself, which was partly responsible for the 'lowering of criteria' and a 'certain stagnation' in Kirghiz literature over recent years.[8] Likewise, at the Moldavian Writers' Congress in May that republic's Ministry of Culture was criticised for having among their staff 'many incidental and incompetent people far removed from art and the theatre', and there was criticism of the way literary prizes were awarded without broad discussion.[9]

Moreover, there were some general points that came out of these Congresses. Literary criticism was taken to task for being too 'complimentary' and 'superficial', and writers were urged to get to grips with real life and the process of 'renewal' going on in Soviet

8. *Literaturnaya gazeta*, 18 June 1986, p. 7.
9. *Literaturnaya gazeta*, 21 May 1986, p. 2.

society as a whole. Thus, the role of literature to reflect and interpret changing social forces was never questioned. However, many delegates were quick to request a greater measure of artistic licence, and the difficulties younger writers experienced in getting their works into print or their plays produced gave rise to recurrent complaints. It is difficult to escape the impression that a middle-aged and stagnating literature was being subjected to critical scrutiny and that writers both young and old were calling for an injection of young blood, not just in personnel, but in ideas and energy.

A succinct expression of the mood of many Soviet writers can be seen in the words of V. Kovalenko at the Belorussian Writers' Congress. He noted that some works of recent Belorussian literature revealed the struggle in men's souls between the 'ideal' and 'inertia'; i.e. the struggle between progress and stagnation, the 'new' and vital Gorbachev morality and the decline characteristic of the later Brezhnev years.[10] The tasks of literature under Gorbachev were perhaps most succinctly summarised in speeches at the Kirghiz Writer's Congress. In his opening address, Dzh. Mamytov, a secretary of the Kirghiz Writers' Union, stressed the educative function, an underlying tenet of stock socialist realism: 'A writer's school,' he said, 'is life itself. . . . and a true artist is one who has passed through this school and has managed to develop into a genuine teacher of his people'. In addition an official from the national Writers' Union, N. Fedorenko, called on writers to be more responsive to the demands of the age: 'Today, as never before, it is essential to heed more keenly the voice of the times'.[11]

To summarise: in the run-up to the All-Union Writers' Congress, delegates to the Republican congresses accepted the social and political criteria of literature without question; i.e. that modern literature, like classical socialist realism, should reflect society 'in its revolutionary development', that is, as it changes and evolves in line with the Party's political programme. Although Soviet society is no longer as militant and dynamic as in the 1930s, when classical socialist realism was required to uphold the causes of construction, collectivisation, and rapid industrialisation, it is still motivated by campaigns initiated from above, and by huge and prestigious projects like BAM (the Trans-Siberian Railway). More recently, the Chernobyl' disaster and subsequent clean-up operation were depicted by the Soviet media with emphasis on the qualities of heroism and self-abnegation on the part of those helping to make the crippled

10. *Literaturnaya gazeta*, 30 April 1986, p. 2.
11. *Literaturnaya gazeta*, 18 June 1986, p. 7.

reactor safe, qualities with which to inspire, in true socialist realist spirit, the population as a whole. Chernobyl', indeed, can be seen as primarily a political issue, demanding human effort, will and the overcoming of adversity. Literature must still be optimistic and end on a positive note, and its criteria are still determined by political imperatives.

The Eighth Soviet Writers' Congress

The Congress was by all accounts, even those published in the Soviet press, a lively affair, with those delegates in favour of Gorbachev's reform plans attacking, and in turn being attacked by, others less sanguine.[12] The most immediately tangible result of the Congress was the reduction of the powers of Glavlit, or to give it its full title, Glavnoye upravleniye po delam literatury i pechati (The Central Board for Literature and Press Affairs). Glavlit's jurisdiction in literary affairs is now restricted to preventing the appearance in print of State and military secrets, pornography, and overt racism. It is the State censorship body set up in 1922 supposedly to safeguard State secrets, but which until now operated as overseer and political watchdog over all areas of publishing in the USSR. It is subordinated to the Central Committee Department of Agitation and Propaganda, headed by Yakovlev, and to the Central Committee Secretary for Ideology, who is currently Yegor Ligachev.[13]

However, it is possible that the restriction of Glavlit's power will not fundamentally alter the nature of political control over publishing policy, and will, in essence, be merely an exercise in editorial rationalisation. Censorship still exists. Editors of the Soviet 'thick' journals have always been keenly aware of what is and what is not politically or ideologically acceptable, even those of 'liberal' outlook such as Tvardovsky. Recent Soviet editors, moreover, have included such Stalinist die-hards as Vsevolod Kochetov, editor of *Oktyabr'* from 1961 until his death in 1974, and Anatoly Sofronov, former editor of *Ogonyok*. Such editors could cause more harm to literary works than Glavlit, and it is significant that the last two years have seen respected writers of talent and integrity appointed as editors of the USSR's most prestigious journals, such as Grigory Baklanov as

12. For a more detailed account of the various speeches and polemics at the Congress, see Cosgrove, 'Thoughts on the Eighth Writers' Congress'.
13. For more information on Glavlit and the scope of its power over Soviet publishing, see Vladimirov, '*Glavlit*: How the Soviet Censor Works', *Index on Censorship*, 1, 3/4, Autumn/Winter 1972, pp. 31–43.

editor of *Znamya* and Sergey Zalygin as editor of *Novyy mir*.

Another noteworthy consequence was the retirement of the dull and conservative Georgy Markov as First Secretary of the Writer's Union, and his replacement by Vladimir Karpov, formerly editor-in-chief of *Novyy mir*, the USSR's leading literary monthly. Karpov was born in 1922 in Orenburg, received his schooling in Tashkent, and was arrested and imprisoned, while still a student at the Tashkent military school, as an 'enemy of the people' just before the outbreak of war in 1941. He was released from camp in 1942 and fought in a penal battalion. In the course of the war he was made a Hero of the Soviet Union. Karpov has been active in Soviet literary life since the mid-1940s, and attended the Gorky Literary Institute. Until 1965 he served in the Soviet Army. His literary output is modest, and his works are mainly concerned with the war. He has been on the editorial boards of the journals *Oktyabr'* and *Novyy mir* (he was editor-in-chief of the latter from 1979 to 1986), and is active in political life: in 1984 he became a member of the Supreme Soviet, and at the Twenty-Seventh Party Congress in 1986 he became a candidate-member of the CPSU Central Committee. It is as yet unclear whether Karpov can be termed a 'liberal', in the Soviet context, but his most recent novel, *Polkovodets* ('The Military Commander') (1982–4), has been praised by Soviet intellectuals. He has also recently published a favourable study of the previously unpublished poet Nikolay Gumilyov.[14] Changes in the literary leadership, therefore, signal changes in literary policy.

Among the interesting speeches at the Congress was that by Boris Mozhayev, a writer on rural themes who has written several controversial works in the past. He asked the question: why had the second part of *Muzhiki i baby* ('Rural Folk'), his novel on collectivisation, not yet been published, the first part having appeared in 1976? He noted also that Vladimir Dudintsev's latest novel was also awaiting publication, and gave the firm impression that the appearance in print of both his own and Dudintsev's works had been delayed for political reasons. (Both of these works have since appeared in print.)[15]

14. See Ernst Orlovsky, ' "Yest' osnovaniya dlya optimizma, no yest' i nemalo osnovaniy dlya skeptitsizma" ', *Russkaya mysl'*, 26 June 1987, p. 12. For Karpov's article on Gumilyov, see *Ogonyok*, 36, 1986, pp. 18–24. The *Guardian's* correspondent in Moscow in 1987, Martin Walker, attributes the 'advent of a new literary thaw' to Karpov's courage when, as editor-in-chief of *Novyy mir*, he published Yevtushenko's controversial *Fuku* in September 1985. See Martin Walker, *The Waking Giant: The Soviet Union Under Gorbachev*, Abacus, London, 1987, pp. 194–6.
15. B. Mozhayev, 'Muzhiki i baby', *Don*, 1–3, 1987, pp. 18–136, 5–129, 62–106;

Other well-established writers such as Valentin Rasputin and Vasily Belov were concerned with issues of ecology: the threat to Lakes Baykal and Sevan, and the much-debated project to reverse the flow of the northern Russian rivers to provide irrigation for the deserts of the South. Elem Klimov's film *Proschaniye* ('Farewell') (1983), based on Rasputin's *Proschaniye s Matyoroy* (*Farewell to Matyora*)(1976), looked at the fate of a village and its inhabitants about to be flooded as part of a hydro-electric project. Both the film and the novel were remarkable for the directness of their denunciation of progress pursued at the expense of ecology. The prominent novelist and literary bureaucrat Yury Bondarev also touched on this theme. Writers such as Daniil Granin, Andrey Voznesensky, Yevgeny Yevtushenko, and the distinguished scholar Dmitry Likhachev called for the publication of long-forgotten or suppressed writers of the 1920s and 1930s, such as Mandel'shtam, Zamyatin, Vvedensky, Khodasevich, Bely, Gumilyov, Sologub, Remizov, Merezhkovsky, Khlebnikov and Kuzmin, as well as complete collections of works by Akhmatova and Pasternak. However, a warning against too much freedom too soon came from Vladimir Karpov, the incoming First Secretary of the Writers' Union, who reminded delegates of previous thaws and the problems they subsequently caused: 'I want to remind you of the situation in the 1950s and 1960s, when we were again talking and arguing a lot. As it was later to turn out, ignoring the boundary separating democracy and demagogy sometimes has unpleasant consequences. It was precisely during these years that we saw the appearance of the literary dissidents'.[16] There is an apparent contradiction here between the views of the political leadership and those of the First Secretary of the Writers' Union: Gorbachev, after all, has been releasing dissidents, thus implying a greater tolerance of critical opinion. Karpov, meanwhile, is expressing the traditional fears of conservative-minded Russians, and his words could also be interpreted as a warning to the political leadership not to go too far in its liberalisation of society.

A word should perhaps be said about the nationality question. A few weeks before the Congress opened, the eminent Russian 'village' writer Viktor Astaf'yev published a short story in the Russian nationalist journal *Nash sovremennik*, in which he described a trip to Soviet Georgia. At the Congress, this story was sharply attacked by the head of the Georgian Writers' Union Tsitsishvili for unduly mocking Georgian habits and customs. Up stepped Valentin Raspu-

---

for publication details of Dudintsev's novel, see note 27.

16. *Literaturnaya gazeta*, 2 July 1986, p. 10.

tin to defend his Russian colleague, at which point the entire Georgian delegation to the Congress apparently staged a demonstrative walk-out.[17]

Feliks Kuznetsov, literary administrator (persecutor of Vasily Aksyonov, for instance), and critic, touched on the thorny issue of literary criticism, attacked at this and Republican Writers' Congresses for its unwillingness to pass harsh judgments (*komplimentarnost'*), lack of analytical power, and its 'cronyism' (*priyatelizm*). He spoke of the relationship of literary criticism, political control and publishing policy:

> We must learn to work in conditions of democracy. But the more democracy there is, the less administrative interference and diktat, the greater the role of literary criticism will be in literature. . . . We must no longer tolerate the state of affairs whereby the publication of a book, the final fruit of the writer's labour, is so estranged from the person who created it, the writer, and completely uncontrolled by the writers' community.[18]

One is tempted to interpret this statement as an appeal for criticism to be less concerned with the ideological content of works and to be able to concentrate and comment on their purely aesthetic (i.e. formal) qualities. Kuznetsov's latter remark is, of course, an attack on Glavlit.

The role of criticism is a key component in the development of a socialist realist literature, for literary criticism in the USSR, especially over the last twenty years or so, has been used to encourage a politically conformist interpretation of reality and social development. It is thus no accident that at this decisive stage in Soviet social and political history the state of literary criticism was discussed at a meeting of the Writers' Union Committee on Literary Criticism, which was held in the course of the Congress in the Gorky Literary Institute. Many speakers called for the further development of socialist realist theory in order to keep up with current practice, along the following lines indicated by Vitaly Ozerov:

> The theory [of socialist realism] as yet is lagging behind the practice. A number of other theoretical problems that are brought directly into

17. This is only a rumour, but Viktor Astaf'yev refers to 'the comedy acted out at the Congress by the Georgians' in his correspondence with the Soviet Jewish historian Natan Eidelman. See 'The Russian Complex: the Eidelman–Astafyev Correspondence', trans. S. Cosgrove, *Detente*, 8, 1987, pp. 5–7 (p. 7). See also note 2 (p. 7) to the above correspondence.

18. *Literaturnaya gazeta*, 2 July 1986, p. 5.

literary practice also need to be given meaning today: the problem of the positive hero, artistic conflict, the precepts of party-mindedness, popular appeal, the class approach to phenomena of life and literature, and the interaction of literatures in creating a socialist and Communist culture.[19]

Arkady El'yashevich echoed Ozerov's words, saying that socialist realism today was still being interpreted by critics on the basis of past judgments because, he concluded, 'there are simply no new developments'.[20] So it is that the practice of socialist realism is taken for granted, but critics lack a theoretical framework. The absence of such criteria is thus why major works published in the last twenty years or so, such as Bulgakov's *Master i Margarita* (*The Master and Margarita*) (1966), Rasputin's *Proshchaniye s Matyoroy* (referred to above) and Trifonov's *Dom na naberezhnoy* ('House on the Embankment') (1976), to name but a few, can be labelled as socialist realist, although no Soviet critic has been able to say convincingly exactly why.

In the spirit of the Republican Writers' Congresses, there was much criticism of the work of the Writers' Union, of its red tape and its inability to secure the publication of suspect or nonconformist works. Daniil Granin called for a restructuring of the Union, saying that they were too many hacks holding responsible positions, and that the editors of prominent literary journals were not bold enough in what they accepted for publication. Andrey Voznesensky said that it was not unusual for a writer to spend ten per cent of his time writing, and ninety per cent trying to get what he has written into print. This was strong stuff indeed for a Soviet Writers' Congress.

As regards the actual practice of socialist realism, the 'basic method' of Soviet *belles-lettres*, the keynote speech came from the outgoing First Secretary of the Writers' Union, Georgy Markov. Stressing the link between Soviet literature and real life in his report on the successes and failures of Soviet writers over the past five years, he went on to say:

We are socialist realists, we see the world in its revolutionary transformation. And it is important that we always hold in our hearts and in our minds the principle of the revolutionary development of the world. Always — both when we write simply and accessibly, and when phantasmagoric and other forms enter our work. . . . But we are, I repeat, realists. We have to understand that artistic depiction may be varied,

19. 'Kritika: Chetkost' kriteriyev, vysota trebovatel'nosti', *Literaturnaya gazeta*, 2 July 1986, p. 14.
20. Ibid.

even unusual in the way it is done, but the historical and social truth of character must always be clearly delineated.[21]

Markov also called upon writers to try and create the new positive hero who would correspond to the changing times. That is to say, the stock rituals of classical socialist realism were still being invoked; i.e. the task of literature remained to exhort people to face up to and tackle the political and social issues facing society, and to reveal 'the historical and social truth' of man and society in everyday life. Likewise, the image of the modern man who would embody the best features of the time (although exactly what these features are is still vague and undefined) was still offered as a model for emulation. There is no question of jettisoning or even modifying the correct ideological and political content of literature (although literary bureaucrats and editors can be replaced). As of old, therefore, writers were still called upon to create works and characters according to the classical socialist realist theoretical mould but which would nevertheless reflect the society and the issues of today. Soviet aesthetics thus remains, therefore, plagued by the discrepancy between its vague theoretical guidelines and actual artistic output.

Glasnost' in Action: The Aftermath of the Congress

The replacement of Brezhnev's trusted and often corrupt old guard by dynamic and committed men who share the current leader's own unease at the stagnation of Soviet society and his views on the need to revitalise it has had a knock-on effect in other walks of Soviet life, with die-hards being replaced by younger or more forward-looking men. A good example is the election of the respected film director Elem Klimov, who has had several brushes with the authorities in the past, as the head of the Cinematographers' Union, at their Congress held just before the Writers' Congress. Similarly, one of the significant things about the Writers' Congress was the election to the Secretariat of the Writer's Union of Valentin Rasputin, Yevgeny Yevtushenko, Andrey Voznesensky, Bella Akhmadulina, and Bulat Okudzhava, all writers of considerable artistic merit and not in any sense time-servers. There is hope for a qualitative improvement in Soviet literary output in the near future, and, furthermore, for a more liberal attitude to writers whose works err on ideological grounds. There are indications of a more liberal attitude even to

---

21. *Literaturnaya gazeta*, 25 June 1986, p. 3.

those who have already emigrated, as can be seen by the fullsome obituaries to Tarkovsky in the Soviet press after his death in emigration at the end of 1986, and the showing of his films in the USSR. Likewise, the appointment of the author Sergey Zalygin as editor of *Novyy mir* brings an internationally respected writer in charge of this prestigious journal for the first time since Aleksandr Tvardovsky was in charge in the 1960s.

1986 and 1987 have seen frenetic activity on the Soviet cultural scene. New films such as *Pokayaniye* ('Repentance') and *Pis'ma myortvogo cheloveka* ('Letters from a Dead Man'), which deal frankly and distressingly with Stalinism and the aftermath of nuclear war respectively, have been released. The Cinematographers' Union Congress has pledged to release many more films that have been suppressed, some of them for up to fifteen years. (Panfilov's *Tema* ('The Theme'), which touches on the issue of emigration and discusses the compromises writers make to achieve success, is now being shown, for instance, and was recently broadcast on Soviet TV.)

The theatre is also experiencing a revival. Rehearsals of the self-exiled Yury Lyubimov's production of Trifonov's *Dom na naberezhnoy* (referred to above) are reportedly again under way at Moscow's Taganka theatre. A controversial play by Mikhail Shatrov, *Brestskiy mir* ('The Brest Peace'), written between the years 1962 and 1987, which shows the formulation of the Brest-Litovsk Treaty which brought Russia out of the First World War, has recently been published in *Novyy mir*. It is notable in that alongside Lenin in the Bolshevik leadership in 1917–18 are the former 'non-persons' Bukharin and Trotsky, although they are depicted as opposed to Lenin's line. Both Bukharin and Trotsky are presented as honest, though wayward, Bolsheviks, dedicated to the cause of revolution.[22]

If we turn to poetry and prose, poetry by Vladimir Nabokov has been published in the journal *Oktyabr'*, and *Novyy mir* has published a long-suppressed poem by Tvardovsky on the evils of Stalinism. Nabokov's novel *Zashchita Luzhina* (*The Defence*) (1930) and his study of Nikolay Gogol have also been published recently. Poetry by Nikolay Gumilyov, the outstanding author married to Anna Akhmatova, was published in April 1986 (i.e. before the Congress) in the journal *Ogonyok*, not hitherto a front-rank literary journal but whose every weekly issue now contains something controversial or interesting. Gumilyov was executed by the Reds in 1921 for alleged participation in a counter-revolutionary plot, and hardly a word of

22. M. Shatrov, 'Brestskiy mir', *Novyy mir*, 4, 1987, pp. 3–51.

his had appeared in print in the USSR between 1923 and 1986 Now hardly a month goes by without either the publication of poems by Gumilyov or critical appreciation of his work. Poetry by another 'non-person', Vladislav Khodasevich, has also been published (he, indeed, has suffered even worse at the hands of the Soviet censors in the past, and hardly a line of his had previously appeared). Thus, appeals at the Writers' Congress seem to have been heeded.[23]

So much for literary rehabilitations. Established (albeit to varying degrees) but now long dead writers have also had major works published that were formerly deemed unacceptable. These include Anna Akhmatova's poetic masterpiece *Rekviyem* ('Requiem') (1938–40), Andrey Platonov's short novel *Kotlovan* ('The Foundation Pit') (1929–30), and Nikolay Klyuyev's long poem on collectivisation *Pogorel'shchina* ('The Burnt Land') (1928).[24] There has also been publication of controversial works by more modern (but also, it must be added, deceased) writers, these works having been refused publication ten or twenty years ago such as Alexander Bek's 'Novoye naznacheniye' ('The New Appointment') (1964). Yury Trifonov's unfinished novel 'Ischeznoveniye' ('The Disappearance'), which had apparently previously been refused publication, was published in January 1987 in the journal *Druzhba narodov*, after extracts from it had appeared in *Ogonyok* the previous month.[25] The talk at the Congress of publishing *Doktor Zhivago* has come nearer reality with an announcement that the novel is being prepared for publication by *Novyy mir*, and the publication in *Ogonyok* of some of Pasternak's correspondence with his cousin Ol'ga Freydenberg and others from the years 1946–60 discussing his progress on the

23. For publication of works by V. Nabokov, see the following: 'Iz literaturnogo nasledstva', *Oktyabr'*, 11, 1986, pp. 111–26; 'Zashchita Luzhina', *Moskva*, 12, 1986, pp. 66–163, and 'Nikolay Gogol'', *Novyy mir*, 4, 1987, pp.173–227. For Tvardovsky, see 'Po pravu pamyati', *Novyy mir*, 3, 1987, pp. 190–203. For publication of works by N. Gumilyov, see 'K 100-letiyu so dnya rozhdeniya N. S. Gumilyova. Stikhi raznykh let', *Ogonyok*, 17, 1986, pp. 26–8; 'Teatr. Tvorchestvo. Otravlennaya tunika', *Teatr*, 9, 1986, pp. 167–88; 'Stikhi i pis'ma. A. Akhmatova. N. Gumilyov', *Novyy mir*, 9, 1986, pp. 196–227; 'Trinadsat' stikhotvoreniy', *Znamya*, 10, 1986, pp. 181–3; 'Afrikanskiy dnevnik', *Ogonyok*, 14–15, 1987, pp. 19-22, 20-23. For publication of works by Khodasevich, see 'Koleblemyy trenozhnik', *Ogonyok*, 6, 1987, pp. 17–19, and 'Iz liriki', *Druzhba narodov*, 2, 1987, pp. 177–82.
24. A. Akhmatova, 'Rekviyem', *Oktyabr'*, 3, 1987, pp. 130–5. A. Platonov, 'Kotlovan', *Novyy mir*, 6, 1987, pp. 50–123; N. Klyuyev, 'Pogorel'shchina', *Novyy mir*, 7, 1987, pp. 78–100.
25. A. Bek, 'Novoye naznacheniye', *Znamya*, 10–11, 1986, pp. 3–72, 3–66; Yu. Trifonov, 'Ischeznoveniye', *Druzhba narodov*, 1, 1987, pp. 6–95; extracts published in *Ogonyok*, 52, 1986, pp. 20–4.
26. *Ogonyok*, 16, 1987, pp. 26–8.

novel.[26] To this end Pasternak's membership of the Writer's Union was posthumously restored early in 1987.

Other interesting and previously suppressed works that have recently appeared in print include works by Vladimir Dudintsev and Anatoly Rybakov, two officially approved Soviet writers still alive and active.[27] These works, too, deal with the past, respectively the Lysenko years in Soviet science in the late 1940s and 1950s, and the events in 1934 leading to the murder of the top Party official Kirov (Rybakov leaves us in no doubt that the murder was carried out on Stalin's order). Perhaps more significantly, however, is the publication of works that had previously been smuggled to the West and published there, such as works by Andrey Bitov, Fazil Iskander, and Yevgeny Popov.[28] One of the first signs, therefore, of the new 'openness' is the publication of works presenting a critical and franker discussion of Soviet history under Stalin. However, the denunciation of the evils of Stalinism is nothing new in Soviet literature and can be viewed essentially as a continuation of Khrushchev's policies of 'de-Stalinisation'. On the other hand, the publication of works by Iskander, Bitov and Popov would seem to herald a franker discussion of the 'stagnation' of society in the Brezhnev years, as well as seeming to do away with the stigma of Western publication (we must not forget that in 1966 the writers Yuly Daniel' and Andrey Sinyavsky were given prison sentences for publishing their satirical works in the West).

It seems fair to add that the rush with which writers and editors are publishing neglected or controversial works is due in some measure to the fear that the present beneficial climate may not last long, and that like those before it, the current thaw may be followed by a sudden freeze. Because this is a 'cultural revolution' from above, no-one doubts that it can be halted at any time.

Mention has already been made of editorial changes in Soviet journals with regard to Grigory Baklanov and Sergey Zalygin. Some words should perhaps also be said about the emergence of the formerly pedestrian and lacklustre *Ogonyok* as a driving force in Soviet letters. *Ogonyok* is not a purely literary journal like *Novyy mir* or *Znamya*, but has always contained stories and articles on social and economic issues to suit the tastes of a broad public. It is a mass circulation journal, and is published weekly. In the past two years,

27. V. Dudintsev, 'Belyye odezhdy', *Neva*, 1–4, 1987; A. Rybakov, 'Deti Arbata', *Druzhba narodov*, 4–6, 1987, pp. 3–133, 67–163, 23–151;
28. A. Bitov, 'Pushkinskiy dom', *Novyy mir*, 10–12, 1987; F. Iskander, 'Kroliki i udavy', *Yunost'*, 9, 1987, pp. 21–62; Ye. Popov, 'Rasskazy', *Novyy mir*, 10, 1987, pp. 97–120.

in addition to the works noted above, *Ogonyok*, under the editorship of Vitaly Korotich since June 1986, has published items on such varied and instantly popular topics as breakdancing in Moscow, drug-pushing, and has exposed the *lyubery* thugs who act as vigilantes in Soviet cities and beat up punks, long-haired teenagers, or *metallisty* (not, as one might expect, sheet-metal workers, but heavy metal rock music fans). On the literary front, the initiative of Yevtushenko has seen the publication of poems by such officially neglected Russian writers from the early part of the century as Nikolay Klyuyev, Sof'ya Parnok, Osip Mandel'shtam, Ryurik Ivnev, Igor' Severyanin, Sasha Cherny and many other poets. It has also responded to modern literary tastes by carrying stories and articles by or about such popular contemporary writers as Fazil' Iskander, Vasily Shukshin, Andrey Bitov, and Valentin Rasputin. At the present time, *Ogonyok* is in the forefront of literary activity in the Soviet Union.

Overall, one can point to some patterns emerging in the period of time since the Writers' Congress. The era of *glasnost'* has brought about the publication of many writers of the early Soviet period previously known to Soviet readers only in *samizdat* or Western editions smuggled into the country (Gumilyov, Khodasevich and Nabokov for instance), and this is likely to continue. Also, more contemporary writers, such as Trifonov, Bek, Iskander, and Bitov, regarded as loyal Soviet citizens, have had their controversial works published (the culmination of this process will be the appearance in the Soviet Union of *Doktor Zhivago*). The appearance in print of Yevgeny Popov, and on the pages of the country's leading literary monthly, *Novyy mir*, at that, shows that young writers who had previously been known almost entirely from publications in *samizdat* (i.e. unofficially produced in the Soviet Union) or *tamizdat* (smuggled out of the Soviet Union and published in the West) can now be officially countenanced. Similarly, the appearance of works by Rybakov, Akhmatova, Tvardovsky and Platonov suggests that the political leadership is giving the green light for a full examination of the 'black spots' of recent Soviet history. After all, Gorbachev is the first Soviet leader who is not tainted by the legacy of Stalinism, his rise to power occurred after Stalin's death, and therefore he himself cannot be implicated in some of the excesses of Stalin's rule, unlike his four predecessors. It remains to be seen whether Gorbachev can dismantle, or 'restructure', the Stalinist edifice in the economic and political spheres, as he is successfully doing in the cultural one.

However, because *glasnost'* in literature and the arts is an initiative from the top, so far the changes in Soviet literary life have not yet touched on fundamentals of literary theory. Literary policy has changed and become more liberal, but political control and ideological criteria remain in force. The heritage of Russian literature has certainly been enriched, and we should not underestimate the significance for the Soviet public and, hopefully, the future of Soviet literature, of the appearance of the works already mentioned. In particular, it would be churlish to understate the importance of the recent publication of Akhmatova's long poem *Rekviyem* (referred to above). There is currently a twofold process: the 'discovery' of new poets and writers from the past, and the publication of formerly proscribed works by writers who have enjoyed success and status within the Soviet literary system. Moreover, we can hope that the literary climate will become sufficiently beneficial for the eventual publication of Vasily Grossman's bitter and harrowing novel on collectivisation *Vsyo techet* (*Forever Flowing*) (1955–64), or his magnificent but deeply subversive epic on the battle of Stalingrad *Zhizn' i sud'ba* (*Life and Fate*) (1960), both of which have only appeared in the West.[29]

Rehabilitations of authors safely dead have been part of the Soviet literary scene since the first thaws of the 1950s, and Solzhenitsyn's quotation from Pushkin to the delegates of the Fourth Writer's Congress in 1967 still rings true twenty years on: 'They are capable of loving only the dead'.[30] The publication of *Doktor Zhivago* will be a major victory for the liberal-minded literary intelligentsia, not to say for the Soviet reading public as a whole. With the appearance in print of Popov, we can also hope that the authorities will publish works by other such 'internal *émigrés*', writers living in the USSR who have published little or nothing in their homeland, and of other younger writers who may view Soviet reality in a satirical or critical vein. Also, it may be possible that ideological distinctions between those 'for' and 'against' the regime become blurred, if writers recently removed to the West are published again. Soviet socialist realism would then encompass such a widely diverging array of talent and ideological conviction that the theory would require a fundamental reformulation.

We are seeing signs that the regime is not only more flexible than

29. An extract from *Zhizn' i sud'ba* appeared in *Ogonyok*, 40, 1987, pp. 19–22, with an announcement that the whole work will appear in the journal *Oktyabr'* in the near future.
30. Labedz (ed.), *Solzhenitsyn: A Documentary Record*, p. 65.

at any other time in Soviet history in its attitude to literary freedom, but that it is positively benevolent. For example, we are seeing the publication not only of manuscripts that have been under lock and key in the Soviet Union for many years, but also of works that have appeared previously only in the West, such as the novels by Bek and Bitov, Iskander's short novel, and the short stories by Popov; all of these had been stigmatised by the charge of anti-Sovietism. An idea of the thinking behind this 'new' policy can be gleaned from an article by Academician Likhachev in *Literaturnaya gazeta* at the beginning of this year. While reading *Doktor Zhivago*, he says, he was reminded of the publication of *Master i Margarita* in 1966, another Soviet literary sensation. He continues:

> Remember: twenty years ago we saw the emergence into our literature of Bulgakov with his razor-sharp but uplifting satire, his novel *The Master and Margarita*. And what happened next? Did anything happen? Yes, it did: we were given a wonderful work of art which 'works' for us, and not against us. We need satire, sharp and uplifting, and which savages our vices. It will help us.[31]

We must assume, therefore, that literature will continue to 'help' the Party push through its radical programme of reform, but we must still remain cautious given that the degree of artistic freedom is determined by, and thus dependent on, the political leadership. In short, socialist realism is still alive and Soviet officials and writers continue to use and work within the stock formulae and terminology; Soviet socialist realism can be seen to be adapting to new conditions and, officially, thereby be able to regenerate itself.

The changes taking place in Soviet literary life are not painless. At the April 1987 Plenary Meeting of the Board of the USSR Writers' Union, which met to discuss the progress made in publishing policy and the 'renewal' of the literary scene, there were several speeches referring to pointed exchanges and differences of opinion within the Board and the Secretariat regarding the direction of Soviet culture. On the eve of the Plenum the writer Pyotr Proskurin, writing in *Pravda*, criticised the continued publication of long-lost writers and works:

> Our thick and thin journals have fallen over each other in seeking out and publishing works from decades past which for one reason or another did

---

31. *Literaturnaya gazeta*, 1 January 1987, p. 11.

not see the light of day or were published in the West. . . . Attempts to include them in the continuous and vital literary process in the context of what is happening today — whether we want to or not — not only retard the flow of this process, but also introduce into it the slight odour of a kind of literary necrophilia.[32]

At the Plenum Proskurin maintained his acerbic tone, asking rhetorically: 'But anyway, do we really need corpses in art, do we need in the literal sense their physical presence?'[33]

Proskurin met with objections from Voznesensky, among others, who not only defended the current policy but also went on to defend rock music and welcomed the re-admittance into the Writers' Union of the poet Semyon Lipkin. Ecology was still a burning topic, and it is the ecological issue which demonstrates the strength of publicism in modern Soviet literature, as Voznesensky pointed out:

> It is exactly literature which can do now what it could never have done before: stop the turning-round of the rivers, stop the construction of the ugly Victory monument on Poklonnaya hill and so on. Literature has begun to have an effect, and in the past we only dreamed of that. Thanks to the times we live in and to our hard struggle.[34]

The power of publicism today in the Soviet Union testifies to the existence and strength of pressure groups independent of Party prerogatives. It may be that we are seeing the emergence in the USSR of what we in the West refer to as 'public opinion'.

In his opening address to the Plenum, First Secretary Vladimir Karpov summed up the developments in Soviet literature since the Congress, discussing changes in the Writers' Union Secretariat and naming those Republican Writers' Unions 'dragging their feet in getting to grips with the tasks of the moment': Armenia, Moldavia, Tadzhikistan, Azerbaidjan. He bemoaned the fact that many writers were using the pretext of *glasnost'* to settle old scores on the pages of the periodical press, but cautiously welcomed the initiative of some Moscow writers to set up cooperative publishing houses (i.e. printing houses independent of the State where writers themselves

32. *Pravda*, 26 April 1987, p. 3.
33. *Literaturnaya gazeta*, 6 May 1987, p. 9. At a meeting of the Secretariat of the Board of the Writers' Union of the RSFSR held in March 1987, Proskurin had already criticised the journal *Ogonyok* for its 'spirit of cliquishness, even a kind of caste exclusiveness . . . in its basic assumptions regarding literature and art', and his criticisms of current literary policy were further echoed by writers such as Sergey Mikhalkov, Mikhail Alekseyev, F. Chuyev, and Yu. Bondarev. See *Literaturnaya Rossiya*, 27 March 1987, pp. 2–4.
34. *Literaturnaya gazeta*, 6 May 1987, p. 7.

decide editorial policy). But developments in literary criticism he nevertheless framed in the terminology and cant of canonical socialist realism:

> In the creation of a work of art the author's civic stance is very important. But in judging works the critic must also have recourse to definite civic positions. From the point of view of dissidents, a great many books of Soviet authors have nothing to do with literature of great artistic merit. But one could hardly expect any other judgment on the part of our ideological enemies. The trouble is that some of our critics, when discussing the achievements and blackspots in our literary affairs, forget that one must be guided by the criteria of ideological correctness, appeal to the masses, and party-mindedness, that one's life must be governed by the concerns of the Soviet people and by concerns which are aimed at eradicating mistakes and shortcomings in the construction of socialism.[35]

So, despite the relative freedom of 1986–87, in official terms the developments are in line with the formula of a 'command literature' drawn up in the 1930s. Consequently, the evolution of 'socialist realist' literature and culture in the Soviet Union is viewed by those who control and propagate it in terms of Soviet teleology: Soviet culture develops by constantly enriching itself and encompassing new influences and works.

We must nevertheless retain some perspective on the new-found literary 'freedom' in the USSR. Real change, and an indication that the new leadership is prepared to equate *glasnost'* with freedom of expression, and not merely see it as a tool in a political campaign, will come about when works critical of the regime and even the very foundations of socialism are allowed into print. It is not enough to publish criticism of Stalin, as was done back in the 1950s. Soviet writers need to be able to look not only at the past, but also at the present. A step in the right direction is the literary rehabilitation of *samizdat* authors, for example, Popov and Semyon Lipkin (the latter relinquished his membership of the Union following his participation, along with Popov and others such as Vysotsky, Aksyonov and Yerofeyev, in the unofficial publication of the *Metropol'* almanac in 1979). Also encouraging is the publication of young writers such as Vyacheslav P'yetsukh, Oleg Bazunov, and Sergey Kaledin.[36] To sum up: the signs are good, but while the development of Soviet literature depends on the political will of the Party, as established with the onset of socialist realism in the 1930s, then we must

35. *Literaturnaya gazeta*, 29 April 1987, p. 2.
36. See Julia Wishnevsky, 'A Survey of Russian Literature Published in the Past Year', *Radio Liberty Research Bulletin*, 3453, 387/87, September 30 1987, pp. 1–7.

conclude that literature and art are still at the mercy of their political overseers. The experience of past 'thaws', however, shows that writers soon overstep the mark of what is acceptable and expedient, that initiatives emerge from below, and eclipse those from above. *Glasnost'* and socialist realism in the long term may yet prove to be quarrelsome bedfellows.

Select Bibliography

The following select bibliography is intended as a guide for further reading. It makes no claims to comprehensiveness, and is offered as an indication of the key texts used by authors in the preparation of individual contributions. Texts are arranged according to chapter sequence.

Introduction

Aesthetics and Politics: Debates between Bloch, Lukács, Brecht, Benjamin, Adornos, ed. R. Taylor, R. Livingstone, P. Anderson and F. Mulhern, New Left Books, London, 1977

Alvarez, A., *Under Pressure — The Writer in Society: Eastern Europe and the USA*, Penguin, Harmondsworth, 1965

Barthes, R., *Le Degré zéro de l'écriture*, Seuil, Paris, 1953

Eagleton, T., *Marxism and Literary Criticism*, Methuen, London, 1976

Fischer, E., *The Necessity of Art: A Marxist Approach*, trans. Anna Bostock, Penguin, Harmondsworth, 1964

Garaudy, R., *D'un réalisme sans rivages*, Plon, Paris, 1963

—— *Une littérature de fossoyeurs*, Editions sociales, Paris, 1948

Goldmann, L., *Pour une sociologie du roman*, Gallimard, Paris, 1964

Jameson, F., *Marxism and Form: Twentieth-Century Dialectical Theories of Literature*, Princeton University Press, Princeton, NJ, 1971

Kundera, M., 'A Kidnapped West or Culture Bows Out', *Granta*, no. 11, 1984, pp. 93–118

Macherey, P., *Pour une théorie de la production littéraire*, François Maspero, Paris, 1966

Rühle, J., *Literature and Revolution: A Critical Study of the Writer and Communism in the Twentieth Century*, trans. Jean Steinberg, Pall Mall Press, London, 1969

Sartre, J.-P., *Situations II: Qu'est-ce que la littérature?*, Gallimard, Paris, 1948

Soviet Writers' Congress 1934: The Debate on Socialist Realism and Modernism in the Soviet Union, Lawrence & Wishart, London, 1977 (facsimile reprint of *Problems of Soviet Literature*, ed. H.G. Scott, Lawrence, London, 1935)

Stern, J.P., *On Realism*, Routledge & Kegan Paul, London, 1973

Weimann, R., 'Realität und Realismus: Über Kunst und Theorie in dieser Zeit', *Sinn und Form*, no. 4, 1984, pp. 924–51

Williams, R., *The Long Revolution*, Penguin, Harmondsworth, 1965

1. Georg Lukács and Socialist Realism

Entries for works by Lukács himself have been arranged thematically (i.e. general works on realism and specific works on Russian literature) rather than chronologically, both as a means of clarifying the distinctions between the various editions and translations and in view of the fact that many volumes are collections covering a wide period of early writing.

Gallas, H., *Marxistische Literaturtheorie: Kontroversen im Bund proletarisch-revolutionärer Schriftsteller*, Luchterhand, Neuwied, 1971

Koch, H. (ed.), *Georg Lukács und der Revisionismus*, Dietz, Berlin, 1966

Löwy, M., *Georg Lukács: From Romanticism to Bolshevism*, New Left Books, London, 1979

Lukács, G., *Wider den mißverstandenen Realismus*, Claassen, Hamburg, 1958 (English edn: *The Meaning of Contemporary Realism*, trans, J. and N. Mander, Merlin, London, 1963)

——, *Probleme des Realismus I (Essays über Realismus)*, *Werke*, vol. 4, Luchterhand, Neuwied, 1971. Includes 'Tendenz oder Parteilichkeit?', 'Die intellektuelle Physiognomie des künstlerischen Gestaltens', 'Erzählen oder Beschreiben?' 'Die Gegenwartsbedeutung des kritischen Realismus'

——, *Writer and Critic*, trans. A. Kahn, Merlin, London, 1978. Includes 'Narrate or Describe?', but without Section VII on socialist realism, and 'The intellectual physiognomy . . .'

——, *Essays on Realism*, trans. D. Fernbach, ed. R. Livingstone, Lawrence & Wishart, London, 1980. Includes '"Tendency" or Partisanship?'

——, *Schriften zur Ideologie und Politik*, ed. P. Ludz, Luchterhand, Neuwied, 1967

——, *Die Moskauer Schriften: Zur Literaturtheorie und Literaturpolitik 1934–40*, ed. F. Benseler, Sendler, Frankfurt, 1981

——, *Der russische Realismus in der Weltliteratur*, Aufbau, Berlin, 1952. Includes essays on Gorky, Fadeyev, Virta, Sholokhov, Makarenko, Bek and Kazakevich

——, *Probleme des Realismus II (Probleme des russischen Realismus)*, *Werke*, vol. 5, Luchterhand, Neuwied, 1964. Omits the essay on Kazakevich from *Der russische Realismus* of 1952 and is supplemented by one of 1937 on Platonov and his first on Solzhenitsyn (*Ivan Denisovich*)

——, *Solzhenitsyn*, trans. W.D. Graf, Merlin, London, 1970. Includes the *Ivan Denisovich* essay from *Werke*, vol. 5, and 'Solzhenitsyn's Novels'

Parkinson, G.H.R., *Georg Lukács*, Routledge & Kegan Paul, London, 1977

2. Gramsci and Cultural Rationalisation

Cirese, A.M., 'Gramsci's Observations on Folklore', in A. Showstack Sassoon (ed.), *Approaches to Gramsci*, Writers and Readers, London, 1982

Fortini, F. 'The Writer's Mandate and the End of Anti-Fascism', *Screen* 15, 1, Spring 1974, pp. 33–70

Gramsci, A., *Selections from the Prison Notebooks*, ed. and trans. Q. Hoare and G. Nowell-Smith, Lawrence & Wishart, London, 1971

——, *Selections from Cultural Writings*, trans. W. Boelhower, ed. D. Forgacs and G. Nowell-Smith, Lawrence & Wishart, London, 1985

Nizan, P., 'Littérature révolutionnaire en France', in *Pour une nouvelle culture*, ed. S. Suleiman, Paris, 1971, pp. 33–43

Serge, V., 'Littérature prolétarienne?' (originally pub. in *Monde*, 3 November 1928) in idem, *Littérature et Révolution*, François Maspero, Paris, 1976, pp. 99–103

3. Soviet Perspectives on Socialist Realism

Bullitt, M., 'Towards a Marxist Theory of Aesthetics: the Development of Socialist Realism in the Soviet Union', *Russian Review*, 35, 1, January 1976, pp. 53–76

Clark, K., *The Soviet Novel: History as Ritual*, University of Chicago Press, Chicago and London, 1985

Crouch, M. and R. Porter, (eds.), *Understanding Soviet Politics through Literature*, Allen & Unwin, London, 1984

Ermolaev, H., *Soviet Literary Theories, 1917–34: The Genesis of Socialist Realism*, University of California Press, Berkeley, 1963

Freeborn, R., *The Rise of the Russian Novel*, Cambridge University Press, Cambridge, 1973

Hayward, M., 'The Decline of Socialist Realism', in idem, *Writers in Russia 1917–1978*, ed. P. Blake, Harvill Press, London, 1983, pp. 149–83

Hosking, G., *Beyond Socialist Realism*, Granada, London, 1980

James, C.V., *Soviet Socialist Realism: Origins and Theory*, Macmillan, London, 1973

Kosík, K., 'Hašek and Kafka', *Cross Currents*, no. 23 1983, pp. 127–36

McLeod, A., 'The Socialist Realist Perspective: A Theoretical Critique', *Irish Slavonic Studies*, 6, 1985, pp. 46–63

Marsh, R., *Soviet Fiction since Stalin*, Croom Helm, London, 1986

Sinyavsky, A. [Abram Tertz], 'Chto takoye sotsialisticheskiy realizm?', in idem, *Fantasticheskiy mir Abrama Tertsa*, YMCA, Paris, 1967, pp. 401–46

——, 'The Literary Process in Russia', trans. M. Glenny, in *Kontinent* I, André Deutsch, London, 1976, pp. 73–110

Soviet Writers' Congress 1934: The Debate on Socialist Realism and Modernism in the

Soviet Union, Lawrence & Wishart, London, 1977 (facsimile reprint of *Problems of Soviet Literature*, ed. H.G. Scott, Lawrence, London, 1935)

Swayze, H., *Political Control of Literature in the USSR 1946–1959*, Harvard University Press, Cambridge, Mass., 1962

Zhdanov, A. A., *On Literature, Music and Philosophy*, trans. Eleanor Fox, Stella Jackson and Harold C. Feldt, Lawrence & Wishart, London, 1950

4. 'Breadth and Diversity': Socialist Realism in the GDR

Benjamin, W., *Understanding Brecht*, New Left Books, London, 1973

Bock, S., *Literatur — Gesellschaft — Nation: Materielle und ideelle Rahmenbedingungen der frühen DDR-Literatur*, Metzler, Stuttgart, 1980

Brecht, B., *Zur Literatur und Kunst, Werke*, vols. 18–19, Suhrkamp, Frankfurt, 1967

Jäger, M., 'Der sozialistische Realismus', in idem, *Kultur und Politik in der DDR: Ein historischer Abriß*, Wissenschaft & Politik, Cologne, 1982, pp. 33–48

Kaufmann, H. (ed.), *Tendenzen und Beispiele: Zur DDR-Literatur der siebziger Jahre*, Reclam, Leipzig, 1981

Lukács, G., *Deutsche Literatur in zwei Jahrhunderten, Werke*, vol. 7, Luchterhand, Neuwied, 1964

Mittenzwei, W., *Der Realismus-Streit um Brecht: Grundriß der Brecht-Rezeption in der DDR 1945–1975*, Aufbau, Berlin and Weimar, 1978

Münz-Koenen, I. (ed.), *Literarisches Leben in der DDR 1945–1960*, Akademie, Berlin, 1979

Pracht, E. et al., *Einführung in den sozialistischen Realismus*, Dietz, Berlin, 1975

Schlenstedt, D., *Wirkungsästhetische Analysen: Poetologie und Prosa in der neueren DDR-Literatur*, Akademie, Berlin, 1979

Tate, D., *The East German Novel: Identity, Community, Continuity*, Bath University Press/St. Martin's Press, Bath and New York, 1984

Wolf, C., *Die Dimension des Autors: Essays und Aufsätze, Reden und Gespräche 1959–1985*, Luchterhand, Darmstadt, 1987

Zur Tradition der deutschen sozialistischen Literatur, 4 vols., Aufbau, Berlin and Weimar, 1979

5. Socialist Realism and the West German Novel

Batt, K., *Revolte Intern. Betrachtungen zur Literatur in der BRD*, Reclam, Leipzig, 1974

Bernhard, H.J. et al., *Geschichte der Literatur der Bundesrepublik Deutschland*, Volk und Wissen, Berlin, 1983

Bullivant, K., *Realism Today: Aspects of the Contemporary West German Novel*,

Berg, Leamington Spa and New York, 1987

Fischbach, P., H. Hensel, and U. Naumann (eds.), *Zehn Jahre Werkkreis Literatur der Arbeitswelt. Dokumente, Analysen, Hintergründe*, Fischer, Frankfurt, 1979

Hüser, F., M. von der Grün, and W. Promies (eds.), *Aus der Welt der Arbeit. Almanach der Gruppe 61 und ihrer Gäste*, Luchterhand, Neuwied and Berlin, 1966

Laemmle, P. (ed.), *Realismus — welcher? Sechzehn Autoren auf der Suche nach einem literarischen Begriff*, Edition Text und Kritik, Munich, 1976

Powroslo, W., *Erkenntnis durch Literatur. Realismus in der westdeutschen Literaturtheorie der Gegenwart*, Kiepenheuer & Witsch, Cologne, 1976

Realistisch Schreiben. Springener Protokolle und Materialien, ed. Werkkreis Literatur der Arbeitswelt, 2nd edn, Werkkreis, Erkenschwick, 1972

Reinhold, U., 'Realismus in der Diskussion. Anmerkungen zum Problemkreis Literatur und Wirklichkeit im literarischen Kontext der BRD', *Weimarer Beiträge* 25, 1979, no. 2, pp. 32–55

Schonauer, F., *Max von der Grün* (Autorenbücher 13), Beck/Edition Text und Kritik, Munich, 1978

Stieg, G., and B. Witte, *Abriß einer Geschichte der deutschen Arbeiterliteratur*, Klett, Stuttgart, 1973

Trommler, F., 'Realismus', in *Kulturpolitisches Wörterbuch Bundesrepublik Deutschland/Deutsche Demokratische Republik im Vergleich*, W.R. Langenbucher, R. Rytlewski, B. Weyergraf, Metzler, Stuttgart, 1983, pp. 596–9

6. Socialist Realism without a Socialist Revolution: The French Experience

Anissimov, I., 'Le Réalisme socialiste dans la littérature mondiale', *La Nouvelle Critique*, Jan. 1955

Aragon, L., *Pour un réalisme socialiste*, Denoël & Steele, Paris, 1935

——, *L'Homme communiste*, 2 vols., Gallimard, Paris, 1946, 1953

——, *La Culture et les hommes*, Editions Sociales, Paris, 1947

——, *Littératures soviétiques*, Editions Denoël, Paris, 1955

Bernard, J.-P., *Le Parti communiste français et la question littéraire, 1921–1939*, Presses universitaires de Grenoble, Grenoble, 1972

Casanova, L., *Le Communisme, la pensée et l'art*, Editions du PCF, Paris, 1947

——, *Le Parti communiste, les intellectuels et la nation*, Editions de la Nouvelle Critique, Paris, 1949

——, *Responsabilités de l'intellectuel communiste*, Editions de la Nouvelle Critique, Paris, 1949

Fréville, J. (ed.), *Les Grands textes du marxisme sur la littérature et l'art*, Editions sociales internationales, Paris, 1936

Select Bibliography

Select Bibliography

Kanapa, J., *Situation de l'intellectuel* (Critique de la Culture, vol. I), Editions Sociales, Paris, 1957
——, *Socialisme et culture (Critique de la Culture*, vol. II), Editions Sociales, Paris, 1957
Prévost, C., *Littérature, politique, idéologie*, Editions Sociales, Paris, 1973
Ragon, M., *Histoire de la littérature prolétarienne en France*, Albin Michel, Paris, 1974
Robin, R., *Le Réalisme socialiste*, Payot, Paris, 1986
Stil, A., *Vers le réalisme socialiste*, Editions de la nouvelle critique, Paris, 1952

7. Persona as Propaganda: Neruda and the Spanish Civil War

Alberti, R., *The Lost Grove*, trans. G. Berns, Berkeley University Press, Berkeley, 1976
Aznar, M. and L.M. Schneider (eds.), *II Congreso Internacional de Escritores Antifascistas (1937)*, Laia, Barcelona, 1979
Butt, J., *Writers and Politics in Modern Spain*, Hodder & Stoughton, London, 1978
Cano Ballesta, J., *La poesía española entre la pureza y la revolución, 1930–1936*, Gredos, Madrid, 1972
Cobb, C., *La Cultura y el pueblo: España 1930–1939*, Laia, Barcelona, 1981
Collard, P., *Ramón J. Sender en los años 1930–1936*, Rijksuniverseit te Gent, Gent, 1980
Grimau, C., *El cartel republicano en la guerra civil*, Cátedra, Madrid, 1979
Hanrez, M. (ed.), *Los escritores y la guerra de España*, Monte Ávila, Barcelona, 1977
Neruda, P., *Memoirs*, trans. Hardie St Martin, Souvenir Press, London, 1977
——, *Residence on Earth*, trans. Donald D. Walsh, Souvenir Press, London, 1976
Salaün, S., *La poesía de la guerra de España*, Castalia, Madrid, 1985

8. Paul Nizan and Socialist Realism: The Example of *Le Cheval de Troie*

Brochier, J.-J. (ed.), *Paul Nizan, intellectuel communiste 1926–1940*, François Maspero, Paris, 1967
Cohen-Solal, A. and H. Nizan, *Paul Nizan: communiste impossible*, Grasset, Paris, 1980
Fé, F., *Paul Nizan un intellettuale comunista*, Edizioni Savelli, Rome, 1973
Ishaghpour, Y., *Paul Nizan: une figure mythique et son temps*, Le Sycomore,

–176–

Paris, 1980

King, A., *Paul Nizan, Écrivain*, Didier, Paris, 1976

Leiner, J., *Le Destin littéraire de Paul Nizan*, Kliencksieck, Paris, 1970

Nizan, P., *Antoine Bloyé*, Grasset, Paris, 1933

——, *Le Cheval de Troie*, Gallimard, Paris, 1935 (English edn: *Trojan Horse*, trans. Charles Ashleigh, Lawrence & Wishart, London, 1937)

——, *La Conspiration*, Gallimard, Paris, 1938

——, *Pour une nouvelle culture*, ed. S. Suleiman, Grasset, Paris, 1971

Ory, P., *Nizan: destin d'un révolté 1905–1940*, Ramsay, Paris, 1980

Redfern, W., *Paul Nizan: Committed Literature in a Conspiratorial World*, Princeton University Press, New Jersey, 1972

Sartre J.-P., *Préface: Aden Arabie*, François Maspero, Paris, 1960

Scriven, M., *Paul Nizan: Communist Novelist*, Macmillan, London, 1988

9. Art, Politics, and *Glasnost*:The Eighth Soviet Writers' Congress and Soviet Literature, 1986–7

Numerous articles and statements have been published in the Soviet periodical press in 1986–7, ranging from reviews of individual works to theoretical critiques. The following examples are arranged in chronological order:

Mozhayev, B., '"No chto zhe my govorim o glasnosti!"', *Literaturnaya gazeta*, 11 February 1987, p. 6

Shugayev, V., 'Moskovskiy roman, ili Muzhestvo pisatelya', *Literaturnaya Rossiya*, 24 April 1987, p. 5

Burtin, Y., '"Real'naya kritika" vchera i segodnya', *Novyy mir*, 6, 1987, pp. 222–39

Karpov, A., 'Istoriya ne terpit suyesloviya', *Literaturnaya gazeta*, 1 July 1987, p. 4

Gachev, G., 'Arsenal dobroy voli. O romane V. Dudintseva "Belyye odezhdy" i v svyazi s nim', *Oktyabr'*, 8, 1987, pp. 183–90

Burtin, Y., '"Vam, iz drugogo pokoleniya . . ." K publikatsii poemy A. Tvardovskogo "Po pravu pamyati"', *Oktyabr'*, 8, 1987, pp. 191–202

Kuznetsov, F. and Y. Polyakov, 'Minuvsheye — polnaya pravda', *Literaturnaya gazeta*, 30 September 1987, p. 3

Karyakin, Y., 'Stoit li nastupat' na grabli?', *Znamya*, 9, 1987, pp. 200–24

Surovtsev, Y., 'Velikiy Oktyabr´ i sovremennaya literatura', *Literaturnaya gazeta*, 14 October 1987, pp. 1, 3

'Literatura i perestroyka', *Literaturnaya gazeta*, 21 October 1987, p. 2

About the Contributors

J.E. Flower is Professor of French at the University of Exeter. He is author of *Writers and Politics in Contemporary France* (Hodder & Stoughton, 1978), and *Literature and the Left in France* (Macmillan, 1983; Methuen, 1985).

David Forgacs is Lecturer in Italian Studies at the University of Sussex. He is author of 'Marxist Literary Theories' in *Modern Literary Theory*, ed. A. Jefferson and D. Robey (Batsford, 1982), and joint editor of *Antonio Gramsci, Selections from Cultural Writings* (Lawrence & Wishart, 1985).

David C. Gillespie is Lecturer in Russian at the University of Bath. He is author of *Valentin Rasputin and Soviet Russian Village Prose* (MHRA, 1986).

Axel Goodbody is Lecturer in German at the University of Bath. He is author of *Natursprache* (Wachholtz, 1984).

Rodney Livingstone is Senior Lecturer in German at the University of Southampton. He is editor of *Georg Lukács: Essays on Realism* (Lawrence & Wishart, 1980), and joint editor of *Aesthetics and Politics: Debates between Bloch, Lukács, Brecht, Benjamin, Adorno* (New Left Books, 1977).

Robert Porter is Lecturer in Russian at the University of Bristol. He is joint editor of *Understanding Soviet Politics Through Literature* (George Allen & Unwin, 1984), and author of *Four Contemporary Russian Writers* (Berg, 1988).

Michael Scriven is Lecturer in French at the University of Bath. He is author of *Sartre's Existential Biographies* (Macmillan, 1984), and *Paul Nizan: Communist Novelist* (Macmillan, 1988).

Dennis Tate is Lecturer in German at the University of Bath. He is author of *The East German Novel: Identity, Community, Continuity* (Bath University Press/St. Martin's Press, 1984).

Robin Warner is Lecturer in Spanish at the University of Sheffield. He is author of 'The Politics of Pablo Neruda's *España en el corazón*', in *Hispanic Studies in Honour of Frank Pierce* (University of Sheffield, 1980).

Index

Abramov, Fyodor, 58
Abusch, Alexander, 22
Adorno, Theodor W., 30
Aitmatov, Chingiz, 58
Akhmadulina, Bella, 161
Akhmatova, Anna, 158, 162, 165
  'Rekviyem', 163, 166
Aksyonov, Vasily, 150, 159, 169
Alberti, Rafael, 114, 118–19, 121–2,
  126
Alvarez, A., 6
Andersch, Alfred, 79, 81, 83
Anderson, Perry, 31
Andreyev, Leonid, 17
Andropov, Yury, 59
Aragon, Louis, 4, 33, 100, 102–5,
  107–8, 129
  Pour un réalisme socialiste, 105, 129
Association des Ecrivains et Artistes
  Révolutionnaires (AEAR), 33–5,
  102–4
Astaf'yev, Viktor, 158–9
Averbakh, Leopold, 19

Baklanov, Grigory, 156, 164
Balzac, Honoré de, 17, 21, 63
Barbusse, Henri, 33, 53, 55–6,
  99–100, 102
Barthel, Max, 85–6
Barthes, Roland, 5
Batt, Kurt, 75, 83–4, 94, 96
Baumgart, Reinhard, 91
Bazunov, Oleg, 169
Beaumarchais, Pierre-Augustin Caron
  de, 53
Becher, Johannes R., 60, 64–5, 66, 86
  Abschied, 63
Beckett, Samuel, 77
Bek, Alexander, 28–9, 163, 165, 167
  Volokolomskoye shosse, 28
  Rezerv generala Panfilova, 29
Belinsky, V.G., 2, 51
Belov, Vasily, 158

Bely, Andrey, 158
Benjamin, Walter, 15
Bergamín, José, 117–18
Berl, Emmanuel, 33
Biermann, Wolf, 74
Bitov, Andrey, 164, 165, 167
Bloch, Ernst, 81
Bloch, Jean-Richard, 103–4
Blok, Alexander, 51, 53
Bobrowski, Johannes, 67, 71
Bock, Stephan, 64 n.8, 65
Böll, Heinrich, 8, 75, 81, 82–5, 98
  Billard um halbzehn, 83
  Gruppenbild mit Dame, 83–4, 94
  Die verlorene Ehre der Katharina Blum,
  94
Bondarev, Yury, 158
Bourgeois, Lucien, 99
Braun, Volker, 72, 73, 81
  Hinze-Kunze-Roman, 76–7
Brecht, Bertolt, 4, 5, 7, 8, 10, 24, 28,
  30, 53, 60, 62, 63, 66, 68–9, 72–3,
  77–8, 81, 82, 93, 96–7
  'Weite und Vielfalt der realistischen
    Schreibweise', 63 n.6
  Herr Puntila und sein Knecht Matti, 77
Bredel, Willi, 62, 87, 90
Bredthauer, Carlo, 92
Brezhnev, Leonid, 1, 59, 150, 155, 161,
  164
Broch, Hermann, 6
Bröger, Karl, 85–6
Bruyn, Günter de, 67, 68, 72
Büchner, Georg, 71
Buehler, Georg, 61
Bukharin, Nikolay, 2 n.3, 9, 103–4,
  127, 162
Bulgakov, Mikhail, 52,
  Master i Margarita, 50 56, 160, 167
Bullivant, Keith, 5, 80, 97
Bund proletarisch-revolutionärer
  Schriftsteller (BPRS), 21, 85–6, 90,
  92, 93

Index

Buñuel, Luis, 33

Camus, Albert, 107
Carpentier, A., 75
Casanova, Laurent, 107
Caute, David, 104
Chernenko, Konstantin, 58, 59
Cherny, Sasha, 165
Chernyshevsky, N.G., 2, 51
class-mindedness, 2, 53, 56, 92, 152, 160
Claudius, Eduard, 66
Courtade, Pierre, 110
Croce, Benedetto, 37
Cwojdrak, Günther, 66

Dabit, Eugène, 106
Daix, Pierre, 106, 108, 110
Daniel', Yuly, 68, 150, 164
Degenhardt, Franz Josef, 90
Delius, F.C., 92
Deutscher, Isaac, 13, 27 n.31
Dickens, Charles, 63
Diderot, Denis, 53, 77
Dieste, Rafael, 118
Döblin, Alfred, 63, 71, 81
Dobrolyubov, N., 2
Dos Passos, John, 33, 63
Dostoevsky, Fyodor, 51, 98, 130
Drews, Jörg, 80, 97 n. 28
Dudintsev, Vladimir, 157, 164
Dymshits, Alexander, 64

Eagleton, Terry, 3, 4
Ehrenburg, Ilya, 66
Elsberg, Ya., 22
Eluard, Paul, 4
El'yashevich, Arkady, 160
Engelke, Gerrit, 85
Engels, Friedrich, 2, 21
engineer of the human soul, 1, 41, 104

Fadeyev, Alexander, 49–50, 58, 65, 103
Razgrom, 21
Fedin, Konstantin, 58
Fedorenko, N., 155
Felipe, Léon, 119
Fischer, Ernst, 4–5
Flaubert, Gustave, 14
France, Anatole, 53
Freeborn, Richard, 59
Fréville, Jean, 105
Freydenberg, Ol'ga, 163

Friedrich, Wolfgang, 88
Fries, Fritz Rudolf, 71
Fuchs, Gerd, 89, 97
Beringer und die lange Wut, 90
Fühmann, Franz, 6 n.21, 67, 68, 71, 72, 76, 81

Gallas, Helga, 82
Garaudy, Roger, 5, 49, 74, 109
Gaulle, Charles de, 106
Gide, André, 104, 118
Gil-Albert, Juan, 118
Gisselbrecht, André, 109
Gladkov, Fyodor: Energiya, 15–16
glasnost', 1, 6, 9, 10, 149, 153–4, 161, 165–6, 168–70
Gluchowski, Bruno, 89
Goethe, Johann Wolfgang von, 14, 53, 63, 72, 104
Gogol, Nikolay, 52, 98, 162
Goldmann, Lucien, 5
Goncourt, Edmond and Jules, 99
González Tuñón, Raul, 126
Gorbachev, Mikhail, 1, 7, 57, 59, 151, 152–3, 155, 156, 158, 165
Gorky, Maxim, 4, 17–18, 26, 51, 58, 103
Mother, 18
Gotsche, Otto, 90
Gramsci, Antonio, 7, 10, 31–45
The Prison Notebooks, 31, 38, 41
Granin, Daniil, 158, 160
Grossman, Vasily, 166
Grün, Max von der, 82, 85–8, 92, 95–6
Irrlicht und Feuer, 86–7
Stellenweise Glatteis, 87–8, 90, 95
Grünberg, Karl, 90
Guéhenno, Jean, 102
Gumilyov, Nikolay, 9, 157, 158, 162–3, 165
Günderrode, Karoline von, 72

Hager, Kurt, 74
Harich, Wolfgang, 13, 66
Hašek, Jaroslav, 6, 57
The Good Soldier Švejk, 54–6
Havel, Václav, 57
Hayward, Max, 50–1
Hegel, G.W.F., 14
Hemingway, Ernest, 56
Hermlin, Stephan, 65, 67, 71, 72, 81
Hernandez, Miguel, 119
Heym, Stefan, 66, 73

Index

'Die Langeweile von Minsk', 68–9
Collin, 74–5
Hoffmann, E.T.A., 71
Honecker, Erich, 62, 69, 72, 73–4
Hosking, Geoffrey, 2, 4, 50, 150
Hugo, Victor, 104
Hüser, Fritz, 85–6

ideological orthodoxy, 2, 57, 152, 169
Illès, Bena, 102
International Union of Revolutionary
  Writers (RAPP), 100–1
Ippers, Josef: *Am Kanthaken*, 90, 92–3
Iskander, Fazil', 164, 165, 167
Ivner, Ryurik, 165

James, C. Vaughan, 2, 51 *n*.6, 53
Jameson, Frederic, 5
Jarmatz, Klaus, 77
Jirásek, Alois, 54
Johnson, Uwe, 67, 75, 81
Jourdain, Francis, 100
Joyce, James, 63

Kafka, Franz, 6, 63, 76, 109
  The Trial, 55
Kaledin, Sergey, 169
Kanapa, Jean, 107
Kant, Hermann, 71
Karpov, Vladimir, 157, 158, 168–9
Kästner, Erich, 79, 81
Kaufmann, Hans, 13, 75
Kazakevich, Emmanuil: *Vesna na Odere*,
  24, 29
Khlebnikov, Velimir, 158
Khodasevich, Vladislav, 158, 163, 165
Khrushchev, Nikita, 50, 59, 66, 150,
  164
Kirov, Sergey, 164
Kirpotin, Vladimir, 101
Kleist, Heinrich von, 72
Klíma, Ivan, 57
Klimov, Elem, 158, 161
Klyuyev, Nikolay, 163, 165
Kochetov, Vsevolod, 156
Koeppen, Wolfgang, 81, 83
Köpping, Walter, 88
Korotich, Vitaly, 165
Kosík, Karel, 55
Kovalenko, V., 155
Kundera, Milan, 6, 57
  Jacques et son maître, 77
Kunert, Günter, 81
Kuzmin, M.A., 158

Kuznetsov, Feliks, 150, 159

Larnac, Jean, 108
Lefebvre, Henri, 105
Lefebvre, Raymond, 100
Léger, Fernand, 53
Lemonnier, Léon, 99
Lenin, Vladimir Il'ich, 2, 23, 51, 53,
  58, 59, 130, 133, 162
Lenz, Siegfried, 81, 83
Léon, Maria Teresa, 114, 118
Lersch, Heinrich, 86
Ligachev, Yegor, 156
Likhachev, Dmitry, 158, 167
Lipkin, Semyon, 168, 169
Loest, Erich
  Es geht seinen Gang, 74
  Der vierte Zensor, 74–5
Lorca, Federico García, 126
Ludkewicz, Z., 102
Lukács, Georg, 4, 5, 7, 8, 10, 13–30,
  31, 52–3, 60, 62–3, 64, 65, 66, 67,
  71–2, 80–1, 82–3, 86–7, 89, 91,
  92–3, 96, 98
  Wider den mißverstandenen Realismus, 4,
    13, 20, 22–3, 24, 26, 63
  'Erzählen oder Beschreiben?',
    14–16, 21
  ' "Tendenz" oder Parteilichkeit?',
    22–3
  *Der russische Realismus in der
    Weltliteratur*, 22, 24
  Probleme de russischen Realismus,
    17–18, 24, 29
  Solzhenitysn, 52–3
Lyubimov, Yury, 162

Machado, Antonio, 119, 126
Macherey, Pierre, 5
Majerová, Marie, 56
Makarenko, Anton, 4
Malinovsky, Rodion, 59
Malraux, André, 33, 103–4, 131 *n*.7,
  143
Mamytov, Dzh, 155
Mandel'shtam, Osip, 158, 165
Mann, Heinrich, 81
Marchwitza, Hans, 62, 90
Marcuse, Herbert, 84
Markov, Georgy, 157, 160–1
Márquez, Gabriel García, 75
Marsh, Rosalind, 50
Marx, Karl, 2, 39, 41, 133
Mayakovsky, Vladimir, 4, 54, 105

181

Index

Mehring, Franz, 16
Merezhkovsky, D., 158
modernism, 7, 15–16, 17, 21, 22, 24, 28, 31, 74, 76, 81, 90
Mondolfo, Rodolfo, 44–5
Morgner, Irmtraud, 67, 71, 76
Morin, Edgar, 106
Moussinac, Léon, 105
Mozhayev, Boris, 157
Musil, Robert, 6, 76

Nabokov, Vladimir, 9, 163 n.23, 165
  Zashchita Luzhina, 162
naturalism, 14–16, 17, 21, 25, 26, 53, 65, 95, 97
Neruda, Pablo, 9, 53, 113–27
  España en el corazón, 9, 113–14, 118–27
Nezval, Vítězslav, 53
Nizan, Paul, 3–4, 7, 9–10, 32–6, 43, 102–3, 106, 128–45
  Aden Arabie, 137
  Antoine Bloyé, 130–3, 139–40, 143–4
  Le Cheval de Troie, 9, 128–45
  La Conspiration, 130
  'Littérature révolutionnaire en France', 32–6
Nossack, Hans Erich, 83

O'Casey, Sean, 4
Okudzhava, Bulat, 161
Olbracht, Ivan, 56
omniscient narrator, 15, 62, 67, 74–5, 81, 94, 132–3, 143
Orlov, Vladimir, 50–1
Ottwalt, Ernst, 30, 87, 90
Ovcharenko, Alexander, 51
Ozerov, Vitaly, 159–60

Panfilov, Gleb, 162
Pankin, Boris, 150
Parnok, Sof'ya, 165
partisanship, 2, 21–4, 53, 56, 57, 58, 59, 61, 62, 67, 70, 82, 83, 92, 93, 96, 152, 160, 169
Pasternak, Boris, 9, 150, 158, 163–4
  Doktor Zhivago, 150, 163, 165, 166–7
Philippe, Charles-Louis, 99
Picasso, Pablo, 53
Platonov, Andrey, 19–20, 24, 26, 165
  Bessmertiye, 19
  Usomnivshiysya Makar, 19
  Kotlovan, 163
Plievier, Theodor, 79

Popov, Yevgeny, 164, 165, 166, 167, 169
popular appeal, 2, 17, 53, 56, 57, 61, 65, 68, 76, 81, 88, 89, 94, 152, 160, 169
Popular Front, 13 n.1, 21, 22, 31, 62, 64, 90, 117–18, 121, 124, 131–2, 134, 137, 139
populism, 33–4, 99–100, 106
positive hero, 2, 18–20, 23, 57, 61, 67, 69–70, 87, 89, 97, 98, 152, 160
Poulaille, Henri, 99–100
Pozner, Vladimir, 103
Prados, Emilio, 119, 122, 124
Prévost, Claude, 13, 109
proletarian literature, 31–2, 62, 82, 85–6, 92, 93, 99–102, 106
Proskurin, Pyotr, 167–8
Proust, Marcel, 76
Pujmanová, Marie, 56
Pushkin, Alexander, 166
P'yetsukh, Vyacheslav, 169

Raabe, Wilhelm, 26
Raddatz, Fritz, 82
Radek, Karl, 103–4, 115
Rákosi, Mátyás, 13
Rasputin, Valentin, 58, 75, 158–9, 161, 165
  Proschaniye s Matyoroy, 51, 158, 160
Reimann, Brigitte, 67
Reinhold, Ursula, 96–7
Remarque, Erich Maria, 56, 81
Remizov, Alexey, 158
Renn, Ludwig, 55
Revai, Joseph, 21–2
revolutionary romanticism, 2, 9, 16, 18, 24, 25, 53, 89, 104, 127
Richter, Hans-Werner, 79, 83
Richter, Jean Paul, 71
Robin, Régine, 110 n.30
Rolland, Romain, 53, 102, 104
Rühle, Jürgen, 3
Runge, Erika, 91
Rybakov, Anatoly, 164, 165

Sadoul, Georges, 100
Saltykov-Shchedrin, M.E., 55
Sánchez Barbudo, Antonio, 118
Sartre, Jean-Paul, 5, 107, 128–9, 140
Schiller, Friedrich, 23, 104
Schlenstedt, Dieter, 75, 77
Schmidt, Arno, 81
Schmitt, Hans-Jürgen, 82

Index

Schneider, Peter, 95, 97
Schöfer, Erasmus, 92
Schroeder, Margot: *Ich stehe meine Frau*, 90, 93, 94, 95
Seghers, Anna, 33, 60, 63, 65, 66, 81
  Das siebte Kreuz, 64
  Die Entscheidung, 67
Serge, Victor, 105
Serrano Plajo, Arturo, 119, 121
Severyanin, Igor', 165
Shakespeare, William, 23, 104
Shatrov, Mikhail: *Bretskiy mir*, 162
Sholokhov, Mikhail, 4, 18–19, 26, 50, 58–9
  And Quiet Flows the Don, 18, 59
  Virgin Soil Upturned, 27–8
Shukshchin, Vasily, 165
Simonov, Konstantin, 29
Sinyavsky, Andrey [Abram Tertz], 18, 52, 68, 150, 164
Sofronov, Anatoly, 156
Sologub, Fyodor, 158
Solzhenitsyn, Alexander, 4, 7, 19, 25–6, 52–3, 150, 152, 166
  One Day in the Life of Ivan Denisovich, 24, 25, 51, 52
  The Gulag Archipelago, 51
  The First Circle, 52, 98
  Cancer Ward, 52, 84–5
Soviet Writers' Congress 1934, 2, 7, 41, 49 *n*.1, 60, 62, 65, 103, 114, 130–1, 150
Spix, Hermann, 94
Stalin, Josef, 1, 2, 3, 4, 9, 23, 25, 27, 29, 50, 58, 59, 60, 62, 66, 103–4, 110, 116, 150, 151, 154, 164, 165, 169
Stendhal [Henri Beyle], 14
Stern, J.P., 3, 4
Sterne, Laurence, 26
Stil, André, 108–10
  Vers le réalisme socialiste, 108
Strittmatter, Erwin, 87
Struck, Karin, 95
Suleiman, Susan, 110
Surkov, Aleksey, 150
Surovtsev, Yury, 57–8
Švorecký, Josef, 57

Tarkovsky, Arkady, 162
Tendryakov, Vladimir, 58
Thérive, André, 99
Thorez, Maurice, 102, 107
Timm, Uwe, 82, 89, 95 *n*.24, 97–8

Heißer Sommer, 89–90
Tolstoy, Leo, 26, 28, 51, 53, 63, 98
totality, 14, 17–18, 23, 62, 63, 78, 80–1, 82, 83, 89, 91, 94, 95
Tret'yakov, Sergey, 15
Trifonov, Yury, 98, 165
  Dom na naberezhnoy, 160, 162
  'Ischeznoveniye', 163
Triolet, Elsa, 106
Trotsky, Leon, 162
Tulpanov, Sergey, 64
Turgenev, Ivan, 51
Tvardovsky, Alexander, 156, 162, 165
typicality, 2, 20, 61, 62, 69, 71, 93, 152

Vailland, Roger, 110
Vaillant-Couturier, Paul, 102
Virta, Nikolay, 23, 28
Vladimov, Georgy, 149
Voynovich, Vladimir, 52, 56, 59, 150
Voznesensky, Andrey, 158, 160, 161, 168
Vvedensky, Alexander, 158
Vysotsky, Vladimir, 169

Wallraff, Günter, 82, 91–2, 93
Walser, Martin, 81, 82, 83, 90, 91, 96, 98
Wander, Maxie, 71
Webb, W.L., 1
Weber, Max, 40–1
Weimann, Robert, 6
Wellershoff, Dieter, 79–80, 81–2
Werner, Wolfgang, 91
Weyrauch, Wolfgang, 79
Williams, Raymond, 5
Wolf, Christa, 5, 61, 67, 69–73, 75, 76, 80 *n*.5, 81, 91, 94–5, 96, 98
  Der geteilte Himmel, 67–8, 69
  Nachdenken über Christa T., 69–71, 72, 75, 78, 91
  'Lesen und Schreiben', 72–3, 81
  Kein Ort. Nirgends, 61, 72
  Kassandra, 76
Wolf, Gerhard, 71
Wurmser, André, 110

Yadin, P., 103
Yakovlev, Alexander, 151, 156
Yerofeyev, Venyamin, 169
Yevtushenko, Yevgeny, 157 *n*.14, 158, 161, 165

Zalygin, Sergey, 157, 162, 164

Zamyatin, Yevgeny, 158
Zhdanov, Andrey, 2, 3, 10, 13, 21, 23,
 60, 62, 103, 107, 115, 128–9, 139,
145
Zola, Emile, 14, 99
Zweig, Arnold, 81

Selections from Cultural Writings -

Armstrong, Tim. Modernism, technology &
the body: a cultural study
Cambridge UP, 1998

Gallop, Jane. Thinking through the
body
Grosz, Elizabeth. Volatile bodies